Dark Vanishings

28/1/08

Dark Vanishings

*Discourse on the Extinction of
Primitive Races, 1800–1930*

Patrick Brantlinger

Cornell University Press
Ithaca and London

First published 2003 by Cornell University Press
First printing, Cornell Paperbacks, 2003

Printed in the United States of America

Library of Congress Cataloging-in-Publication Data

Brantlinger, Patrick, 1941–
    Dark vanishings : discourse on the extinction of primitive races,
1800–1930 / Patrick Brantlinger.
        p. cm.
Includes bibliographical references and index.
    ISBN 0-8014-3809-8 (cloth : alk. paper)—ISBN 0-8014-8876-1 (pbk. : alk. paper)
    1. Indigenous peoples.   2. Social Darwinism.   3. Genocide.   4.
Eurocentrism.   I. Title.
    GN380.B73 2003
    306'.08—dc21

                            2003004117

Cornell University Press strives to use environmentally responsible suppliers and materials to the fullest extent possible in the publishing of its books. Such materials include vegetable-based, low-VOC inks and acid-free papers that are recycled, totally chlorine-free, or partly composed of nonwood fibers. For further information, visit our website at www.cornellpress.cornell.edu.

Cloth printing   10 9 8 7 6 5 4 3 2 1
Paperback printing   10 9 8 7 6 5 4 3 2 1

To Leroy and Jayla

When they died, there the road ended.
—Eavan Boland, "That the Science of Cartography Is Limited"

Contents

Acknowledgments

Over the ten or twelve years it has taken me to research and write various parts of this book, more students and colleagues have helped in one way or another than I can remember. So this list is selective. Among those at Indiana University I am especially grateful to Bob Arnove, Todd Avery, Purnima Bose, Ellen Brantlinger, Eva Cherniavsky, John Eakin, Jonathan Elmer, Tom Foster, Richard Higgins, Renata Kobetts-Miller, Todd Kuchta, Andrew Libby, Chris Lohmann, Joss Marsh, Sara Maurer, Andrew Miller, Brook Miller, Jim Naremore, Sylvia Pamboukian, Janet Sorensen, Steve Watt, and Perry Willett.

Jan Nederveen Pieterse invited me to participate in his "Decolonization of the Imagination" conference in Amersterdam in 1991, where I gave an account of the "first and last" Tasmanians; a version of this later reappeared in his and Bhikhu Parekh's collection *The Decolonization of Imagination: Culture, Knowledge, and Power*, and I am grateful to both of them. I gave a version of my analysis of James Fenimore Cooper's "sentimental racism" at the University of Montana in 1993, and I have John Glendening to thank for inviting me to do so; I presented another version at the "(Un)fixing Representation" conference at the University of North Carolina in 1994, and later this appeared in a special issue of *Cultural Studies* (1998), guest-edited by Judith Farquhar, Tomoko Masuzawa, and Carol Mavor, whom I also thank. My friends and colleagues who organized the Victorians Institute Conference in 1998 and who invited me to speak at the University of Victoria, Gettysburg College, and the City University of New York in 1999 heard and responded to early versions of the chapter on the Irish Famine; I appreciate the many helpful questions and comments I received. I am also grateful to Judith Johnstone, Hilary Fraser, and the other organizers of the Australasian Victorian Studies Association conference for 2000 for inviting me to speak, again on the Irish Famine, and for their wonderful hospitality while I was in Perth. I could not give the editors of the *Australasian Victorian Studies Journal* a copy of my lecture to publish, but they accepted instead a short account of pre-Darwinian ideas about the extinction of primitive races; my thanks go to them for doing so.

There are many others—too many others—for me to thank, including Janice Carlisle, Mary Jean Corbett, Deirdre David, Gaurav Desai, Regenia Gagnier, Anne Humpherys, Gerhard Joseph, Christopher Keep, John Kucich, Carolyn Mitchell, Donald Randall, John Reed, Bill Thesing, and Martha Vicinus. And, as always, I am thankful to Bernie Kendler and the staff of Cornell University Press for their patience and editorial excellence.

Dark Vanishings

1. Introduction

Aboriginal Matters

"When civilised nations come into contact with barbarians the struggle is short, except where a deadly climate gives its aid to the native race." So writes Darwin in the section on "the extinction of races" in *The Descent of Man* (190). His account is one of many: from the late 1700s on, an enormous literature has been devoted to the "doom" of "primitive races" caused by "fatal impact" with white, Western civilization. While *Dark Vanishings* includes evidence about populations of indigenous peoples around the world and about the tragic histories of their decimations, its primary focus is on the assumptions and theories that arose to explain those decimations.

Extinction discourse is a specific branch of the dual ideologies of imperialism and racism—a "discursive formation," to use Foucauldian terminology. Like Orientalism and other versions of racism, it does not respect the boundaries of disciplines or the cultural hierarchies of high and low; instead, it is found wherever and whenever Europeans and white Americans encountered indigenous peoples. A remarkable feature of extinction discourse is its uniformity across other ideological fault lines: whatever their disagreements, humanitarians, missionaries, scientists, government officials, explorers, colonists, soldiers, journalists, novelists, and poets were in basic agreement about the inevitable disappearance of some or all primitive races. This massive and rarely questioned consensus made ex-

1

tinction discourse extremely potent, working inexorably toward the very outcome it often opposed.

Understood and sometimes celebrated as necessary for social progress, the demise of "savagery" throughout the world also inspired mourning; in many versions, celebration and mourning are fused. The fusion expresses a sentimental racism, evident, for example, in James Fenimore Cooper's Leatherstocking novels, characteristic of the literatures of the new and emerging nation-states in North America, Australia, New Zealand, and South Africa, and also of much writing about the South Pacific. In all these places, as well as in Latin America and some parts of Asia, the advent of Europeans meant steep declines in indigenous populations. One of the main causes for these declines was not mysterious: violence, warfare, genocide. The other main cause, disease, though just as evident, was somewhat mysterious, because its deadly operations were not yet well understood. In many accounts, a third cause took precedence over violence and disease. Often viewed as the main or even sole cause, this third factor was savage customs: nomadism, warfare, superstition, infanticide, human sacrifice, cannibalism. Savagery, in short, was frequently treated as self-extinguishing. The fantasy of auto-genocide or racial suicide is an extreme version of blaming the victim, which throughout the last three centuries has helped to rationalize or occlude the genocidal aspects of European conquest and colonization.

Any combination of savage customs could imply a temporal limit—the primitive past and passing versus the civilized present and future—beyond which those trapped in such customs could not progress. Natural historians and "race scientists" from Carl von Linnaeus and Georges Buffon through Darwin down to World War II hierarchized the races, with the white, European, Germanic, or Anglo-Saxon race at the pinnacle of progress and civilization, and the "dark races" ranged beneath it in various degrees of inferiority. The temporal hierarchy or limit—assigning primitive races to a futureless past—reinforced the vertical, spatial hierarchy. The anthropologist Johannes Fabian writes of the "denial of coevalness" to those identified as primitive or savage.[1] The term "Stone Age" applied to modern Australians or Bushmen is an obvious example: the illusion that certain peoples, races, or cultures are unable to speak the present and future tenses of history is implicit in the words *primitive* and *savage*, which mean archaic, belated, even dead to the present or the modern.

Shadowing the romantic stereotype of the Noble Savage is its ghostly twin, the self-exterminating savage. It is no exaggeration to include this Gothic stereotype among the causes—and not just effects—of the global decimation of many indigenous peoples.[2] The belief that savagery was vanishing of its own accord from the world of progress and light mitigated guilt and sometimes excused or even encouraged violence toward those deemed savage. Even when savagery was not identified as causing its own extinction, it was frequently held that some races could not be civilized and were thus doomed to fall by the wayside no matter what customs they practiced. And "doomed," of course, means inevitable: no amount of humanitarian sentiment or scientific expertise, even when supported by the correct political will, could come to the rescue. The most ardent humanitarianism—that of the British Aborigines Protection Society, for example—could speak only of preventing future violence and of saving by civilizing the sad remnants of the dying races.

The pervasive concept of race reinforced assumptions of biological necessity while lending a supposedly scientific legitimacy to Western ideas about non-Western peoples. Race also homogenized the great diversity of peoples—into the uncivilized stages of savagery and barbarism but also into the stereotypic molds of separate, radically unequal types of mankind.[3] Thus, for example, the Incas and the Iroquois, the Hopis and the Kwakiutls constituted one "red race" with one ultimate destiny. Through its unifications of widely divergent cultures and societies, racial theory and its subset, extinction discourse, downplayed or ignored the possibility that there might be many degrees, levels, or types of progress toward (or degeneration away from) civilization—or, more radically yet, that there were diverse cultures and civilizations pursuing different but equally legitimate histories.

In art, literature, journalism, science, and governmental rhetoric, extinction discourse often takes the form of proleptic elegy, sentimentally or mournfully expressing, even in its most humane versions, the confidence of self-fulfilling prophecy, according to which new, white colonies and nations arise as savagery and wilderness recede. Proleptic elegy is thus simultaneously funereal and epic's corollary— like epic, a nation-founding genre. Thus, in the American context, several of Philip Freneau's poems from the 1780s illustrate the general pattern. According to the last lines of "The Indian Burial Ground" (1788), with the Indian "hunter" now a "shade,"

long shall timorous fancy see
The painted chief, and pointed spear,
And Reason's self shall bow the knee
To shadows and delusions here.

(356)

And Freneau's "The Dying Indian: Tomo-Chequi" (1784) is a good example of that staple of early American literature, the Indian death song:

I too must be a fleeting ghost! —no more—
None, none but shadows to those mansions go;
I leave my woods, I leave the Huron shore,
For emptier groves below!

(329)

In Australia, South Africa, and elsewhere, many other nineteenth-century writers adopted the form of the lament of the dying, often last aboriginal.[4]

Everywhere the future-perfect mode of proleptic elegy mourns the lost object before it is completely lost. The work of cultural, national mourning occurs not because the aboriginals are already extinct but because they will sooner or later become extinct. If, from a psychoanalytic perspective, the identities of both individuals and nation-states are founded on lacks, then the nation-founding discourse of proleptic elegy is founded on the lack of a lack or, in other words, on a wished-for lack that is instead an all-too-real obstacle to identification.[5] Rather than absences, primitive races such as the Australian "blackfellows" were and remain presences disturbing the process of national unification and identification.

Whatever else it may have been, extinction discourse was performative in the sense that it acted on the world as well as described it. Thus, for instance, in the United States it served as the ideological basis for the passage of the Indian Removal Act of 1830 and, more generally, for official "Indian policy" down to World War II. On the other side of the planet, it underwrote the intense scientific scrutiny of the final Tasmanians and the distressing but convenient myth of their total extinction by 1876. It spurred home governments, responsive to the opinion that a stronger imperial and military presence would protect indigenous peoples, to support colonizing projects, as in New Zealand and South Africa, they might otherwise have opposed. It inspired missionary efforts to save at least the souls of the last members of perishing races. From the 1860s on, it lent support to social Darwinism and its offshoot, the eugenics movement. Extinction discourse has been a mainstay of the literature, art, advertising, and cinema of the new nations spawned by European imperialism from the eighteenth century on. And it has served as a primary motivation for the funereal but very modern science of anthropology in its attempt to learn as much as possible about primitive societies and cultures before they vanish forever.

From the start, anthropology has been a science of mourning. Its "disappearing object is," writes James Clifford, "a rhetorical construct legitimating a representational practice: 'salvage' ethnography. . . . The other is lost, in disintegrating time and space, but saved in the text" ("Allegory," 112). In other words, this is a salvation in the words and museums of Western science, not in deed. "The modern anthropologist," Clifford declares, "lamenting the passing of human diversity, collects and values its survivals"—and, for survivals, one might as well substitute ghosts (*Predicament*, 244). So, too, writing of the "imperialist nostalgia" that informs anthropology as well as much recent popular culture, Renato Rosaldo characterizes his science as "mourning for what one has destroyed" (69). Although such "nostalgia" or "mourning" is frequently an ideological ruse, assuaging guilt for the destruction wrought by empire and its driving force—capitalist, industrial modernization—Rosaldo points out that "anthropologists have often used the notion of the 'vanishing savage' to criticize the destructive intrusions of imperialism" (82).[6]

The main focus of *Dark Vanishings* is on sites within the British Empire and North America, but extinction discourse has been influential in the contexts of other modern empires and nation-states. Bartolomé de Las Casas's *Devastation of the Indies* (1552) shows that there were versions of the discourse—in his case, a humanitarian and religious one—long before the 1800s. But extinction discourse in British and North American contexts reached its crescendo between the early 1800s and World War I. Taking 1880 and 1939 as the starting and end points for his study of the Australian version of extinction discourse, Russell McGregor notes that "the former date marks not the beginnings of the doomed race theory but its consolidation, by the evolutionary science of the late nineteenth century." However, World War II and the reaction against fascism and Nazism led to widespread questioning of race-based theories. By the 1940s, McGregor writes, "the inevitability of extinction" of the Australian aboriginals "was as much contested as conceded," and the "doomed race theory was itself heading toward extinction" (x–xii).

Between the early 1800s and the 1930s the belief that most or all primitive races were doomed, rarely contested even by would-be saviors of indigenous peoples, became a mantra for the advocates of British imperial expansion and American manifest destiny. It is, for instance, virtually an axiom in *The Colonies of England* (1849), by the parliamentary radical J. A. Roebuck:

> I say, that for the mass, the sum of human enjoyment to be derived from this globe which God has given to us, it is requisite for us to pass over the original tribes that we find existing in the separate lands which we colonize. . . . When the European comes in contact with any other type of man, that other type disappears. . . . Let us not shade our eyes, and pretend not to see this result. (138)

It is also a key theme in more conservative paeans to "Anglo-Saxondom" and the British Empire, including Charles Wentworth Dilke's *Greater Britain* (1868) and James Anthony Froude's *Oceana* (1886). For Dilke, a necessary result of "the grandeur of our race" and the salutary spread of "Saxondom" around the globe is the disappearance of the Australian, Tasmanian, New Zealand, and North American aboriginals (1:vii–viii). In Canada and the United States "the Red Indians have no future. In twenty years there will scarcely be one of pure blood alive" (1:125). In New Zealand, the Maori "numbered 200,000" in 1840, but "they number 20,000" thirty years later (1:126).[7] Because of their faculty for imitation, Africans fare better than the "conservative" and rigid "American savage" (1:128); it is more difficult for Dilke to explain the vanishing of the Maori, both because he believes them to be more flexible than "the Red Indians" and because, in his view, they have not been subjected to genocide as have the Tasmanian and Australian aboriginals.

For his part, Froude contemplates with apparent equanimity a future in which the entire planet has been tamed and Anglo-Saxonized:

> It is with the wild races of human beings as with wild animals, and birds, and trees, and plants. Those only will survive who can domesticate themselves into

servants of the modern forms of social development. The lion and the leopard, the eagle and the hawk, every creature of earth or air, which is wildly free, dies off or disappears; the sheep, the ox, the horse, the ass accepts his bondage and thrives and multiplies. So it is with man. The negro submits to the conditions, becomes useful, and rises to a higher level. The Red Indian and the Maori pine away as in a cage, sink first into apathy and moral degradation, and then vanish. (300)

Froude expresses an astounding faith in "social development" or progress, according to which slavery improves "the negro." What cannot be tamed will have to "vanish." The telos of "social development" is the total subjugation of nature, entailing the disappearance of wilderness and all wild creatures, including "wildly free" human beings.

Partly by refusing to elegize the vanishing tribes and wilderness, the colonial surveys by Roebuck, Froude, and Dilke sing the praises of the all-conquering Anglo-Saxon race in epic mode. In 1872 the Reverend John George Wood published a different sort of survey, his "comprehensive" *Uncivilized Races of Men in All Countries of the World*. Perhaps more reliably than works that aim to be original, popular surveys like Wood's express widely held assumptions and beliefs about race, culture, and progress.[8] In any event, Wood expresses an elegiac urgency about his project, one shared by many other experts and observers: because "the uncivilized races" are rapidly disappearing, ethnology becomes a salvage enterprise, just as Clifford declares it to be, aiming to record as much information as possible about doomed peoples and cultures. "For many reasons we cannot but regret that entire races of men," writes Wood, "possessing many fine qualities, should be thus passing away; but it is impossible not to perceive that they are but following the order of the world, the lower race preparing a home for the higher" (790). Here nature itself ("the order of the world," whether divine or Darwinian) has ordained a course of events whereby the blameless progress of civilization can occur only through the vanishing of "the lower race."

Like Froude and countless others, Wood compares "savages" to wild animals. About the Australian aboriginals, Wood says "they occupied precisely the same relative position toward the human race as do the lion, tiger, and leopard toward the lower animals, and suffered in consequence from the same law of extinction" (790). Wood's logic is fuzzy in more ways than one (for instance, "lower animals" such as toads or lice do not disappear just because they are "lower"), but his meaning is clear enough. The coming of Europeans to Australia has not caused or even hastened the destruction of the aboriginals, Wood thinks, but might instead have been beneficial to them—if they had only been willing and able to take advantage of "the superior knowledge of the white man" (790). Alas, the aboriginals were unwilling and perhaps unable to do so:

> Instead of seizing upon these new [European] means of procuring the three great necessaries of human life, food, clothing, and lodging, they not only refused to employ them, but did their best to drive them out of the country, murdering the colonists, killing their cattle, destroying their crops, and burning their houses. (790)

Savages, in short, practice savagery; the Australian aboriginals, because they are so very savage, are destroying themselves, something they were in the process of doing even before the advent of Europeans:

> I have . . . shown that we can introduce no vice in which the savage is not [already] profoundly versed, *and feel sure that the cause of extinction lies within the savage himself,* and ought not to be attributed to the white man, who comes to take the place which the savage has practically vacated. (Wood, 791; my emphasis)

According to Wood, savagery everywhere is self-exterminating, a mournful but also hopeful view for a clergyman who identifies savagery with sin.

In his multivolume *Races of Mankind* (1873), another popularizer, Robert Brown, indicates that disease and infertility are causes of "the decay of wild races," but he also makes it plain that violence from whites is an equally important cause. Brown quotes George Augustus Selwyn, Bishop of New Zealand:

> They had heard it said that it was a law of Nature that the coloured race should melt away before the advance of civilisation. He would tell them where

that law was registered: it was registered in hell, and its agents were those
whom Satan made twofold more the children of hell than himself. (3:199)

Although Selwyn's "language is somewhat forcible, even for a Colonial bishop," Brown writes, it is nevertheless true: "The disappearance
of wild races before the civilised is, for the greater part, as explicable
as the destruction of wild animals before civilised sportsmen" (3:199).
After examining the main causes of their "disappearance" including
what is today called genocide, Brown writes that the only way to preserve "savage races" would be "by keeping away from them, and leaving them in that condition . . . which they are best able to occupy; for
where one is benefited and ameliorated by civilisation a thousand are
ruined . . . resulting sooner or later in . . . utter extinction" (3:220–21).

Those who, like Brown and Darwin, carefully examined the "fate"
of primitive races, stressed several factors besides savage customs: the
violence of the colonizers, of course; disease; infertility; and alter-
ations in environments and ways of living. Culturally, as well as biologically, the races seemed to be very different from one another; perhaps not all of them were doomed, so perhaps some could be saved or
could save themselves. Thus, to many observers, Native Americans
seemed destined for extinction because they were wild, free, and apparently incapable of becoming civilized. In contrast, African slaves
were often held to be thriving in slavery, though that did not prevent
many observers from believing that "the blacks" would also eventually vanish—at least from the United States or the Western Hemisphere (Frederickson, 154–59, 245–52). But most sub-Saharan African
"tribes" or "races" such as the Ashantis and Zulus were not usually
viewed as slated for extinction.

Especially on colonial frontiers in Australia, New Zealand, South
Africa, and North America, there were many rationalizers and even
advocates of the extermination of native populations. Their racist and
imperialist arguments frequently entail denunciations of humanitarian attempts to protect indigenous peoples as misguided sentimentalism. Clergymen and missionaries such as Selwyn and the Reverend
John Philip in South Africa were often the bane of white colonizers.
The rationalizers and sometimes proponents of genocide, however,
included many who were humane on other issues such as slavery.
Thus, though highly critical of slavery in his *American Notes*, Charles
Dickens, in his 1853 article "The Noble Savage," declared: "a savage

[is] something highly desirable to be civilized off the face of the earth" (337). So, too, in 1872, Anthony Trollope wrote that the "doom" of the Australian aboriginals "is to be exterminated; and the sooner that their doom be accomplished,—so that there be no cruelty—the better it will be for civilisation" (*Australia*, 2:87). And in his 1870 essay "The Noble Red Man," Mark Twain denied any nobility to the ordinary "Indian," declaring him to be "nothing but a poor, filthy, naked scurvy vagabond, whom to exterminate were a charity to the Creator's worthier insects and reptiles" (443).

Like Dilke, Trollope traveled to all the major outposts of the British Empire and wrote several hefty travelogues, in which he repeated the claim that most aboriginals were inevitably perishing, not so much through violence and disease as apparently through mere proximity to civilization. The one exception, Trollope thought, was South Africa, which "is a country of black men,—and not of white men . . . and it will continue to be so" (*South Africa*, 2:332). But in Australia, Canada, and New Zealand the reverse was the case:

> There we have gone with our ploughs and with our brandy, with all the good and with all the evil which our civilization has produced, and throughout the lands the native races have perished by their contact with us. They have withered by commune with us as the weaker weedy grasses of Nature's first planting wither and die wherever come the hardier plants, which science added to nature has produced. (*South Africa*, 2:332).

Like the Reverend John Wood, Trollope treats "Nature" rather than imperialism as the primary gardener or weeder of peoples ("science" comes later). And also like Wood, he adds that he is "not among those who say that this [perishing] has been caused by our cruelty":

> It has often been that we have struggled our very best to make our landing on a shore an unmixed blessing to those to whom we have come. In New Zealand we strove hard for this;—but in New Zealand the middle of the next century will probably hear of the existence of some solitary last Maori. (*South Africa*, 2:332–33)

Today's minimizers of what Zygmunt Bauman calls "modern genocide" echo Trollope and Wood when they attribute most of the "withering away" of indigenous populations to factors other than violence and imperialism.[9] Smallpox and other diseases did indeed kill millions, but, as Jared Diamond argues in *Guns, Germs, and Steel*, so, too, did modern technology, especially guns.[10] Further, minimizers often underestimate the initial size of indigenous populations.[11] One long-accepted minimalist estimate of the population of North American Indians was a mere 1 million. More accurate estimates today multiply that number by at least nine and perhaps as much as eighteen times or more, so that, Ward Churchill declares, "there may have been as many as 18.5 million people inhabiting pre-invasion North America" (*A Little Matter*, 135). Thus, too, well into the twentieth century, the standard figure for the number of Australian aboriginals at the time of the First Fleet in 1788 was 150,000. According to the economic historian Ned Butlin, however, we should perhaps multiply that estimate by ten. Though Butlin's estimate may, as he acknowledges, be too high, it is certainly closer to the mark than was *terra nullius*, the Latin phrase for "nobody's land," which became legal doctrine in Australia until it was struck down by the High Court in the Eddie Mabo land rights case of 1992 (Reynolds, *Law*, 12–14, 186–88).[12]

Minimizers insist, however, that extinction discourse was and is hyperbolic. Certainly it claimed both fatality and finality for its predictions. In part, such exaggeration reflects the rapidity and magnitude of indigenous population declines; in many contexts it seemed sadly realistic to expect demographic collapse to be total. Moreover, in specific cases—the Tasmanians, for example—total extinction did occur.[13] In part, however, the emphasis on fatality and finality also expressed the utopianism of "modern genocide." As in Froude's *Oceana*, once rid of savagery, the world would be a better place, entirely civilized.[14]

The passages from Dilke, Froude, Wood, and Trollope exemplify Bauman's claim that "modern genocide, like modern culture in general, is a gardener's job":

> It [genocide] is just one of the many chores that people who treat society as a garden need to undertake. If garden design defines its weeds, there are weeds wherever there is a garden. And weeds are to be exterminated. . . . All visions of society-as-garden define parts of the social habitat as human weeds. (92)

Just so, in *Evolution and Ethics* (1890), Thomas Henry Huxley employs gardening as a metaphor for colonization. Huxley's key example is Tasmania, a colony from which the aboriginals were supposedly totally eradicated by 1876, so he clearly has in mind the elimination of unwanted savages, along with unwanted flora and fauna. Huxley was far from alone among Victorian scientists and intellectuals in believing that "the process of colonisation presents analogies to the formation of a garden which are highly instructive" (Huxley, 9:16).

Huxley's use of the gardening trope is not ironic, just standard social Darwinism. In *Modernity and the Holocaust*, Bauman's stress on the significance of that metaphor points to both the ordinariness and the utopianism involved in Nazism and, more generally, in "modern genocide," which is

> *genocide with a purpose*. Getting rid of the adversary is not an end in itself. It is a means to an end: a necessity that stems from the ultimate objective, a step that one has to take if one wants ever to reach the end of the road. *The end itself is a grand vision of a better, and radically different, society*. Modern genocide is an element of social engineering, meant to bring about a social order conforming to the design of the perfect society. (91)

Bauman believes that the Nazi holocaust was unique in several ways but not that "modern genocide" was a one-time affair or that it has ended. On the contrary, it has been and is likely to continue to be "an element" in the process of modernization, or what Froude calls "social development."

Bauman suggests that modernization or "social development" as such is genocidal.[15] Others—Frantz Fanon, Jean-Paul Sartre, Hannah Arendt—have claimed that imperialism is genocidal. These two large-scale, inexorable historical processes cannot be easily differentiated from each other. Further, while the gardening metaphor implies intention on the part of the gardeners, and while many definitions of genocide stress intentionality (typically the conscious decision of a government or state to eliminate an unwanted race or group from its territory), the idea that imperialist expansion and globalizing modernization are inherently genocidal renders moot the legalistic question of intention. Certainly in the British and North American contexts, governments ordinarily did not plan or promote racial exterminations. On the contrary, though often to little or no effect, they typically opposed the violence that white colonizers inflicted on indigenous peoples.

Dark Vanishings analyzes extinction discourse in the contexts of several major British colonies, the United States, and Polynesia. The next chapter analyzes the three main types of scientific discourse that, prior to Darwinism, shaped the discourse about primitive races and their "doom": natural history, political economy, and early ethnology or race-science. Buffon and other Enlightenment natural historians constructed hierarchic taxonomies of the races that continued to be influential, albeit hotly debated, down to Darwin and beyond. Geology, moreover, was turning up massive evidence about the age of the world and of mankind which did not square with the Bible and which also indicated that thousands of species existed only in the fossil record. In his best-selling *Vestiges of the Natural History of Creation* (1844), Robert Chambers summarized many of these new discoveries and ideas and gave currency to the "development" of species and races; among other notions, Chambers believed that the "lower" races were the evolutionary stepping-stones to the "higher," Caucasian race. Early ethnologists such as James Cowles Prichard and Robert Knox also believed that primitive races were inevitably perishing. And political economy, especially through the influence of Malthus's *Essay on Population*, depicted savagery as supremely irrational and, indeed, self-extinguishing.

Chapter 3 turns to North America and the vast literature about "the vanishing Indian." It samples white responses to the "red race" from Puritan times through the revolutionary era and on to the development of an American tradition of ethnology. It notes the importance of extinction discourse in the debates on the Indian removal policy of the 1830s and then focuses on treatments of the "vanishing tribes" theme in fictional form, notably in Cooper's *Last of the Mohicans*.

The fourth chapter examines the emergence of the humanitarian variety of extinction discourse in the context of British debates over slavery and South Africa. Key figures include the parliamentary leader of the abolitionist crusade, Thomas Fowell Buxton; the Reverend John Philip, who in 1819 went to South Africa to superintend the outposts of the London Missionary Society; and Thomas Hodgkin, the Quaker founder and mainstay of the Aborigines Protection Society. Although the Bushmen and Hottentots were often declared to be en route to extinction, other African "races"—the Xhosas, the Zulus, Bantu peoples more generally—were clearly not vanishing; on the contrary, their alleged invasions of South African space were held by some defenders of both Boer and British colonization to be a main cause of the demise of their supposedly "weaker" or "unfit" neighbors.

I then turn, in chapter 5, to Ireland and the Irish Famine of 1845–50. English and Scottish commentators often likened the Irish to primitive races elsewhere in the world. Further, some, especially Irish nationalists, have viewed the Famine as a genocidal event. Both before and after the Famine, many of the elements of extinction discourse were applied to Ireland, as in Trollope's novel *Castle Richmond*. And the Famine, which killed more than one million people and caused the emigration of perhaps two million, was a glaring instance of mass extinction—indeed, one right on the doorstep of the same governmental officials who were worrying about the fate of other races besides the Irish.

In the case of Australia, the subject of chapter 6, the Tasmanian genocide in particular was both well publicized and seemingly clear-cut. It served as the key example for Darwin when he turned to the issue of the extinction of primitive races in *Descent of Man*. And it involved an important case of humanitarian intervention—the so-called "friendly mission" of George Augustus Robinson—as well as various scientific efforts both to understand what had happened and to preserve the remains of the last Tasmanians. On the mainland, meanwhile, efforts to protect and convert the aboriginals proved extraordinarily difficult, as the failure of the Reverend Lancelot Threlkeld's mission illustrates.

Chapter 7 deals with the New Zealand Maori and other Pacific Island peoples. Tahiti, Hawaii, Samoa, and the Marquesas were often at first viewed as tropical paradises, as in Herman Melville's *Typee*. From the 1790s missionaries to Polynesia and Melanesia encountered and tried to eradicate savage customs—infanticide, cannibalism, human sacrifice—that they saw as diabolical and as a primary reason for depopulation. In the late 1800s and early 1900s literary travelers—Robert Louis Stevenson, Jack London, Mark Twain among them—depicted ruined paradises, decimated by imported diseases, firearms, and alcohol. In the case of New Zealand, according to the historian James Belich, "It was sometimes argued that Europeans had no role at all to play in the fading away of the Maori; that the process was well advanced before Europeans arrived" (*Victorian Interpretation*, 324). But this was no different, except in emphasis, from extinction discourse elsewhere in the British Empire.

The theories about the races of mankind and their evolution espoused by Darwin, Huxley, Alfred Russel Wallace, and their followers are the topic of the chapter 8. Instead of affirming the biological essentialism of the earlier race scientists, Darwin and his allies did just the reverse: evolution by natural selection meant that species, races, and even individuals were the creatures of contingency rather than of either design or biological essence. Moreover, the races were one species, not several, and the similarities among the races were far greater than the differences. Nevertheless, the Darwinian view of the future of primitive races was just as grim as that of most of the pre-Darwinians. Social Darwinists argued that nature's constant laws mandated the extinction of all unfit creatures and species to make room for new, supposedly fitter ones.

Paradoxically one end point of extinction discourse, from the late nineteenth century on, was widespread anxiety about the degeneration or even extinction of the white race, as in Madison Grant's *Passing of the Great Race* (1908). Evident in the eugenics movement, this anxiety is the focus of the concluding chapter. Anxiety about the future of all the races of mankind—indeed, of the entire human species—was always implicit in extinction discourse. The pervasiveness of that anxiety in the 1800s can be suggested by a glance at novels by two authors, Mary Shelley and H. G. Wells, from opposite ends of the century. In Shelley's *The Last Man* (1826), the protagonist, Lionel Verney, witnesses the extinction of the entire human race. This catastrophe takes the form of imperialist expansion running in reverse: the plague that exterminates all mankind is, as Verney puts it, "of old a native of the East, sister of the tornado, the earthquake, and the simoom" (184). Further, Verney catches the plague from a dying "negro" in London. Soon there is no longer any escape to such "colonies" as "New Holland [Australia], Van Diemen's Land [Tasmania], and the Cape of Good Hope" (185). With England already "desolate," an invasion by diseased and starving Irish paupers commences, "burning—laying waste—murdering. . . . They talked of taking London, conquering England" (233). Shelley's tale of Gothic horror, in short, returns the "fatal impact" of imperialism abroad to its home base; *The Last Man* is in part an early instance of a reverse invasion story, as well as a fantasy about the ultimate extinction of the human species.

In *The War of the Worlds* (1896), Wells imagines another "last man" scenario involving an invasion of Martians. The extraterrestrials threaten to extinguish mankind before falling prey themselves to a disease to which they have no immunity. Wells declared that the inspiration for *War of the Worlds* came from a conversation with his

brother, Frank, about "the discovery of Tasmania by the Europeans—
a very frightful discovery for the native Tasmanians!" (quoted in
Bergonzi, 124).

At the start of the twenty-first century, with as many genocidal conflicts occurring around the world as at any time in the past, and with
various apocalyptic scenarios and predictions of the extinction of the
entire human race a familiar feature of global mass culture, "last of
the race" and "last man" fantasies such as those by Shelley and Wells
do not seem far-fetched.[16] They certainly would not have seemed far-
fetched to the Tasmanians or to members of other "primitive races"
over the last several centuries.

2. Pre-Darwinian Theories on the Extinction of Primitive Races

Before the publication of Darwin's *Origin of Species* (1859), three types of supposedly scientific discourse dealt with the extinction of primitive races. The first was "natural history," a broad rubric that embraced both geology and biology. The taxonomies of organisms offered by Carl von Linneaus, Georges-Louis Leclerc de Buffon, Johann Friedrich Blumenbach, and Georges Cuvier included hierarchizing accounts of the human races, with the white or "Caucasian" race leading the parade. Further, through the geological "record of the rocks," massive evidence of the extinction of numerous nonhuman species was being unearthed, though Linnaeus, Thomas Jefferson, and many others resisted it well into the nineteenth century (Banton, 3–4). For Darwin and the Victorians, the key text about the geological history of the earth, about fossils, and therefore about the extinction of species was Charles Lyell's *Principles of Geology* (1830–33).

The second, emergent science that contributed to extinction discourse was economics. Especially in the second, 1803 edition of his *Essay on Population*, the Reverend Thomas Robert Malthus offers a wide range of information and speculation about the population dynamics of both civilized and primitive societies. Although he does not emphasize race, Malthus has, for good reason, been called "the founding father of scientific racism" (Chase, 6). For Malthus, both "savages" and the feckless, starving Irish are key examples. Because of its emphasis on the causes of depopulation as well as overpopulation, Malthus's *Essay* has much to say about human mass extinctions. In the preface to *Origin*, moreover, Darwin credits Malthus as the main source for his own central theme of "the struggle for existence" among both human and nonhuman populations.

The third, at least nascent science concerned with racial extinctions was anthropology. In the eighteenth century the study of human cultures and customs took the form of moral philosophy or natural history or some combination of the two, as in Scottish Enlightenment history. But it gained increasing disciplinary distinctness and influence from the 1830s on, partly through the pressures of colonial expansion, which lent urgency to attempts to understand the behaviors of indigenous peoples throughout the world. Through roughly the first half of the nineteenth century, however, anthropology was mainly concerned with the physical, mental, and hierarchical differences among the races (whether considered as separate species or not). In 1842 the Ethnological Society of London emerged as a separate enterprise from the Aborigines Protection Society, and the same year saw the founding of the American Ethnological Society. In both contexts, the shift toward science entailed a move away from earlier humanitarian interest in the fates of primitive peoples (Stocking, 273; Stepan, 45–46).

All three of these supposedly scientific, often overlapping discourses supported a view of savagery as a Hobbesian state of nature, a *bellum omnium contra omnes* in which the strong exterminated or enslaved the weak. For natural historians, economists, and ethnologists alike, savagery itself was often, by definition, a sufficient explanation for the extinction of some, if not all, savage races. Writing about scientific attempts to explain or explain away the extinction of the Tasmanian aborigines, John Cove notes that, in terms of their ideological meaning and utility, there was no difference between those attempts and "religious explanations." What the two types of explanation, scientific and religious, "had in common was a kind of fatalism which underwrote an uncritical stance toward European colonization and government policy. If any human agency had to be blamed for negative consequences, it was the Aborigines themselves who either rejected God's commands or were innately inferior and therefore unable to compete successfully with Europeans" (Cove, 44–45).

Eighteenth-century natural history posed four basic questions about human races. First, were the different races mere varieties of a single species or were they separately created, multiple species? Monogenesis or the single-species thesis was consistent with the biblical account of creation; the different races could then be seen as originating at the time of the flood, with Noah's curse on his son Ham producing, by degeneration, the Negro or African race. But polygenesis could also be reconciled with the Bible, though not so easily, by positing the existence of "pre-Adamite" peoples (Popkin, 140–42). The Bible, then, only pertained to Semitic and Caucasian peoples, not to Africans, Native Americans, Mongolians, and so on. Second, just how many distinct races were there? Were some races primary and relatively unchanging, while others were mixed, intermediate, and changing or even dwindling away of their own accord? Third, what were the laws or natural causes governing the purity versus the hybridization of races? Was racial mixing a version of degeneration and also, perhaps, of the dying out of certain races, as these were absorbed into the "blood" or "stock" of vigorous, more populous races? And fourth, what was the hierarchy of races in historical, moral, intellectual, and religious terms? Which were the superior and which the inferior races? Correlatively, and most important in relation to extinction discourse, were some or all the inferior races incapable of progress—that is, of becoming civilized?

In *On the Natural History of Mankind* (1775) Blumenbach opined, partly through comparing the shapes of skulls from various races, that there were five primary races: "Caucasian, Mongolian, Ethiopian, American, and Malay" (264). That the different races all formed one species he saw no reason to doubt (276). He was also less inclined than many later natural historians to attribute simplistic moral or intellectual traits to the different races. Thus, about Africans, Blumenbach writes:

> The assertion that is made about the Ethiopians, that they come nearer the apes than other men, I willingly allow so far as this, that it is in the same way that the solid-hoofed . . . variety of the domestic sow may be said to come nearer to the horse than other sows. But how little weight is for the most part to be attached to this sort of comparison is clear from this, that there is scarcely any other out of the principal varieties of mankind, of which one nation or

other, and that too by careful observers, has not been compared, as far as the face goes, with the apes. (271)

Blumenbach's version of craniology and physical anthropology served as a model for other pre-Darwinian natural historians, including Georges Cuvier, Peter Camper, Anders Retzius, Count Gobineau, Charles Hamilton Smith, James Prichard, Robert Knox, and the "American School" of Samuel Morton, Josiah Nott, and George Glidden. Camper contributed the measurement of facial angle as a supposedly scientific way to distinguish the races, and Retzius added the "cephalic index," the basis for later craniology or the measurement of skulls and hence supposedly of intelligence (Haller; Gould, *Mismeasure*; Jahoda, 71–74). Published in the mid-1850s, Gobineau's multivolume *Inequality of Human Races* represents one "culmination of pre-Darwinian ideas" (Barkan, 16), whereas, in the United States, Nott and Glidden's *Types of Mankind* (1854) represents another. These works point ahead to social Darwinism and the eugenics movement, which carried over into the first half of the twentieth century and are still evident in versions of sociobiology, as in the recent controversy over the "bell curve."[1]

Cuvier, less cautious than Blumenbach about attributing moral and intellectual traits to the different races, identifies three primary "varieties" of the single species, *Homo sapiens*, ranging a number of secondary types among these. His three main varieties are "1, the fair, or Caucasian variety; 2, the yellow, or Mongolian; 3, the Negro, or Ethiopian" (1:97). He is not sure whether "the American" variety is primary or intermediate, between Mongolian and Caucasian, and so, too, regarding the Malays and Papuans. For Cuvier, the Caucasian variety "is chiefly distinguished by the beautiful form of the head," and from it "have sprung the most civilized nations, and such as have most generally exercised dominion over the rest of mankind" (1:97). In contrast, though the Mongolian "race" has "formed mighty empires" in the past, "its civilization has long appeared stationary" (1:97). And the "negro race," with its "compressed cranium," "manifestly approaches to the monkey tribe. The hordes of which this variety is composed have always remained in a state of complete barbarism" (1:97). As with Adam Smith and the economists, for Cuvier there are three basic social conditions, correlated with his three primary races: progressive (civilized); stationary (semi-civilized); and nonprogressive (savage or completely "barbaric").

Cuvier rejected notions of evolution, but, given the temporal hierarchy involved in any conception of progress, it was easy for later race scientists to assume that one stage or "race" might develop into the next, though also that regression could occur as readily as progress. History, it seemed, was primarily the tale of the rise and fall of civilizations, which could be explained in terms of racial difference. Even if present-day savages had not developed, the barbaric ancestors of civilized peoples—the Anglo-Saxons, for example—had had the ability to progress to civilization, which made the seemingly nonprogressive status of present-day savages appear all the more permanent and hopeless.

The temporal paradigm also suggested to some theorists that the different races of humanity were, so to speak, mere stepping-stones along a linear, progressive route the white race alone was able to travel. Thus, in *Vestiges of Creation* (1844), Robert Chambers speculated that the Negro, Malay, Indian, and Mongolian races were all obsolescent stages in "the development of the highest, or Caucasian type" (307).[2] Why those lower races should continue to exist after their primary function—the emergence of the Caucasian race—had been fulfilled, Chambers did not try to explain. Nevertheless, he believed that the human races belonged to a single species and that civilizations had many independent points of origin among all the races (and not just in the "Caucasian type").

Chambers also argued that the general tendency of human as of cosmic history was progressive and not retrogressive, though he maintained that the development of the human races (as opposed to stages of civilization) had been retrogressive. "The greater part" of humanity, he writes, "must be considered as having lapsed or declined from the original type":

In the Caucasian or Indo European family alone has the primitive organization been improved upon. The Mongolian, Malay, American, and Negro, comprehending perhaps five-sixths of mankind, are degenerate. (309)

Chambers based this opinion partly on a racialized version of embryology, which demonstrated, to his satisfaction at least, that embryos recapitulated not only the phylogeny of different species of animals but also of the different races of humans, starting with the most infantile (the Negro race) and ending with the most mature (the Caucasian) (308). This argument suggested, in turn, that the outcome of historical "development" or "progress" involved the Caucasian race supplanting the earlier, less "perfect" races:

> Look at the progress even now making over the barbaric parts of the earth by the best examples of the Caucasian type, promising not only to fill up the waste places, but to supersede the imperfect nations already existing. Who can tell what progress may be made, even in a single century, towards reversing the proportions of the perfect and imperfect types? (310)

Here imperialist expansion and the extermination of indigenous populations is quite explicitly identified with the biological progress of the human species.

During or perhaps before the voyage of the *Beagle*, Darwin concluded that "the varieties of man seem to act on each other in the same way as different species of animals—the stronger always extirpating the weaker" (*Voyage*, 434). Writing about the fossil remains of numerous extinct creatures in South America, Darwin declares: "Certainly, no fact in the history of the world is so startling as the wide and repeated exterminations of its inhabitants" (*Voyage*, 175). Reading Lyell's *Principles of Geology* while studying those fossils, Darwin must have been all the more startled, because the extinction of species is one of Lyell's main themes. With Lyell clearly in mind, Darwin, in *The Origin of Species*, writes:

> No one can have marvelled more than I have done at the extinction of species. When I found in La Plata [Argentina] the tooth of a horse embedded with the remains of Mastadon, Megatherium, Toxodon, and other extinct monsters, which all co-existed with still living shells at a very late geological period, I was filled with astonishment. (450)

Fossils made the extinction of entire species and, indeed, genera highly legible, so Lyell and other geologists and natural historians, including Darwin, had to deal with that distressing issue. And for Lyell, as later for Darwin, it seemed logical to view the problem of the decline and possible extinction of primitive races in the same light as the extinction of species.

In his history of the concept of evolution, Peter Bowler notes that discoveries of the fossils of animals and plants for which there were no living counterparts, coupled with increasing geological knowledge about the "revolutions" or "catastrophes" that had altered the earth's surface, aroused great interest in the late eighteenth and early nineteenth centuries. "From Siberia came the remains of the woolly mammoth," writes Bowler, "an elephantlike creature so recently extinct that its bones were not truly fossilized" (115). At about the same time, the discovery in North America of the fossil remains of mastodons, creatures distinct from both mammoths and elephants, helped make "the fact of extinction . . . inescapable" (115).[3] Moreover, the "mammoth came from superficial gravel deposits that were very recent by geological standards, only a few thousand years old; but other fossils came from lower (and hence older) deposits, building up a picture of a *sequence* of extinct populations corresponding to each period of rock formation" (115). The most spectacular of extinct species were, however, the dinosaurs. Although the first recorded discovery of their remains occurred in the 1670s, they were clearly identified only in 1824, when the British geologist William Buckland described the gigantic carnivore that he dubbed *Megalosaurus* (Colbert, 12). Richard Owen provided the name for the lost species of giant lizards in 1841 (Colbert, 32–33), and ever since, Bowler notes, "Dinosauria" have been "symbols of the exotic nature of prehistoric life" (122).

The "sequence" of extinction among animal and plant populations implied a corresponding sequence, perhaps a progressive one, of their generation or origin (see Bowler, *Fossils and Progress*). But the explicit "record of the rocks" spoke of death, not life. In the chapters of *Principles of Geology* that deal with the extinction of numerous species through the "deep time" of natural history, Lyell stresses the propagation and diffusion of new, rival species as a primary cause of the diminution and, at times, total destruction of older ones. Although he does not cite Malthus, Lyell sees the biological realm in terms of an unavoidable "struggle" or "conflict" between competing organisms for territory and scarce resources. War and empire are two of Lyell's most frequent metaphors, even for competition among plants. For Lyell as for Malthus, moreover, the struggle over scarce resources is neither inherently progressive nor regressive (though it is nonetheless providential, the result of God's sagacious design). The "struggle for existence" is instead a zero-sum game interrupted only by the introduction of mankind into the well-designed but otherwise blind interplay of forces (mankind is a higher order of being because of the capacity to reason). But in general, according to Lyell, "the successive destruction of species [is] part of the regular and constant order of Nature" (265), and even mankind is not exempt from this destruction. Because it is simultaneously creative and destructive, however, Lyell is able to conclude, comfortingly, that nature is "a perfect harmony of design and unity of purpose" produced by "an Infinite and Eternal Being" (438).

If the stress of *Principles* is more on destruction than creativity, that is partly because "it is obviously more easy to prove that a species, once numerously represented in a given district, has ceased to be, than that some other which did not pre-exist has made its appearance" (295), but also partly because the divine plan is wrapped in mystery. Like other geologists of his time (including "catastrophists" such as Cuvier), Lyell accepts "deep time" rather than the foreshortened, miraculous account of creation in the Bible (Gould, *Time's Arrow*, 112–17). But "deep time" also means that the origins of the earth and life and their ultimate destination are beyond the reach of science, which can only formulate positive conclusions about what it can observe, inferring what occurred in the past and projecting into the future only on the basis of causes operative in the present. Lyell holds that the origin of new varieties within species, if not the origin of species themselves, can sometimes be observed, as can the general causes operative throughout both nature and time. But he was implacably opposed to the theory of the "transmutation" or evolution of species, at least as this theory was presented by Jean-Baptiste Lamarck. And he remained opposed to notions of species evolving or devolving into new species until Darwin's *Origin* persuaded him that species did indeed evolve through "natural selection"—though he still held out, in his 1863 *Antiquity of Man*, for a special dispensation for the human species, an exception that made Darwin "groan" (Bowler, 229).

Although in *Principles* the "perfect harmony" of nature is neither inherently progressive nor regressive, it undergoes, like a huge kaleidoscope, immense albeit mostly gradual changes using and re-using the same materials and causal agencies. Lyell is a proponent of "time's cycle" rather than "time's arrow," as Gould points out: "We may see, Lyell argues, an advance in design from fish to ichthyosaur to whale, but we view only the rising arc of a great circle that will come round again, not a linear path to progress" (*Time's Arrow*, 104). This makes Lyell's speculation about the future regeneration of extinct species intelligible, Gould notes, albeit closer to science fiction than to science. Writing about "the great year" or possible seasonal cycles of "deep time," Lyell opines:

> We might expect, therefore, in the summer of the "great year," . . . that there would be a great predominance of tree-ferns and plants allied to palms . . . [while] other forms now most common in temperate regions would almost disappear from the earth. Then might those genera of animals return, of which the memorials are preserved in the ancient rocks of our continents. The huge iguanodon might reappear in the woods, and the ichthyosaur in the sea, while the pterodactyle might flit again through umbrageous groves of tree-ferns. (67)

Lyell imagines the future, at least in this passage, as an edenic Jurassic Park. Whether Lyell's vision of the return of the dinosaurs provided him or any of his readers with some sort of reassurance, especially when acknowledging the overwhelming evidence of the extinction of numerous species throughout the earth's history, it did provide Sir Henry de la Beche with an opportunity for satire. Gould reproduces de la Beche's caricature of Lyell as "the future Professor Ichthyosaurus," lecturing to other ichthyosaurs about the skull of an extinct "lower order of animals." The skull is human, as the title caption of the cartoon emphasizes: "AWFUL CHANGES. Man Found Only in a Fossil State. — Reappearance of Ichthyosauri" (*Time's Arrow*, 98, fig. 4.1).

Though perhaps some consolation could be derived from fantasizing about the resurrection of the dinosaurs, and also from mankind's special status as the only reasoning animal, Lyell's uniformitarianism meant that the causes of the extinction of dinosaurs and other animal and plant species were operative on the human species and its various races. The main cause Lyell cites is "war," or violent inter-species competition, which operates also between human races. In one hypothetical example that Darwin in South America may have found "startling," Lyell asks his readers to "suppose every living thing to be destroyed in the western hemisphere, both on the land and in the ocean." "Permission" is then "given to man to people this great desert, by transporting into it animals and plants from the eastern hemisphere." This thought-experiment seems to be a revision of the story of Noah. In any event, Lyell proceeds: "Now the result . . . of such a mode of colonizing would correspond exactly, so far as regards the grouping of animals and plants, with that now observed throughout the globe" (252). Lyell reinforces the idea of colonization in various ways, including his frequent use of "races" as a synonym for "species"—perhaps most tellingly in the phrase "lost races" (255).

The subject of "lost races" was, no doubt, more the province of archaeology than of geology. But like the fossil "record of the rocks," with its insistence on the extinction of numerous species of plants and animals, early archaeology unearthed the remains of entire societies and even civilizations that had perished. The *memento mori* theme that is so prevalent a feature of romantic literature reflected both geological and archaeological discoveries, as in Volney's *Ruins* and Shelley's "Ozymandias." Even the "prehistoric" forerunners of the English race were mysterious, lost tribes, who, for some apocalyptic speculators, were none other than the lost tribes of Israel. Writing about "the very high antiquity of the Wiltshire barrows," Sir Richard Colt Hoare declared at the start of the nineteenth century that there was no evidence "respecting the tribes to whom they appertained" (quoted in Daniel, 28). So, too, according to Colt Hoare, the ancient remains at New Grange in Ireland were a mystery involving a lost or, at least, non-identifiable race or "tribe":

> I shall not unnecessarily trespass upon the time and patience of my readers in endeavouring to ascertain what tribes first peopled this country; nor to what nation the construction of this singular monument may reasonably be attributed for, I fear, both its authors and its original destination will ever remain unknown. (Quoted in Daniel, 28)

And so also for Stonehenge.

If the ancient history of Great Britain was a "prehistory," occupied by unknown, vanished "tribes" and perhaps races, then it was only to be expected that the history of modern primitive races would also be a story of vanishing into the ruins, if they were capable even of producing ruins. Moreover, for later reconstructors of human "deep time" and "prehistory" such as John Lubbock, Edward Burnett Tylor, Henry Maine, and J. F. McLennan, surviving primitive races *were* prehistory, or at any rate were the best evidence of what prehistory had been like. As Lubbock put it in *Pre-Historic Times*, "the Van Diemaner [Tasmanian] and South American are to the antiquary what the opossum and the sloth are to the geologist" (429–30). And sometimes when primitive peoples did produce ruins, such as the North American Indian mounds and the remains of Great Zimbabwe, it was often held that these could not have been constructed by existing savages—that they must instead be the relics of superior races which the existing savages had somehow expelled or exterminated. The motif of the discovery of savages living in the midst of a lost civilization whose origin and demise they do not understand became a staple of imperialist adventure fiction and its spin-offs into early science fiction, as in several of the romances of H. Rider Haggard (Becker).

To return to Lyell, the literal colonization of new territory by human populations is, he asserts, a major cause of the "extirpation" of many species and the introduction of new ones. "The kangaroo and the emu are retreating rapidly before the progress of colonization in Australia," he writes; "and it scarcely admits of doubt, that the general cultivation of that country must lead to the extirpation of both" (272). Lyell does not explicitly conclude that the "extirpation" of kangaroos would contribute to the extirpation of the aboriginals. In *The Voyage of the Beagle*, however, Darwin draws that conclusion when he notes that "the number of aborigines is rapidly decreasing" and then links their decline to "the gradual extinction of the wild animals" (433). But besides the destruction especially of kangaroos, besides the great importance of diseases as extinguishers of the aboriginals, besides the bad influence and violence of Europeans, and even besides such savage customs as infanticide, Darwin believes that there is also "some more mysterious agency [of destruction] generally at work" in Australia, a mystery he would attempt to solve in *Descent of Man*.

After mentioning the destruction of kangaroos, Lyell briefly considers the destruction of "savage tribes," including the aboriginals of Australia or "New Holland":

A faint image of the certain doom of a species less fitted to struggle with some new condition in a region which it previously inhabited, and where it has to contend with a more vigorous species, is presented by the extirpation of savage tribes of men by the advancing colony of some civilized nation. In this case the contest is merely between two different *races*, each gifted with equal capacities of improvement—between two varieties . . . of a species which exceeds all others in its aptitude to accommodate its habits to the most extraordinary variations of circumstances. (291)

The phrase "gifted with equal capacities of improvement" suggests a humanitarian inclination in Lyell, and yet the extinction of the aboriginals is only a "faint image" of what goes on in nature all the time: it is "merely" a matter of the destruction of one "race" or "variety" of mankind by another. Lyell's understatements are an aspect of his rhetoric of scientific objectivity. He means, in part, that the extermination of a "race" of any species is not so serious a matter as the extermination of an entire species. He also implies that the "extirpation of savage tribes" by civilization is an aspect of the historical development or progress of the human species (presumably growing from worse to better, even though Lyell does not see progress as part of the general "order" of nature). Lyell concludes:

> Yet few future events are more certain than the speedy extermination of the Indians of North America and the savages of New Holland in the course of a few centuries, when these tribes will be remembered only in poetry and tradition. (291)

Although Lyell's uniformitarianism meant that the causes of the extinction of dinosaurs and other plants and animals were operative at least on the inferior, "savage" races of mankind, competition between the races through war and imperialism might seem to be a different, even a higher form of causation (because of mankind's great difference from all other animals). But not so: Lyell treats the extermination of one human race by another as no different in kind from the extermination of one animal or plant species by another. At the same time, he insists that, because such exterminations are going on all the time in the "perfect harmony" of nature, there is nothing to "repine" or feel guilty about in regard to war and empire. Although "the annihilation of a multitude of species has already been effected, and will continue to go on hereafter, in certain regions, in a still more rapid ratio, as the colonies of highly-civilized nations spread themselves over unoccupied lands" (276), it is all for the best, all part of the divine plan. Therefore, Lyell continues, "if we wield the sword of extermination as we advance, we have no reason to repine at the havoc committed" (276).

> We have only to reflect, that in thus obtaining possession of the earth by conquest, and defending our acquisitions by force, we exercise no exclusive prerogative. Every species which has spread itself from a small point over a wide

area, must, in like manner, have marked its progress by the diminution, or
the entire extirpation, of some other, and must maintain its ground by a successful struggle against the encroachments of other plants and animals.
(277)

If Lyell intended this argument to be consolatory or to absolve
himself and his readers from guilt about the liquidation of, say, the
Australian aboriginals, one reader whom he failed to console was
Tennyson. As is well known, Tennyson's vision of "nature red in tooth
and claw" in his great elegy, *In Memoriam* (1850), is a response largely
to Lyell's *Principles* with its lengthy and often graphic examination of
the "extirpation" of many species and also of "savage tribes." Tennyson writes:

> Are God and Nature then at strife,
>   That Nature lends such evil dreams?
>   So careful of the type she seems,
> So carcless of the single life.
>   (910)

But no! As Lyell demonstrated so thoroughly, "Nature" destroyed
"typcs" or species as well as "single lives" or individuals. Like Mary
Shelley's mad scientist, Nature created, apparently, only to destroy
her own creatures. Lyell may have been trying to affirm the cyclic
processes of nature as opposed to "time's arrow," or linear notions of
Lamarckian "transmutation," but Tennyson saw the endless cycles of
natural violcnce, of countless births leading only to countless deaths,
as his worst nightmare. And the demise of entire species compounded the nightmare:

> "So careful of the type?" but no.
>   From scarpèd cliff and quarried stone
>   She cries, "A thousand types are gone:
> I care for nothing, all shall go."
>   (911)

Even man, Nature's "last work, who seemed so fair," appears, from
the nadir of Tennyson's grief and despair, to be only

A monster then, a dream,
A discord. Dragons of the prime,
That tare each other in their slime,
Were mellow music matched with him.
(912)

In Memoriam thus offers another version of Jurassic Park, only this time the dinosaurs have not returned; they have been replaced by that greater monstrosity, mankind. Tennyson asks the obvious question that Lyell raises but, because of the limits he sets on scientific observation, declines to answer. What is the destiny of *Homo sapiens* in general? Is it, too, even in its supposedly superior, European form, headed inevitably to total extinction, albeit at some date so far in the future that this prospect did not seem particularly threatening to Lyell, accustomed as he was to geological "deep time" and "the great year" of nature? Or is *Homo sapiens*, though a single species, destined to evolve into a higher species? This is the consoling solution Tennyson reaches at the end of *In Memoriam*, by translating evolution into progress and his dead friend, Hallam, into the harbinger of "the crowning race." Or instead, is *Homo sapiens* destined to subdivide along racial lines—a possibility that Tennyson does not consider—so that supposedly inferior or "less fit" races like the Australian aboriginals will die out, while supposedly superior, "fit" races like the Anglo-Saxon will continue evolving until humanity surpasses itself and turns into what Edward Bulwer-Lytton called "the coming race"? Whatever the answers to these questions, Lyell's *Principles of Geology* had brought the evidence of the extinction of numerous animal and plant species to public notice. And he had applied that evidence to the Australian aboriginals in a way which suggested that their extinction, at least, if not that of *Homo sapiens* in general, was inevitable.

In *Dawn Island*, her 1845 propaganda fable for the Anti-Corn Law League, Harriet Martineau depicts a South Seas society starkly different from the happy, peaceful islanders in Herman Melville's *Typee*. Through their savage customs—warfare, infanticide, cannibalism—Martineau's savages have nearly succeeded in exterminating themselves. As the old priest Miava says, "The forest-tree shall grow; the coral shall spread . . . but man shall cease." Luckily, however, the "Higher Disclosure" arrives in the form of a British ship carrying seemingly miraculous commodities and the gospel of free trade. The conversion of the natives is nearly instantaneous, their bloody superstitions and customs giving way to commodity fetishism.

Like Martineau's other tales illustrating political economy, *Dawn Island* is a faithful if simplistic rendering of ideas drawn from Adam Smith, Malthus, Ricardo, and James Mill. Thus, in the fourth paragraph of *The Wealth of Nations*, Smith describes "the savage nations of hunters and fishers" as hard-working but extremely inefficient—so inefficient or "savage" that they are killing themselves off: "Such nations . . . are so miserably poor that, from mere want, they are frequently reduced . . . to the necessity sometimes of directly destroying, and sometimes of abandoning their infants, their old people, and those afflicted with diseases, to perish with hunger, or to be devoured by wild beasts" (1:2). Savagery, in short, is not just the poverty of nations; it is also the depopulation of them.

In the second, 1803 edition of his *Essay on Population*, Malthus's list of savage customs includes warfare, cannibalism, infanticide, and human sacrifice. It is small wonder that, from the perspective of political economy, savages are disappearing from a modernizing world. Given their savage customs, the only surprise is that they have not already depopulated. Though neither the natural historians nor the ethnologists reduce savage customs to a violent function of population control, well before Darwin they also, as in Lyell's *Principles*, portray social life, whether savage or civilized, as a "struggle for existence" that renders the liquidation of entire races normal rather than exceptional. In the antisocial condition called "savagery," the clash of races leads to the extermination of many populations. But civilization only completes the grim picture, because it perfects what savagery has already started—that is, the techniques of mass slaughter.

In much early economics as in *Dawn Island*, however, one supposedly peaceful antithesis of savagery that is also synonymous with civilization is "commerce," which, by definition, entails the use of money. Smith, David Ricardo, and James Mill treat precivilized peoples either as doomed or as proto-capitalists. Through the ages, notes Smith, "many different commodities" have been used as money: cattle, salt, shells, and so forth. But he adds: "there is at this day a village in Scotland where it is not uncommon . . . for a workman to carry nails *instead of money* to the baker's shop or the ale-house" (1:27; my emphasis). So, are the nails money or not? Smith usually identifies money with the precious metals and the bars or coins made from them. Money is only modern money, not nails or wampum; "savages" do not know the value of gold and silver (1:211); money is thus the measure not only of all values in exchange but also of civilization: "in this manner . . . money has become in all civilized nations the universal instrument of commerce" (1:32).

Ricardo also treats the use of money as dividing civilization from savagery (Stocking, 32). But he projects money onto savagery when, for instance, he imagines a hunter and a fisherman bartering a deer for a fish: "If a salmon were worth £1 and a deer £2, one deer would be worth two salmon," and so on (Ricardo, 16). Though Smith does not include price tags in his examples of barter, like Ricardo he treats precivilized peoples as proto-capitalists. "Every man . . . lives by exchanging, or becomes in some measure a merchant," he writes; hence every society "grows to be what is properly a commercial society" (1:26), unless it stalls or regresses in the universal march to capitalism. But if every individual pursues rational self-interest through exchange, then how can any society fail to progress? For Smith, there are three types of society: progressive, stationary, and declining. Many societies fall into one of the nonprogressive modes by failing to shed irrational customs that interfere with the natural impulse "to truck, barter, and exchange one thing for another" (1:17).[4]

When the early economists do not represent savage customs as impediments to progress, that is sometimes because they represent savages as having no customs, no law and order, no social organization. According to this old stereotype, savages ironically behave too much like capitalists—each looking out for himself alone—to advance toward civilization. Thus, in his 1836 essay, "Civilization," John Stuart Mill identifies savagery with an extreme sort of individualism: "The savage cannot bear to sacrifice, for any purpose, the satisfaction of his individual will" (152). In contrast, "the progress of civilization" is identical with "the progress of the power of cooperation" and "combination" (152). According to Mill:

> A savage tribe consists of a handful of individuals, wandering or thinly scattered over a vast tract of country. . . . In savage life there is no commerce, no manufactures, no agriculture, or next to none . . . each person shifts for himself; except in war (and even then very imperfectly), we seldom see any joint operations carried on by the union of many; nor do savages, in general, find much pleasure in each other's society. (149)

On what evidence the young Mill based his portrait of "savage life" is unclear, but he had plenty of precedents, including his father and Jeremy Bentham as well as the other early economists.

The 1798 edition of Malthus's *Essay on Population* devotes only a brief chapter to "the rudest state of mankind"; its main example is the "clouds of Barbarians" who overthrew Rome. But the second, 1803 edition offers a much fuller account of precivilized societies, based on extensive reading in such sources as Captain Cook's *Voyages* and David Collins's *Account of the Colony in New South Wales*. Malthus asks how primitive populations stay in balance with subsistence; his answer rebuts the glowing accounts of noble savages in Rousseau, Diderot, and others (Godelier, 134–35, 144–45).

Smith viewed population growth as a sign of progress, but Malthus rejects this old idea. For Malthus and later economists, there are two primary forms of negative value, antithetical to national wealth: debt and overpopulation. If it represents investment in productive forces, debt can become positive. But overpopulation is sheer waste. It was easy, moreover, to observe population exceeding subsistence just across the Irish Sea, and in the slums of London or Glasgow. But savage populations were not bursting at the seams. Bizarrely, in savagery, the problem of overpopulation took the shape of underpopulation, as on Martineau's Dawn Island. Malthus argues that, if it were not for their savage customs, savages would overpopulate just like the feckless Irish. For Malthus, savagery is that social condition in which population is brought violently into line with the subsistence available— barely—through hunting and gathering. When starvation does not do the job, then most of the other "checks" to population are at work, and the preventive checks equal savage customs: warfare, cannibalism, infanticide, human sacrifice. The purpose of savage customs is to ward off the positive checks of nature, especially famine. Savage customs, in short, are simultaneously irrational and strictly functionalist: to level population with subsistence.

For none of the early economists do savage customs instantiate value schemes different from that of capitalist Europe; there is no tropical paradise or primitive communism in any of them (cf. Herskovits, 230–31). Savage customs, bolstered by superstition, entail a suicidal pattern of brutality and self-extermination, counteracting reproduction. Thus the "constant state of warfare" among the Maori, Malthus says, would lead to race suicide if the Maori could manage it (174). Among the Australian aboriginals, the near self-destruction of that race is also the consequence of its savage customs. Malthus claims that the Australians "forcibly repress the rising generation" through "frequent wars ... and their perpetual contests with each other; [through] their strange spirit of retaliation and revenge, which prompts the midnight murder, and the frequent shedding of innocent blood" (171). But paradoxically, in attributing the function of population control to savage customs, Malthus also sees savages as behaving, albeit blindly and violently, according to economic reason. Malthus's savages, too, are proto-capitalists; they are on the road to civilization—that is, capitalism—though they will probably exterminate themselves before they get there.

"Under such powerful causes of depopulation," as Malthus calls savage customs, savages in a stationary condition are found only in precarious balance "with the average food supply," whereas savages in a declining condition are "in great want," with "some of the natives ... reduced to skeletons" and starving (171). In contrast to the savage alternatives of starvation or self-extermination, the famished masses usually evoked by Malthus's idea of "surplus populations" are European. Like savagery, civilization is subject to the same "law of nature" that causes population, unless checked, always to overpopulate. For Malthus, the ultimate measure of progress is not the use of money but the degree to which a population limits its size through nonviolent self-restraint. Even Europe, however, fails to meet this severe standard, so poverty and starvation are omnipresent, at least among workers and peasants. "To remove the wants of the lower classes" is impossible, writes Malthus; "the pressure of distress on this part of a community is an evil so deeply seated that no human ingenuity can reach it" (38). Money only adds to the dilemma, because the more money the poor possess, the greater their inducement to overpopulate.

The tendency toward overpopulation, unchecked, whether in civilization or in savagery, leads to catastrophe. But bleak though the prospect of depopulation, caused by overpopulation, may be, for Malthus the deadly workings of "nature's laws" are the result of divine wisdom. Just as Lyell could see even in the extinction of entire species the "perfect harmony" of God's design, so, for Malthus, that population increases more rapidly than subsistence "tend[s] rather to promote than impede the general purpose of Providence" (132). The "law of population" is at once the spur to industry and to rational self-restraint that Malthus identifies both as the causes of progress and as the main values of civilization (Malthus differs from Lyell in stressing progress). This is the "dismal science" of economics as fortunate fall.

Malthus provided later economists with a scientific theodicy that saw progress as the outcome of disaster. They could rationalize the extermination of the Tasmanians, the Mohicans, and the Irish from a seemingly scientific perspective that said, in effect, both savagery and improvidence are self-exterminating, less than valueless. Like over-populating Ireland, depopulating savagery, if it could not be converted to civilization, was so counterproductive that it deserved its suicide. For some economists, moreover, colonization was strictly a matter of occupying and rendering productive "waste" or "unoccupied" lands. In his various treatises on "systematic colonization," Edward Gibbon Wakefield refers only fleetingly to resistance from indigenous peoples; the major threat of "savagery" comes instead from convicts and the indiscriminate "shovelling out of paupers" (Wakefield, 153–54, 39). What is threatened by white savagery, moreover, is peaceful, productive settlement by respectable colonists.

Starting in the 1830s, many economists—Malthus, J. R. McCulloch, Nassau Senior, and John Stuart Mill among them—agreed with most of Wakefield's ideas about "systematic colonization," including the old notion, going back to John Locke's *Two Treatises on Government*, that the lands to be colonized were unowned and virtually uninhabited (Winch, 90–143). In "Chartism" and *Past and Present*, Thomas Carlyle also recommended emigration to "waste lands" as a solution to poverty and unemployment at home. Among economists, a notable exception is Herman Merivale, who, in his 1839–41 Oxford lectures on colonization, devoted two lectures to the question of protecting indigenous peoples from the violence of white settlers (487–553). Merivale largely agrees with Wakefield but also voices many of the concerns of the newly founded Aborigines Protection Society. He claims, however, that there are only three possible outcomes for "natives": extermination; civilization, which he deems "impossible" (510); and "amalgamation," meaning both a sort of lower-class assimilation to white ways and intermarriage. But "amalgamation" is "the only possible Euthanasia of savage communities" (511); extinction is otherwise merely brutal.

From the insular but imperializing perspective of orthodox economics, the elimination of savagery, whether through extermination or conversion to civilization, meant progress. Modernization into or through the capitalist mode of production was the road that precivilized societies had to travel to reach a condition of positive value, measured by modern money rather than by cattle, yams, or cowrie shells. This is not news, of course: non-Western societies that fail to adapt to capitalist conceptions of value are still being bulldozed to make way for the trucking, bartering, and exchanging of transnational corporations. From Smith and Malthus down to the present, the fate of "savages" everywhere has been the same: if not outright extermination, then the transformation, whether violently forced or otherwise, into the inferior simulacrum of civilization. The anachronistic representations of savages as proto-capitalists in Smith and Ricardo turn out to have been prophetic—at least, for those remnants of "savage races" that have managed to escape extinction.

According to James Cowles Prichard, early member of the Aborigines Protection Society and pioneer of British ethnology: "Certain it is, that many vast regions of the earth . . . were formerly the abode of tribes which have long ago perished" (167).[5] In his 1839 essay, "On the Extinction of Human Races," Prichard does not view all savage "tribes" as warlike, much less as self-exterminating, but he notes that "the extermination of human races is still going on" (168), a tragic fact he attributes largely to imperialism—that is, to the relentless "progress" of civilization. "Wherever Europeans have settled, their arrival has been the harbinger of extermination to the native tribes" (169). It seems likely, Prichard thinks, that another century of the "progress of colonization" will entirely liquidate "the aboriginal nations of most parts of the world" (169). Prichard sounds the alarm for two reasons. First, he considers it a matter of scientific urgency "to record the history of the perishing tribes." Savages and savage customs are survivals from the remote past that are both rapidly vanishing from the modern world (the doctrine of survivals would become a key factor in the cultural anthropology of Edward Burnett Tylor). And, second, in common with Thomas Hodgkin and the Aborigines Protection Society, Prichard takes it to be a moral imperative to see "whether any thing can be done . . . to prevent the extermination of the aboriginal tribes" (170), though he clearly thinks this is unlikely.

In his 1845 *Natural History of Man*, Prichard seems less concerned about the "extermination" question. Yet he concludes his global survey of the human "races" or "tribes" with an assertion that their similarities are more significant than their differences: "We are entitled to draw confidently the conclusion that all human races are of one species and one family" (546). Further, Prichard charges that those who insist that the non-white races of the world are distinct species are both pro-slavery and unconcerned about "human sufferings" and the "extirpation" of Australians and other aboriginal "races" (5–7).

For Prichard, the humanitarian imperative was at least as important as science, but it was the other way around for many of the ethnologists who came after him. In 1839 the American physician Samuel G. Morton published *Crania Americana*, examining skulls via the pseudo-science of craniology, to argue that neither Indians nor Africans had the brainpower to become civilized (Bieder, 55–103; Gould, *Mismeasure*, 50–69). Morton's work provided the basis for the supposedly scientific racism of Josiah Nott and George Glidden, whose *Types of Mankind* appeared in 1854. Morton, Nott, and Glidden were not interested in attempting to preserve primitive races from their fates, whether of extinction or slavery, but were very interested in preserving slavery. Thus they held that slavery was good for Africans and that emancipation would lead to the extinction of the former slaves (Frederickson, 233).[6]

In common with the American race scientists, in his 1848 *Natural History of the Human Species*, Charles Hamilton Smith, a main contributor to "racial typology" in Britain (Banton, 52), treats the liquidation of many races as a matter of scientific inevitability. He does so without Prichard's explicitly humanitarian concern; yet occasionally he acknowledges the violence that European "monsters" have inflicted, on, for instance, the Incas of Peru (257). Such occasions are moments of explicit guilt, but guilt without remedy: what a superior race inflicts on its inferiors is just a matter of tragic reality.

Following Cuvier, Smith contends that there are three great, primary races: the woolly-haired Negro, based in central Africa; the beardless Mongolian from central Asia; and the bearded Caucasian or European. Conquest and miscegenation have spawned numerous intermediate varieties or "abnormal" races, as Smith calls them; these mixed races may flourish for decades or even centuries, at least through admixtures from the pure races. If isolated, however, these abnormal races are doomed to extinction through eventual failure to reproduce—that is, through infertility. Echoing Cuvier, Smith claims that mulattoes become infertile, if not in the third or fourth generations, then later. Along with miscegenation, infertility was the least violent of the causes of racial extermination, and, though the thesis about mulattoes was false, it offered a relatively comforting explanation for some vague but large fraction of mass extinctions.

Smith is ambivalent about whether the three great races had a single origin, though he is more inclined to monogeny than polygeny. In any event, throughout history the three main races expand outward, collide with one another in war, enslave or exterminate one another, yet gradually form the intermediate, mixed races. Though he says that mixed or abnormal races tend to die out through infertility or through conquest by the pure races, Smith nevertheless believes that the progress of civilization depends on the mixing of races (157–58).

Smith's basic model of history is the barbarian hordes that swept over the Roman Empire.[7] Though he does not claim that "savages" have fallen from a previously civilized condition, the downfall of Rome, like the evidence of the extinction of animal species, gives him a precedent for his model of history as a universal "struggle for existence" among warring races. "From the occasional destruction of whole tribes and races," writes Smith, "caused, even in modern ages, by the sword, by contagious diseases, or by new modes of life . . . it is evident, that numerous populations of the human family have disappeared, [often] without leaving a record of their ancient existence" (150). Only the three primary races are permanent, and then only in the great centers where their purity and domination have remained stable throughout history: central Africa, central Asia, and Europe. Beyond these centers, members of the three races can only survive as slaves—the fate of Africans in the Americas—or as a "master race," the imperializing Caucasians (124).

Smith, however, hardly endorses either slavery or European imperialism. For him, civilization is too often a continuation of barbarism by other, more effective means. "We must allow that all men, and all races, bear within them the elements of a measured perfectibility," he writes, "probably as high as the Caucasian; and it would be revolting to believe, that the less gifted tribes were predestined to perish beneath the conquering and all-absorbing covetousness of European civilization, without an enormous load of responsibility resting on the perpetrators." Nevertheless, Smith adds that the "fate" of the "less gifted tribes" "appears to be sealed in many quarters, and seems, by a pre-ordained law, to be an effect of more mysterious import than human reason can grasp" (168).[8] This is Darwin's "mystery" about the extinction of primitive races writ large. Smith tries to distinguish between "conquest that brings amelioration with it to the masses of the vanquished, and extermination, which leaves no remnant of a broken people." But "amelioration" is "only awardable to the great typical stocks, effecting incorporations among themselves," presumably like African slavery in the Americas. Extermination, on the other hand, is "almost invariably the lot of the intermediate," "abnormal" races, like the American Indians.

For complicated reasons, Smith thinks that the indigenous "American races . . . are not a typical people," and a key reason is their evident "decay, amounting to prospective extinction," which in turn proves that they are not one of the three primary races (258). This tautological argument does not prevent him from condemning "the white Man's insatiable cupidity" and cruelty. But the Europeans are doing to the Indians only a more effective version of what the Indians were doing to one another well before Columbus. The "stern Indian," "on all occasions where he can glut his passion for bloodshed," does so "unmercifully" (284). In short, Native Americans are self-exterminating; the European invasion only speeds up that lugubrious process.

In *The Races of Men*, first published in 1850, Robert Knox echoes many of Smith's ideas. The chief differences are that Knox inclines toward polygeny rather than monogeny and rejects any notion of social progress (on the somewhat ambiguous character of Knox's polygenism, see Stocking, 65). Foreshadowing Gobineau's *Essay on the Inequality of Human Races* and Nott and Glidden's *Types of Mankind*, Knox argues that the mainspring of history is the physical and mental inequalities among races; that race hatred and conflict are inbred factors in human nature; that war and imperial expansion are the results of this hatred; that, despite the claims of religion and morality, might makes right; and, finally, that, where climate does not affect the outcome, the fair, stronger races invariably defeat and either enslave or exterminate the dark, weaker races. Knox indicates that he does not approve of this bloody dynamic but rather is merely describing, on the basis of the best scientific evidence available, the objective pattern of world history.

It would be comforting to dismiss Knox as a crackpot. He had turned to ethnological lecturing and writing after the derailment of his medical career by the Burke-and-Hare, body-snatching scandal of 1828. Knox had been a prime customer for the corpses that Burke and Hare supplied, occasionally by suffocation, to use in teaching anatomy. The crackpot label is all the more tempting when Knox, despite his claims to neutrality and unlike Charles Hamilton Smith, gloats sadistically over the prospect of new race wars and killing fields. But, unlike Smith who is not often cited by later writers, Knox had a "considerable" influence on theories of race in the 1850s and 1860s (Stepan, 43; Dubow, 27). Darwin cites Knox respectfully, and he was a key figure for James Hunt and the Anthropological Society that Hunt founded in 1863 (Stocking, 247).[9] Perhaps we should even view Knox as a minor Victorian sage, albeit not the equal of Carlyle or Ruskin. After all, both Carlyle and Ruskin held opinions about slavery, racial inequality, war, and empire similar to Knox's. So did Disraeli, Dickens, the Reverend Charles Kingsley, and Anthony Trollope; and Matthew Arnold's ethnological claims about the Celtic race share much with Knox's views.[10] Arnold's racial theory of culture, including his famous Hellenism-Hebraism distinction, may owe something to Knox (Faverty, 73; Young, 55–82). In short, whether Knox was a main cause or just one of many contributors to the upsurge of race-based ideas in Britain from the 1840s on, such thinking was hegemonic or becoming so, even for supposedly liberal intellectuals such as Dickens, Darwin, and Arnold.

Racial theories of history were, however, not just British but European as well as American—that is, white and Western. So, for example, Smith's and Knox's theories of world history as race war can be read as simplified versions of Hegel's philosophy of history. This is not to say that Hegel directly influenced either Smith or Knox, though that is a possibility. Rather, the ideas about history that all three propound were outcomes of Enlightenment theories under the impact of warfare, slavery, and empire during and after the Napoleonic era. Hegel writes of "the slaughter-bench of history" (21), upon which nations and races are sacrificed to the juggernaut of the World Spirit.[11] For Hegel as for Smith and Knox, entire races—indeed, continents—lie beyond the pale of world history, their populations doomed to fall by the wayside. Thus Africa, according to Hegel, has no history: "It is the Gold-land, compressed within itself—the land of childhood, which lying beyond the day of self-conscious history is enveloped in the dark mantle of night" (91). And as to "Negroes" being "enslaved and sold to America," writes Hegel, "bad as this may be, their lot in their own land is even worse" (96). How Hegel knew this, especially since, according to him, the entire continent of Africa had no history, is unclear. But for Marx and Engels also, though the primary engine of history is class conflict both causing and caused by transformations in economic modes of production, war and empire are inevitable results of these cataclysms, and primitive peoples around the world are fated either to extinction or to undergo what today is called economic "development."

In any event, Knox's insistence on race as historical causality and his account of war, slavery, and racial extermination can be seen as a crude but nevertheless realistic version of world history. It is at least a materialist (and in that sense only, perhaps, a scientific) version of that history. No more than Marx, moreover, is Knox a jingoist or an advocate of white supremacy. Unlike Smith, Knox does not express any sympathy for humanitarian views on the subject of race and the "slaughter bench" of history. However, he treats the conquering and colonizing Anglo-Saxon race—which he claims to be his own—with contempt: they are at once money-grubbing pirates, ruthless exterminators of the weaker races, and hypocrites. They are especially hypocritical, Knox thinks, when, in the guise of humanitarianism or philanthropy, they try to protect the weaker races from enslavement or extermination. Knox believes that efforts like those of the Aborigines Protection Society are too little too late, as well as ignorant attempts to interfere with the workings of nature, which for him is most decidedly "nature red in tooth and claw."

Contemptuous of history's victors, Knox is equally contemptuous of the victims, and his sarcastic irony is often hard to distinguish from sadistic celebration of genocide:

What a field of extermination lies before the Saxon Celtic and Sarmatian races! The Saxon will not mingle with any dark race, nor will he allow him to hold an acre of land in the country occupied by him; this, at least, is the law of Anglo-Saxon America. (153)

Knox goes on to say that "the fate" of the American aboriginals is "in no shape doubtful. Extinction of the race—sure extinction—it is not even denied" (153). What is true of history as race war in the Americas is true around the world. Everywhere "the destroying angel walks abroad . . . striking even at the races of men" (314). Knox attributes the extinction of the dark races of the world to a malign, murderous antipathy on the part of their supposedly civilized exterminators:

Already, in a few years, we have cleared Van Diemen's Land [Tasmania] of every *human* aboriginal; Australia, of course, follows, and New Zealand next; there is no denying the fact, that the Saxon . . . has a perfect horror for his darker brethren (153)

and hence liquidates him at every possible opportunity.

In contrast to both Australasia and the Americas, the vast continents of Africa and Asia contain many different races, and some of these, Knox claims, are more resistant to invasion, enslavement, and extermination than others. Central Africa remains impenetrable to the murderous, piratical Saxon. In the world-historical war of races, the fair always conquer the dark; but the fair races cannot survive long in, and therefore cannot colonize, the tropics. The enslavement of the dark races becomes necessary because whites cannot labor in hot climates. The Saxon Boers have occupied South Africa for three hundred years, but Knox argues that all European colonies or former colonies can sustain themselves only through immigration. As in Smith's *Natural History*, transplanted races, whether dark or fair, may be doomed to expire without fresh transfusions of blood. This is the situation in India, where the fair, conquering race encounters several dark but very populous and at least semi-civilized races. Both climate and race dictate against the Saxon's permanent settlement of India. The piratical Saxon can plunder India to his heart's content; but he cannot colonize it, which for Knox means moving large populations: the seizure and settlement of territory by a conquering race and the enslavement, eviction, or extermination of the original inhabitants.[12]

To return to South Africa, where Knox spent three years as an army surgeon while conducting anatomical research on Africans, the weaker dark races—the Hottentots and the "Boesjmen"—are nearing extinction; the stronger race of "the Kaffirs" (by which he probably means all the Bantu peoples) may survive longer, but their "fate" is also "certain." In short, all "the dark races" are doomed, sooner or later. Some, like Native Americans, may have been self-extinguishing even before the arrival of the "fair" race; but the main mechanism of extinction is the hatred that propels the fair to destroy the dark races. Quite bluntly, "the aim of the Saxon man" today, Knox declares, "is the extermination of the dark races of men—the aborigines—the men of the desert and of the forest" (314).

Relations among the fair, European races, moreover, are no differ-

ent: for Knox, the key to European history is also race war and genocide. The eventual outcome of the conflict between the Saxon and
the Celtic races will be just the same as that between the Maori and
both these "fair" races in New Zealand. But because, just as Matthew
Arnold would later do, Knox defines the Celtic race as including the
French, and because in 1850 European history was still overshadowed
by the Napoleonic wars, which might have ended in a French victory, the long-range outcome of the race war between Saxons and
Celts is uncertain.

Though of the same race, however, the French, according to Knox,
are very different from the Irish. The French are close to the pinnacle,
whereas the Irish are the lowest dregs of civilization and seem fated to
go the way of the dark races of the world. Writing during the Great
Famine of the late 1840s, Knox views the mass extinction of the Irish
peasantry as similar to that of the dark races in Africa, Asia, the Americas, and Australasia. Even emigration is no solution, because the Irish
abroad, like other transplanted races, will be absorbed by other populations or else gradually killed off by disease and climate. For Knox,
the Irish are "children of the mist," who like Cooper's expiring Mohicans, cannot look to "the darkening future" but can only "dream of
the past."[13]

Although elegizing the expiring race of the Irish, Knox believes
that the starving Irish peasant himself is the cause of the Famine—or,
rather, his race is the cause. Knox may have been the only non-Irish
intellectual who interpreted the Famine, while it was happening, in
terms of racial extermination. (Young Irelanders such as John
Mitchel did not hesitate to accuse the English of pursuing a policy of
deliberate genocide.) True, Knox says that the main cause of the
Famine is the Irish race rather than English misrule, a form of blaming the victim just as glaring as Malthus's version of "savage customs,"
and a position antithetical to the Irish nationalist charge of genocide.
But Knox suggests that the weaknesses of the Celtic race permitted
the Saxon race to dominate and exploit Ireland over the centuries in
ways that culminated in the Famine, a view of the negative results of
imperialism rarely expressed in other Victorian accounts either of the
Famine or more generally of Irish-English relations.

Despite his cynical comments about stuffed Hottentots and broad
killing fields, Knox sounds an elegiac note both for the Irish peasantry and, on the opposite side of the world, for the Tasmanian and

Australian aboriginals. Knox writes that the Saxon and Celtic settlers of Australia have discovered "a ready way . . . of extinguishing" the "miserable" aboriginals: "the Anglo-Saxon has already cleared out Tasmania. It was a cruel, cold blooded, heartless deed. Australia is too large to attempt the same plan there; but by shooting the natives as freely as we do crows in other countries, the population must become thin and scarce in time" (99).

The pre-Darwinian race scientists—Prichard, Smith, Knox, Morton, Nott and Glidden, and others—insisted that the dark races were everywhere in retreat from the onslaught of white civilization or imperialism and that many, perhaps all, of those races were doomed to extinction. In making this claim, however, they questioned easy equations between European domination, racial extermination, and progress. Despite their stress on racial difference as the causal mechanism of world history, and even though neither Smith nor Knox shared Prichard's humanitarianism, all three offer accounts of the violence of the so-called civilizing process that are more unblinkingly honest about the global conflict among "the races of men" than do most of the defenders of empire, who ordinarily treat savagery just as they treat the starving Irish, as deserving its self-extinction.

Surveying the mighty works of nature in South Africa, its wildlife including its wild races, Knox declares that that portion of the world has "remained seemingly unaltered for countless ages" until the advent of "the Dutch-Saxon and the Anglo-Saxon," with their "firearms, discipline, and laws. [Given] this new element, [nature's] works are doomed to destruction, in as far as man can destroy" (311). But that is, Knox believes, all man—at least, Saxon man—is capable of doing: "Man's gift is to destroy, not to create; he cannot even produce . . . a new and permanent variety of a barn-door fowl, of a pheasant, of a sheep or horse. This, then, is the antagonism of man . . . to nature's works," including other men (312). Whatever one makes of such a strange, gloomy assertion, Knox offers a vivid contrast to those Whiggish interpretations of the civilizing process, according to which the "fading away" of primitive races and even the Irish Famine were signs both of progress and of God's infinite benevolence.

3. Vanishing Americans

Toward the beginning of *The Maine Woods* (1864), his posthumously published account of treks that he made in 1846 and again in the 1850s, Henry David Thoreau describes a "woebegone" Indian disembarking from his canoe near Oldtown with "a bundle of skins . . . and an empty keg" to fill with whiskey. "This picture will do to put before [the reader] the Indian's history," Thoreau declares; "that is, the history of his extinction" (6). On a later trip, the killing and butchering of a moose by his Indian guide suggests to Thoreau "how base or coarse are the motives which commonly carry men into the wilderness":

> For one that comes with a pencil to sketch or sing, a thousand come with an axe or rifle. What a coarse and imperfect use Indians and hunters make of Nature! No wonder that their race is so soon exterminated. (161–62)

Like many other white Americans of his era, Thoreau finds it easy to claim that the "race" of Indians would be "soon exterminated." At the same time, he depicts Indians and presumably white hunters (who obviously are not being "exterminated") engaged in the same activity: slaughtering animals, exploiting the wilderness. Surprisingly, for someone who takes a keen interest in Indian cultures and archaeology (see Sayre), Thoreau suggests that Indians deserve their extinction because they do *not* appreciate nature. But this suggestion is coupled with the contrary and much more standard idea that they are so closely bound to nature (the moose, the Maine woods) that they must retreat as it retreats before the inexorable advance of white civilization, which knows how to turn both Indians and wilderness into works of art—into sketches and songs, into cigar store icons, and, more recently, into movies, sports teams, and TV commercials.

In *The National Uncanny: Indian Ghosts and American Subjects*, Renée Bergland writes that "the birth of the American nation and the death of the Native American were as closely related as light and shadow" (40). For more than half a century after the American Revolution, Independence Day orations employed the elegiac trope of the dying Indian to help celebrate the creation and progress of the new republic (Lubbers, 26–48). Even as the citizens of the new nation rejoiced in their rights, freedom, and radiant future, the dying Indian became the object of national sympathy and mourning. The world of savagery—noble, perhaps, but still savage—was passing away into darkness; the world of white civilization and progress, with its vanguard in the new United States, was emerging into the full light of day.

Native Americans were not totally exterminated, of course; a recent estimate places the decline in their population at 95 percent, but their numbers have been increasing since World War II.[1] Yet so engrained in the dominant culture is the ghosting of "the Indians" that extinction remains the imaginary telos and to some extent even the standard history of Native America.[2] David Stannard's *American Holocaust*, Ward Churchill's *A Little Matter of Genocide*, and many other recent studies emphasize that, although total extinction did not happen, it almost happened. They also demonstrate that the colonizers have almost, but not entirely, succeeded in eradicating the cultural identities and languages of the colonized. Near-extinction and the vanishing of many tribes, cultures, and languages have been paralleled by the rise and flourishing of "the white man's Indian," a phantasm that has played an enormous role in the construction of modern American culture.[3]

In his *Autobiography*, which he began writing in 1771, Benjamin Franklin recounts serving as a commissioner for Pennsylvania at a treaty-signing "with the Indians at Carlisle." No liquor was given to the Indians before the signing, but "we would give them plenty of rum when business was over." After the signing, the Indians got very drunk and began "quarreling and fighting" among themselves. The following day the Indians apologized, but declared:

> The Great Spirit, who made all things, made every thing for some use, and whatever use he design'd any thing for, that use it should always be put to. Now, when he made rum, he said, "Let this be for the Indians to get drunk with," and it must be so.

To this bit of pagan theology, Franklin responds that if indeed "it be the design of Providence to extirpate these savages in order to make room for cultivators of the earth, it seems not improbable that rum may be the appointed means. It has already annihilated all the tribes who formerly inhabited the sea-coast" (136–37).

Franklin's response to the Carlisle Indians illustrates several aspects of extinction discourse as applied to Native America. First, extinction discourse extends well back into the eighteenth century and beyond (Franklin is obviously invoking earlier claims—John Locke's, for instance—about cultivators versus non-cultivators "of the earth," and so on).[4] Second, Franklin sees Indian misbehavior—here, drunkenness—as a main cause of their demise (savagery is its own undoing). Third, he treats the fact that the coastal "tribes" have been "annihilated" as evidence that all Indians will ultimately share that fate: the vanishing of a portion serves as synecdochal evidence that the entire race will vanish. Fourth, though an Enlightenment deist, Franklin echoes the Puritans of New England in at least suggesting that the demise of the Indians is "the design of Providence." And finally, Franklin sees one purpose of that "design" to be the elimination of "savages . . . to make room for cultivators of the earth" (137) or, in other words, for white settlers. It hardly matters that the Carlisle Indians were themselves cultivators, as were most Native Americans in the eastern portion of North America. Franklin treats them as hunters with no involvement in what most commentators on "savagery" viewed as one of its antitheses: farming. As nomadic hunter-gatherers, savages, it was held, had no conception of property and no stake in improving and living permanently on the land.[5]

Hector St. John Crèvecoeur, in *Letters of an American Farmer* (1781), also expresses all of Franklin's ideas about "the Indians." Crèvecoeur acknowledges that many Indian "nations" have been "extirpated by fraud, violence, or injustice" (119), but this has not been so for the Indians of Nantucket. They have been well treated by the white islanders, so "if their numbers are now so decreased, it must not be attributed either to tyranny or violence, but to some of those causes, which have uninterruptedly produced the same effects from one end of the continent to the other, wherever both nations have been mixed" (119). Prior to the coming of Europeans, the Indians were in danger of annihilating themselves through "perpetual war," Crèvecoeur claims; but "both parties became so thin and depopulated that the few who remained, fearing lest their race should become totally extinct, fortunately thought of an expedient which prevented their entire annihilation." They drew a boundary through the middle of the island, agreeing not to trespass on each other's territory, and, as a result, "they multiplied greatly" (120–21). The idyll of the Nantucket Indians was interrupted, however, by the arrival of the Europeans, who brought with them two new causes of extinction, smallpox and rum (123). The result is that they are now "hastening towards a total annihilation" (119), along with Native Americans throughout the continent.

The certainty with which Franklin and Crèvecoeur forecast "total annihilation" of all Indians everywhere in America suggests that that prediction was a key ingredient of the nation-forging ideology of the new United States. Nevertheless, both writers share the Enlightenment tendency to view the Indians—and, indeed, aboriginal peoples elsewhere in the world—as Noble Savages. Franklin's account of the Carlisle Indians in the *Autobiography* is mainly negative, but on other occasions he notes that Indians must be doing something right, because whites captured by them often do not want to return to white society. Crèvecoeur makes the same point, and says: "there must be in their social bond something singularly captivating and far superior to anything to be boasted of among us; for thousands of Europeans are Indians, and we have no examples of even one of those aborigines having from choice become Europeans!" (214). Crèvecoeur adds:

> Without temples, without priests, without kings, and without laws, they are in many instances superior to us; and the proofs of what I advance are that they live without care, sleep without inquietude, take life as it comes, bearing all its asperities with unparalleled patience. . . . They most certainly are much more closely connected to Nature than we are; they are her immediate children. (215)

What Franklin and Crèvecoeur say about whites "going native" has been largely confirmed by the historian James Axtell, who notes that, from the 1600s on, hundreds of white captives were assimilated into Indian families and societies, and that many of these, when given opportunities for rescue or escape, chose to remain with the Indians. But the idea of a benign, close-to-nature alternative to civilization was most certainly not expressed in the first captivity narratives written by Puritans such as Mary Rowlandson. During her captivity, she believed herself in hell—if not literally, then the next closest thing to it, because Indians were the demonic agents of Satan. In taking this view, Rowlandson agreed with Cotton Mather, who, in *Magnalia Christi Americana*, opines:

> probably, the devil seducing the first inhabitants of America into it, therein aimed at the having of them and their posterity out of the sound of the *silver trumpets* of the *Gospel*, then to be heard through the Roman Empire. (1:42)

In his account of the Pequot War of the 1630s, Mather treats all Indians as "nations of wretches, whose whole *religion* [is] the most explicit sort of *devil-worship*" and who aim at "the extinction of a plantation so contrary to [Satan's] interests, as that of New-England" (2:552). In other words, it is not the Indians who are threatened with extinction, but the Puritans. This threat, however, coupled with the belief that the Indians are the irreclaimable creatures of Satan, prompts Mather to advocate their extermination: "So . . . the infant colonies of New-England, finding themselves necessitated unto the *crushing of serpents*, while they were but yet in the *cradle*, unanimously resolved, that with the assistance of Heaven they would root this 'nest of serpents' out of the world" (2:553).

In this earliest of white–Indian wars in New England, the intention of the Puritans turned genocidal: during if not before the conflict, they aimed to destroy the Pequots root and branch (Drinnon, 43–44). Captain John Mason celebrated the burning of a Pequot stronghold in 1637 in terms of God's "laugh[ing] his Enemies and the Enemies of his People to Scorn, making them as a Fiery Oven. . . . Thus did the Lord Judge among the Heathen, filling the Place with dead Bodies!" (quoted in Drinnon, 43). The Pequots and, a few decades later, the Wampanoags, who were defeated by the New Englanders in King Philip's War (1675–77), served as examples of what would eventually happen to all Indians everywhere who resisted white colonization. From the Puritan perspective, moreover, God's assistance in the good work of extirpating "the serpents" could be observed not only in the results of war but also in the more mysterious workings of disease. No Puritan himself but a worldly person who befriended the Indians, Thomas Morton nevertheless shared with Mather the belief that "the plague" that was causing the tribes to die out was God's handiwork: "the place is made so much the more fitt, for the English Nation to inhabit in, and erect in it Temples to the Glory of God" (quoted in Kupperman, 32).

Versions of the Puritan belief that God would extirpate "the savages" either by plague or by fire and sword recur in later Indian-hating formulations, including the innumerable captivity-as-atrocity stories that became a staple of early American literature. As Franklin and Crèvecoeur illustrate, however, during the 1700s less negative, fanatical, and, indeed, more scientific ideas about Native Americans were developing. Nevertheless, science did not remake the image of the Indian in an entirely positive mode. Though their theories relegated God or Providence to the role of witness of the unfolding of His unalterable, constant laws, natural historians such as Buffon and Blumenbach adhered to the biblical version of creation. They thus viewed mankind as a single species with one origin and considered the dark races as degenerate offspring of the original, white race. The degeneration hypothesis took a number of eccentric twists and turns in the eighteenth century and after. Buffon, for instance, argued that the conditions for life in America were harsh, and that therefore the plants and animals as well as the human inhabitants of the New World were degenerate, a theory that early American intellectuals such as Thomas Jefferson sought to refute (Bieder, 6, 61; Dippie, 33). But even among American intellectuals, writes Robert Bieder, by the 1830s "the view that Indians had degenerated from a more advanced state of civilization had received wide acceptance" (33).

The discovery of Indian burial mounds led to the idea that North America had once supported a nascent civilization, perhaps equivalent to those of Mexico and Peru. This quasi-civilization had, however, declined and fallen, as had those of the Incas and Mexicans. Because they did not construct mounds, existing Indians, it was often claimed, were either the degenerate offspring of the mound builders or an altogether different race. According to the second possibility, the Indians were the barbarian destroyers of the perhaps white race that had constructed the mounds. In his 1832 poem, "The Prairies," William Cullen Bryant writes of "the mighty mounds" in Illinois:

A race, that long has passed away,
Built them;—a disciplined and populous race
Heaped, with long toil, the earth, while yet the Greek
Was hewing the Pentelicus to forms
Of symmetry, and rearing on its rock
The glittering Parthenon.

But then "the red man came—"

The roaming hunter tribes, warlike and fierce,
And the mound-builders vanished from the earth.
(132)

As with the barbarian invasions of the Roman Empire, the red bar-
barians, though apparently an inferior race, managed to defeat and
exterminate the superior, perhaps white race of mound builders
(Kennedy; Dippie, 17–18). Such was also the thesis of Cornelius
Matthews's 1846 romance, *Behemoth: A Legend of the Mound-
Builders* (Maddox, 40).

To many white Americans, "the Indians whose culture was being
destroyed," writes Roger Kennedy, "could not be the same people as
those who accomplished such prodigies" as the mounds. The addi-
tional notion that the present-day "savages were the descendants of the
barbarians who had swept down upon [the] kindly mound builders"
was "solacing," because then white Americans, "redressing an ancient
crime," could be seen as "agents of delayed retribution. Better than
that—theirs was retribution at the hands of a master race" (Kennedy,
30). At least what was happening in the 1800s had happened before,
one race defeating and exterminating another. In defending the policy
of Indian removal from Georgia and elsewhere east of the Mississippi,
President Andrew Jackson contended that the government was only
doing to the Indians what they had done to the earlier, mysterious,
quite possibly white race of mound builders (Dippie, 17).

In the new United States, both archaeology and anthropology took
root in investigations of Indian burial mounds and bones. In his 1787
Notes on the State of Virginia, Jefferson tried to analyze the available
evidence about Native Americans scientifically and to add to that evidence through his own exploration of burial mounds and their con-
tents. For Jefferson and many later white investigators, Indian graves

and relics possess an evidentiary significance consonant with the belief in the future extinction of all Native Americans. Jefferson provides statistics about tribal populations and their rapid declines. He emphasizes the urgency of understanding and preserving Indian languages before they disappear along with their speakers. Writing about the eminent vanishing of those languages, Jefferson turns to the vanishing of the Indians themselves:

> It is to be lamented then, very much to be lamented, that we have suffered so many of the Indian tribes already to extinguish, without our having previously collected and deposited in the records of literature, the general rudiments at least of the languages they spoke. (143)

Despite Jefferson's manifest sympathy and also his desire to understand the Indians scientifically, this astonishing sentence announces that "many of the Indian tribes" have already vanished, apparently of their own accord (they have been allowed "to extinguish"), and moreover that it is white America that has "suffered" (or perhaps suffered *from?*) this disappearance, mainly because white science (or scientific "literature" especially about language) will suffer. The double note of mourning in the sentence ("lamented . . . lamented") expresses the elegiac attitude toward Native Americans that characterizes dominant white discourse from the 1700s to the present: anthropology in general as a form of ghosting the primitive.

Concerning the causes of the decimation of "the tribes" of Virginia through the 1600s and beyond, Jefferson writes:

> What would be the melancholy sequel of their history, may . . . be augured from the census of 1669; by which we discover that the tribes therein enumerated were, in the space of 62 years, reduced to about one-third of their former numbers. Spiritous liquors, the small-pox, war, and an abridgment of territory, to a people who lived principally on the spontaneous productions of nature, had committed terrible havock among them. (135)

As does Franklin, Jefferson views the Indians of the Atlantic seaboard as mere hunter-gatherers, rather than also farmers. The "abridgment of territory" from which they suffer is the penalty for not having a more settled, productive way of life. And as in Franklin, alcoholism leads the list of causes. Whenever alcohol is emphasized as a cause of extinction, it is an instance of savagery's inability to cope with civilization; Indians learn the vices, but not the virtues, of the whites. Finally, "war" in Jefferson's list is ambiguous; he does not say whether he means whites warring against Indians or Indians warring against themselves, though probably he means both. In any event, repeatedly in extinction discourse about Native America, the Indians of all types and tribes are treated as having atavistically warlike natures. This idea has two main implications: that when whites go to war against Indians, they are only defending themselves against a naturally warlike race; and that Indians, like savages elsewhere in the world, are self-exterminating. Jefferson does not make these points explicitly, but by the time he wrote *Notes on Virginia* he did not need to—they were already among the commonplaces of extinction discourse.

In his commission to Lewis and Clark, Jefferson set forth an extensive list of questions to ask about the various tribes the explorers would encounter on their expedition. The story of American anthropology perhaps begins with that famous expedition. A related point of origin is the work of Albert Gallatin, who served as Secretary of the Treasury under both Jefferson and James Madison and who helped found the American Ethnological Society in 1842. Gallatin's 1836 *Synopsis of the Indian Tribes of North America* offered an encyclopedic amount of information about Indian languages and cultures. He saw, as did Alexis de Tocqueville in *Democracy in America*, the incompatibility between democracy and belief in the inferiority of the non-white races, whether African, Native American, or Asian. And he recognized claims about the inevitable extinction of the Indians for what they were: ideological rationalization for "unbounded cupidity and ambition" (quoted in Bieder, 49). Yet Gallatin also thought that the Indian "disappears before the white man, simply because he will not work." The chief factor in their destruction was neither disease nor white violence but their own "inveterate indolence" (quoted in Dippie, 41). For all his sympathy toward and knowledge about Native America, Gallatin offers a version of the stereotype of "the lazy native," in which that laziness is treated as a prime cause of racial extinction.

Besides Jefferson and Gallatin, before mid-century many others contributed to an American tradition of ethnological observation and theory. As in Britain, France, and elsewhere, there were two major trends: the beginnings of modern cultural anthropology are evident in the work of Gallatin, Henry Schoolcraft, and Lewis Henry Morgan, while Samuel Morton's *Crania Americana* (1839) promoted a version of race science, insistent on polygenesis and the biological determinants of racial differences, that supported both Indian removal (or extermination) and slavery.

Throughout his numerous accounts of Indian customs and mythology, Schoolcraft expresses the standard beliefs and assumptions of the first trend before mid-century. Compared to later anthropologists including Morgan, Schoolcraft seems unmethodical, more an amateur folklorist and collector than a scientist. Nevertheless, in 1846 he sent the newly opened Smithsonian Institution a *Plan for the Investigation of American Ethnology*, which he already understood as "salvage" work, because "America is the tomb of the Red man" (quoted in Hinsley, 20). For Schoolcraft, as for many other commentators before the 1850s, the Indians were doomed because their "race" was, in contrast to whites, nonprogressive. Thus, in *The American Indians, Their History, Condition and Prospects*, Schoolcraft writes:

> Two types of human race, more fully and completely antagonistical, in all respects, never came in contact on the globe. They were the alpha and omega of the ethnological chain. If, therefore, the Red Race declined, and the white increased, it was because civilisation had more of the principles of endurance and progress than barbarism; because Christianity was superior to paganism; industry to idleness; agriculture to hunting; letters to hieroglyphics; truth to error. Here lie the true secrets of the Red Men's decline. (369)

In contrast to Schoolcraft and most other early, white commentators on the future of Native Americans, Morgan rejects racial determinism.[6] His 1854 *League of the Iroquois* offers a highly positive account of the societies and cultures that belonged to the League, and notes optimistically that, after steep declines, their populations are stabilizing and even beginning to increase (35, 446). "The League of the Iroquois," Morgan declares, "exhibited the highest development of the Indian ever reached by him in the hunter state" (55). The question of the survival of the Iroquois and of other extant "Indian races" depends, Morgan asserts, on whether the white public and the government of the United States will behave responsibly and aid them "towards their final elevation to the rights and privileges of American citizens" (445). This he believes is certainly possible, though not exactly probable, because "civilization" in general has a destructive as well as constructive side (444). The note of caution suggests also that, for Morgan, the "primitive" condition of Native America is in many ways superior to the white "civilization" that has overtaken it. Of life among the Iroquois, Morgan writes:

> It would be difficult to describe any political society, in which there was less of oppression and discontent, more of individual independence and boundless freedom. The absence of family distinctions, and of all property, together with the irresistible inclination for the chase . . . secured to them an exemption from the evils, as well as denied to them the refinements, which flow from the possession of wealth, and the indulgence of the social relations. (139)

Evidently Morgan does not have much regard either for civilized "refinements" or for "the possession of wealth." This Rousseauistic emphasis helped to make him a key influence on the anthropological ideas of Marx and Engels, including their conception of a pre-state, quasi-utopian, primitive communism.[7]

Nevertheless, as do Marx and Engels, Morgan sees progress toward civilization as inexorable and as operative on all savage and barbarian peoples around the world. In his 1877 *Ancient Society*, Morgan elaborates on the evolutionary paradigm of primary stages—savagery, barbarism, and civilization—by identifying a series of substages through which, given favorable conditions, all societies and cultures progress, unless impeded by warfare or natural catastrophes. As in the writings of the British cultural anthropologist Edward Burnett Tylor, Morgan's evolutionism counters notions of racial essentialism, basic to most pre-Darwinian versions of extinction discourse, by insisting that progress from savagery to civilization is universal: all races are branches of a single species and all are following the same upward trajectory.

In contrast to the more liberal strain of early cultural anthropology from Jefferson to Morgan, Samuel Morton's *Crania Americana* stresses the fixed, physiological inequalities among the races. He accepts the biblical account of creation but argues that, after the Flood, God gave the different races very different abilities, fitted to the locations in which they came to dwell (Stanton, 31). Morton combines two sciences or pseudo-sciences, craniology and phrenology, in a peculiarly lethal mix that correlates physical attributes (primarily of skulls) with mental and moral characteristics (for non-white races, mostly negative). According to Morton's miscalculations (Gould, *Mismeasure*, 50–69), Caucasian or white skulls are the largest, and hence the white race is the only truly intelligent and progressive one. The smaller brain size of Native Americans proves that they are creatures of the wilderness incapable of becoming civilized. And it is the necessary, beneficent advance of white civilization, Morton believes, that dooms both the Indians and the wilderness.

Morton next authored *Crania Aegyptica* (1844), in which he proves, to his satisfaction at least, that the skulls of black Africans have remained small since the days of the pharoahs, who had enslaved them. Hence slavery in the southern United States is justified, as is white supremacy from the pyramids to the present (Stanton, 51–53; Bieder, 55–103). Morton's theories were a main influence on Josiah Nott and George Glidden, whose 1854 *Types of Mankind* also espouses the fixity of races in an ahistorical hierarchy: the superiority of the white race to all others; the stupid docility of Negroes (hence their inevitable role as slaves—slavery is good for them, and they will perish if emancipated); and the wild untamability and therefore doom of the Indians. Nott and Glidden sidestep the question of "the common origin of races" while insisting, with Morton, on the "permanence of moral and intellectual peculiarities of [the] types" of mankind (50). Whether they formed a single species, the races were very unequal, and the dark races could not be improved. In an 1846 essay arguing against "the unity of the human race," Nott declares that the Indians are "incapable of development" and that "their earthly destiny is now so rapidly fulfilling, that, after a few generations, the red men will all be gathered to the tombs of their forefathers, in darkness" (quoted in Bieder, 96).

From the 1780s through World War I, the consensus among white experts and observers was that "the red race" would sooner or later completely vanish. In the 1820s and 1830s, "removal" of all Indians to lands west of the Mississippi River became the panacea that would prolong the existence of the race at least for another generation or two. Thomas McKenney, first superintendent of the Bureau of Indian Affairs, supported removal in these terms in his 1828 Report:

> But the question occurs—*What are humanity and justice in reference to this unfortunate race?* Are these found to lie in a policy that would leave them to linger out a wretched and degraded existence, within districts of country already surrounded and pressed upon by a population whose anxiety and efforts to get rid of them are not less restless and persevering, than is that law of nature immutable, which has decreed, that, under such circumstances, if con-

tinued in, *they must perish?* Or does it not rather consist in withdrawing them from this certain destruction? (Washburn, 9–10)

And McKenney's successor as superintendent, Elbert Herring, opined in 1831 that removal was the only "humane policy," one that he hoped would soon be "crowned with complete success." Otherwise, once again, the Indians were doomed:

> Gradually diminishing in numbers and deteriorating in condition; incapable of coping with the superior intelligence of the white man, ready to fall into the vices, but unapt to appropriate the benefits of the social state; the increasing tide of white population threatened soon to engulf them, and finally to cause their total extinction. (Washburn, 18)

Predictions of "total extinction" such as these by McKenney and Herring underwrote official policy toward the Indians from the 1820s well into the twentieth century.

In the debates leading up to the Removal Act of 1830, it hardly mattered that the opponents of that act insisted that the Cherokees, for example, were already literate, Christian farmers.[8] Congressman Peleg Sprague pointed out that the Cherokees "now live by the cultivation of the soil, and the mechanic arts. [But it] is proposed to send them from their cotton fields, their farms and their gardens, to a distant and . . . unsubdued wilderness—to make them tillers of the earth!—to remove them from their looms, their work-shops, their printing press, their schools, and churches . . . to frowning forests, surrounded with naked savages—that they may become enlightened and civilized!" (Congress, 65). No matter how much civilization the Cherokees or any other group of Indians exhibited, the proponents of removal insisted they were savages and were doomed by mere contact with white civilization. Removal, it was claimed, meant that the date of final extinction could be postponed, and this in turn meant that its advocates could see removal as "philanthropy" rather than tyranny, forced diaspora, or genocide.

The emphasis on philanthropy is evident, for instance, in Andrew Jackson's presidential message of 1830:

> Humanity has often wept over the fate of the aborigines of this country [Jackson declares], and Philanthropy has been long busily employed in devising means to avert it, but its progress has never for a moment been arrested, and one by one have many powerful tribes disappeared from the earth. To follow to the tomb the

last of his race and to tread on the graves of extinct nations excite melancholy reflections. But true philanthropy reconciles the mind to these vicissitudes as it
does to the extinction of one generation to make room for another.

Besides, Jackson continues, "What good man would prefer a country
covered with forests and ranged by a few thousand savages to our extensive Republic, studded with cities, towns, and prosperous farms?"
(quoted in Pearce, 57). Jackson was hardly the best spokesman for
"philanthropy," however; according to Michael Rogin, he "was the
single figure most responsible for Indian destruction in pre-Civil War
America" (Rogin, 13; and see Wallace).[9]

Among early American historians, Francis Parkman penned several
elaborate elegies for the Indians—ones that double as opening chapters, at least, of the epic history of the new United States. Parkman
himself had traveled throughout the west, studying Indians firsthand,
so he was just as knowledgeable as other early ethnological observers
about the differences between Native American societies and cultures. Nevertheless, he also treats all Indians as belonging to one race
with one ultimate, negative destiny. Thus, in his 1851 *Conspiracy of
Pontiac*, Parkman writes:

> Some of the races of men seem moulded in wax, soft and melting, at once
> plastic and feeble. Some races, like some metals, combine the greatest flexi-
> bility with the greatest strength. But the Indian is hewn out of a rock. You can
> rarely change the form without destruction of the substance.

The Indian, Parkman explains, is "fixed and rigid," and this rigidity
"has proved his ruin. He will not learn the arts of civilization, and he
and his forest must perish together" (63). Parkman adds that while
there is something admirable in his "wild love of freedom, and impa-
tience of all control" (160), there is "nothing progressive in the rigid
inflexible nature of an Indian. He will not open his mind to the idea
of improvement; and nearly every change that has been forced upon
him has been a change for the worse" (169). To view Native America
in this stereotypic, "fixed and rigid" manner is, of course, to blame
them, along with nature or the laws of nature, for their inevitable annihilation.[10]

Even as they celebrated the westward expansion of the United
States, early American historians, novelists, poets, and artists grieved

over the inevitable vanishing, whether through extinction or removal, of the Indians. According to Bergland, from Puritan times to the present, Native Americans have always already been figuratively dead but also, for that very reason, hauntingly central, "possessing" the political, cultural imaginary of white America. The attempt to put the ghostly Indian to rest is evident in the elegiac quality of almost all the literature and art of the United States and Canada that deals with them, from the poetry of Philip Freneau and novels of Charles Brockden Brown to such movies as *Cheyenne Autumn*, *Dances with Wolves*, and *The Last of the Mohicans*.

In the preface to *Edgar Huntly* (1801), Brown had asserted that one way for American fiction to avoid imitating "puerile" European models was to employ "incidents of Indian hostility, and the perils of the western wilderness" (3). To that end, Brown recast the Gothic romance or tale of terror in a peculiarly subversive manner. The narrator-protagonist of *Edgar Huntly*, in pursuit of a murderer whom he suspects is the sleepwalking Irishman Clithero, discovers both that he also is a sleepwalker and that, despite his loathing and fear of bloodshed, he must turn Indian-killer to save himself. The irrationality of somnambulism and Indian-killing fuse in a murky narrative in which Huntly's sanity is called into question and therewith, as Bergland notes, the sanity of "the American nation itself" (51). But *Edgar Huntly* is not an overtly political novel; Brown's main aim appears to be simply to terrify his readers. Nevertheless, situating Indian-killing (and Indians killing whites) on the nightmare side of early American experience, as something white Americans were living through in a terrorized, somnambulistic way, established a powerful pattern for later frontier romances.

From Philip Freneau's Indian death songs through John Wadsworth Longfellow's *Hiawatha*, early American poetry often also takes the form of proleptic elegy. The most famous nineteenth-century attempt to turn the Indians and their destiny into poetry ends in death, with the departure of Hiawatha "To the land of the Hereafter" (Longfellow, 266). In Freneau's relatively short poems, there is no indication as to why the Indians are dead or dying, except (it seems) through natural causes. But in Longfellow's 1855 poem, the final section, "Hiawatha's Departure," follows one entitled "The White Man's Foot," in which Hiawatha has a "vision" of the triumphant westward march of white civilization and religion, taming the wilderness and perhaps also the Indian:

Then a darker, drearer vision
Passed before me, vague and cloudlike
I beheld our nations scattered,
All forgetful of my counsels,
Weakened, warring with each other;
Saw the remnants of our people
Sweeping westward, wild and woful,
Like the cloud-rack of a tempest,
Like the withered leaves of Autumn!
(259–60)

In Longfellow's poem, the explanation for Hiawatha's "departure" and the future sad fate of all the Indians is the advent and spread of white civilization. Like Hiawatha, creature of Indian legends that Longfellow drew from the works of Henry Schoolcraft, Native Americans in general are creatures of the past—a race with no future. This treatment of the Indians as trapped in the past, as always already dead because they are futureless, reached an apotheosis in the Leatherstocking novels of James Fenimore Cooper, the first of which were published in the 1820s, just when the national debates over Indian removal were heating up.

Romances such as *Edgar Huntly* were a literary staple for the new nation by the time Cooper began his Leatherstocking series.[11] No author did more than Cooper, however, to establish proleptic elegy as a generic pattern for American literature, one that is intrinsically both racist and sentimental. "Where are the blossoms of those summers!—fallen, one by one: so all of my family departed . . . to the land of spirits. I am on the hill-top, and must go down into the valley; and when Uncas follows in my footsteps, there will no longer be any of the blood of the sagamores, for my boy is the last of the Mohicans." So says Chingachgook, sounding the *ubi sunt* theme early in Cooper's novel (28). By the end of the story, Uncas precedes Chingachgook "into the valley" of death, slain by the evil Huron Magua. The death of the son rather than of the father reinforces the sense of finality: for the Mohican *race*, to use the term Cooper prefers to *tribe*, this is also the death of the future. The future will not even contain half-breed Mohicans, assuming that Uncas might have mated with a non-Mohican like the hybrid Cora, the dark daughter of Colonel Munro.

Her West Indian blood is tainted by that of slaves through her mixed-race mother (159), but olive-skinned, raven-haired Cora is nevertheless—or, rather, is therefore—attractive both to Magua, who kidnaps her for his wife, and to Uncas. She is an example of the "tragic mulatta" figure in American literature; but not through miscegenation lies the future of any "race" for Cooper. Racial as opposed to cultural identity depends on a fantasy of purity, of unmixed blood. Natty Bumppo as a "man without a cross" is a man without a *racial* "cross" or mixture with his Mohican adoptive family.[12] It is above all this fantasy of racial purity that makes Cooper's Leatherstocking novels racist: the fantasy involves the ideas that there is a natural hierarchy of races; that the sexual intermingling of races is wrong or unnatural, because it can only degrade the superior without improving the inferior; and also that certain inferior races like the Mohicans (or like all Indians) are doomed to extinction by some innate flaw—the flaw identical with savagery itself.

Miscegenation from such a racist perspective can only be tragic; the tragic mulatta—if she is not sterile—can only degrade, not uplift. Moreover, Cora herself is horrified by the prospect of mating with an Indian. And even though she has done nothing to encourage Magua's attentions, she is slain in the grand finale by one of Magua's warriors just as Uncas is trying to rescue her. Magua then kills Uncas just before Hawkeye kills Magua. This bloody climax leads to the portrayal of the double funeral for Cora and Uncas, "last of the Mohicans," in the final chapter—a funeral performed by the friendly Delawares. The grief-imbued last chapter underscores the elegiac character of the entire novel, which is saturated with blood and death—the bloodiest of the Leatherstocking series. In a final passage that echoes his opening *ubi sunt* eloquence, Chingachgook mourns his son:

> Why hast thou left us, pride of the Wapanachki? . . . Thou art gone, youthful warrior. . . . Who that saw thee in battle would believe that thou couldst die!
> (344)

Chingachgook's opening and closing *ubi sunt* statements serve as symmetrical bookends between which Cooper narrates a history that, for the Mohicans, goes precisely nowhere.

Cooper's elegy to the Mohicans is also an epic. Like Sir Walter Scott's historical romances about the origins of modern Great Britain, Cooper depicts central or typical events—battles, migrations, political conflicts, and genocides—in the formation of the new American nation-state. That Cooper chose to write *historical* romances after Scott's manner, with Indians in the role of Scott's defeated Jacobite highlanders, is noteworthy in part because, according to some commentators, the new nation was too new to have either a literature or a history. But obviously it had a prerevolutionary, pre-national past, which is when Cooper sets his plot. Cooper, like Scott, offers a future-oriented history or prophecy by hindsight, according to which the past of the new nation-state of America lies all in the future—in contrast to the Mohicans who have no history. The elegiac loss of both history and future experienced by the Mohicans (and all Indians) is the negative or Great Zero from which springs the future-perfect, epic history of the United States.[13]

Throughout the Leatherstocking series, writes Robert F. Sayre, "The dying good Indians aid in the destruction of their bad-Indian enemies, then give way themselves to their initiated white brother Leatherstocking, who in turn, gives way to civilization" (13). *The Last of the Mohicans* represents the emergence of the modern United States out of the colonial past as the process of defeating those of its enemies who were prior to Britain, namely, the French and their Indian allies. But the French are never much of a factor; at the center, instead, are the Indians and their fate, which is already inherent in their racial identity as savages. The extinction of the Mohicans adumbrates the total extinction that Cooper believed was the inevitable future of all Indians. In Cooper's fantasy this funereal future is doubly displaced into the past and represented as having, in a sense, always already taken place. That the Mohicans have never been totally extinguished is beside the point; in *The Mohicans of Stockbridge*, Patrick Frazier ends his history of the struggles and survival of a remnant of the Mohicans by noting that their "contribution . . . to American history was soon forgotten, as was their very identity. Generations of Americans preferred to believe in a novelist's invention—that the Mohicans were noble, mythic knights of the forest, as romanticized, elusive, and extinct as the men of King Arthur's Round Table" (245).

Cooper offers a fictional rendition of the common early American opinion, expressed, for instance, by Washington Irving, that "there appears to be a tendency to extinction among all the savage nations, and this tendency would seem to have been in operation among the aboriginals of this country long before the advent of the white men" (*Astoria*, 158).[14] Cooper may not have shared Irving's view that the Indians were on their way to extinction *before* the arrival of Europeans, but he clearly did believe that they were doomed to extinction because they were savages, and he also believed that, no matter how the white man behaved, savagery, by definition, would cause the Indians' auto-genocide. In the 1831 introduction to *The Last of the Mohicans*, Cooper mentions "the seemingly inevitable fate of all these people, who disappear before the advances . . . of civilisation, as the verdure of their native forests falls before the nipping frost" (6–7). Like many other white Americans, both before and after the Civil War, Cooper applied extinction discourse also to other races, including Africans. Thus, in *Notions of the Americans*, Cooper writes: "As a rule the red man disappears before the superior moral and physical influence of the White, just as I believe the black man will eventually do" (483).[15]

That Cooper's attitude toward the vanishing "redskins" is philan-thropically sentimental is evident in his treatment of them through-out the Leatherstocking novels as "the ancient, and perhaps more lawful, occupants" of North America (*The Prairie*, 107). Reared by the friendly Delaware Indians, Natty Bumppo views them from a seem-ingly egalitarian and antiracist perspective. Thus, in *The Deerslayer*, Hurry Harry tells the young Natty that there are "three colours on 'arth: white, black and red":

> White is the highest colour, and therefore the best man; black comes next, and is put to live in the neighborhood of the white man, as tolerable, and fit to be made use of; and red comes last, which shows that those that made 'em never expected an Indian to be accounted as more than half human. (49–50)

To this evidently racist statement, which places the Indian on a lower rung of the hierarchy of races than the more useful "black," Natty re-sponds:"God made all three alike, Hurry." But Natty quickly qualifies what appears to be his racial egalitarianism:"God made us all, white, black and red . . . much the same in feelin's; though I'll not deny that he gave each race its gifts. A white man's gifts are christianized, while a redskin's are more for the wilderness" (50). Thus, Natty adds, it is natural and even "lawful" for an Indian to attack women and chil-dren and to scalp his victims, though these are unnatural and unlaw-ful "sins" for whites.

Later in *The Deerslayer*, scalping, according to the narrator, is "the peculiar art of [the red] race" (231). Natty elaborates on his doctrine of differing racial "gifts"—one that he maintains throughout his life on the frontier—by saying,"Revenge is an Injin gift, and forgiveness a white-man's" (*Deerslayer*, 89).[16] Or, as William Gilmore Simms puts it in his 1835 "American romance," *The Yemassee*, "The vengeance of the red man never sleeps, and is never satisfied while there is still a victim" (14). For both Simms and Cooper, as earlier for Brown, the "red man" is, first and foremost, a killing machine, unlikely to be salvageable through the Christian "gifts" of justice and mercy. For all three novelists, as for many other early American writers, ultimately the only way to deal with "the savages," assuming that removal is just a temporizing measure, is through their own method—that is, through the savagery of warfare and extermination.

Cooper is able to represent Natty Bumppo as an almost saintly figure, even in the midst of slaughtering "redskins," partly because of Natty's seeming impartiality and acceptance of differences between the races in terms of God's differential "gifts." But scalping and revenge, two Indian "gifts," are obviously mere stereotypic traits, ones that whites also abundantly exhibited in their combats with Indians. Other writers, including Brown and Simms, were more forthright than Cooper about "Indian hating," white vindictiveness, and white "savagery"; Brown and Simms express views close to those depicted by Herman Melville in his ironic meditation on "the metaphysics of Indian hating" in *The Confidence Man* (chaps. 23–25). And in *Nick of the Woods* (1835), Robert Montgomery Bird, while portraying all Indians as unredeemable savages, also portrays the appropriately named, insanely vindictive—indeed, genocidal—Nathan Slaughter, pious Quaker turned killing machine, who terrorizes the Indians in his single-handed obsession to exterminate as many as possible. Bird's white Indian-killer may be insane, but the Indians in *Nick of the Woods* deserve what they get; Bird's racism is not qualified by Cooper's brand of sentimentalism.

According to Cooper's sentimental racism, there are good Indians as well as bad ones, and the bad ones are exterminating the good. For Natty Bumppo—though himself half-savage in behavior—savagery is almost synonymous with evil, even while it is also almost synonymous with a state of nature that equals the innocence of childhood (and the past).[17] While Natty can insist that the "savage warfare" he and his Mohican allies are engaged in is an "evil [that] has been mainly done by men with white skins," he adds that "it has ended in turning the tomahawk of brother against brother" (*Last*, 227). Between Chingachgook's early *ubi sunt* pronouncement and the funereal last chapter, the story is crowded with battle scenes that mostly involve Indians killing Indians—brother against brother—just as in the grand finale, when Magua kills Uncas.

The main occasion for warfare is the conflict in the 1760s between the French and the British for the territory around Lake George. But apart from the siege and surrender of Fort William Henry, the French and British struggle hardly seems important. What Cooper foregrounds is quite specifically Indian warfare, announced as such in the opening paragraph: the "colonial wars of North America" were fought in "the wilderness" with the techniques of "the practised native warriors" (11); the story offers a "picture of the cruelty and fierceness of the savage warfare of those periods" (11). Cooper then describes the "savage" violence the Indians practiced against the isolated white colonists:

> The terrific character of their merciless enemies, increased, immeasurably, the natural horrors of warfare. Numberless recent massacres were still vivid in [the colonists'] recollections; nor was there any ear . . . so deaf as not to have drunk in with avidity the narrative of some fearful tale of midnight murder, in which the natives of the forest were the principal and barbarous actors. (13)

Cooper's novel echoes the countless captivity narratives that formed a major sort of "fearful tale" that the early American reading public "drunk in with avidity." These were typically atrocity stories like Mary Rowlandson's narrative, illustrating why savagery had to be extinguished.[18] Cora and Alice must be rescued from captivity twice; the second time, Cora dies along with Uncas and Magua. Captivity and rescue are basic elements in the plots of all the Leatherstocking novels and always entail the threats of rape, torture, and death but, perhaps even more terrifyingly, the threat of regression from civilization to savagery. Poised on the frontier (both figuratively and literally) between the irreconcilable extremes of the white and red races, the near-saintly Natty is able to treat both with equanimity and apparent objectivity toward the racial "gifts" on each side. But in *Last of the Mohicans*, as the war between the French and British fades from view, the main scenes show Indians exterminating Indians, with help from Natty's "long carbeen." Violence seems to be one of Natty's gifts, as it is also a gift of both bad and good Indians.[19]

Natty helps the cause of civilization—helps the white future begin to blossom in the howling wilderness—by fighting savagery with savagery, which might otherwise take too long to exterminate itself, so to speak. The slaying of Uncas by Magua is just the final touch, necessitating that the culturally half-savage Natty end the racial savagery by slaying Magua. That the slaughter is already part of history, located in the prerevolutionary past, underscores the inevitability of the future extinction of all Indians. Cooper's ascription of the Indians to a futureless past is most evident when Chingachgook mourns his son and his entire race; he can speak only in the sentimentalized past tense of elegy. But "denial of coevalness" can also paradoxically be figured by childhood, as when Cooper, Jefferson, Jackson, and many others refer to Indians as "the children of the forest."[20] Lora Romero notes that "Cooper incorporates the racial other as an earlier and now irretrievably lost version of the self" (392). Cooper's Indians are doomed children, stillborn in relation to white American history. Their prehistorical status is registered partly by their childishness; Chingachgook and Uncas are savage Peter Pans, "children of the forest" who do not, because they cannot, grow up.

The metaphor of the savage as futureless child is related to discourse about economic development, based on the assumption that societies, like individuals, grow up or mature.[21] But Cooper does not expect his Indians to develop or mature; he expects them to die. His "children of the forest" are frozen in a pre-state immaturity, apparently without government and almost without law, as Jefferson, for one, declared them to be (Drinnon, 78–98; Sheehan). For Cooper, the metaphor of the savage as futureless child crystallizes in the death of the man-child Uncas, the last child and the last hope of the Mohicans. This metaphor is underscored by the final words of the novel, in which Natty comforts Chingachgook for the loss of his child, and hence the loss of the future of his race: "I have no kin, and I may also say, like you, no people. He was your son, and a red-skin by nature . . . but if ever I forget the lad . . . may He who made us all, whatever may be our colour or our gifts, forget me!" (349). Here the story dissolves into philanthropic tears:

> Chingachgook grasped the hand that, in the warmth of feeling, the scout had stretched across the fresh earth, and in that attitude of friendship, these two sturdy and intrepid woodsmen bowed their heads together, while scalding tears fell to their feet, watering the grave of Uncas, like drops of rain. (349)

Michael Mann's 1992 film adaptation of *Last of the Mohicans* botches Cooper's philanthropically tearful ending, as it botches almost everything else in the novel, by having Russell Means speak these incongruous last words: "I, Chingachgook, last of the Mohicans . . ." Of course Chingachgook is literally the last of his race, but to identify him, rather than Uncas, as the final Mohican obliterates the sentimentally racist metaphor at the heart of Cooper's fantasy— the savage as futureless child. After the first rescue of Cora and Alice from the evil Hurons, Uncas—futureless child and last child of the childlike Mohicans—expresses an "instinctive delicacy" and "sympathy" that, the narrator says, "elevated him far above the intelligence, and advanced him probably centuries before the practices of his nation" (115). So the last Mohican is also the best, the exemplar of a future civilization that his race, already extinct but for Uncas and Chingachgook, will never achieve. Racist though it is, the poignancy of this displacement in time, this loss of both history and future, is the central message of Cooper's elegy-epic. The movie is unfaithful to the novel precisely because it erases Cooper's—and nineteenth-century America's—racist but elegiac understanding of savagery.[22]

The movie continues the ideological project of Cooper's novel, however, because Cooper himself was inventing ways to alter history, especially by insisting that the extinction of all Native Americans was inevitable. In a sense, Mann's film adaptation perfects Cooper's sentimental racism by obliterating that racism (and, with it, the imperialist and racist roots of United States nation building). Mann thus also helps to perfect Cooper's canonization as a classic American author—a canonization rendered possible only through minimizing or denying Cooper's sentimental racism.[23] The movie looks remorselessly, cynically on the historical violence it portrays, and yet it identifies nothing whatsoever racist about that violence. Perhaps there is even an implicit antiracism in the movie: Indians and whites are equals in combat, and maybe also in love, although the Indians lose—not clearly because they are Indians but rather just because that is the story line. So, too, the sentimentalism of Cooper's brand of racism already initiated the process of mystification whereby racism interprets itself as having the best interest of the Indians at heart, as with Jackson's "Philanthropy" and the cynical policy of Indian removal starting in the 1830s.

4. Humanitarian Causes

Antislavery and Saving Aboriginals

Until the American Civil War in the 1860s, humanitarianism concerning other races focused on slavery. But that issue could not be disentangled from questions of imperialism, economic exploitation, and the impact of white colonization on indigenous populations in Africa, the Americas, and elsewhere. Within the British Empire, the abolitionist struggle culminated in the outlawing of the slave trade in 1807 and then of slavery itself in 1833. The condition of the ex-slaves and the continuation of slavery in the southern United States, Brazil, Cuba, and parts of Africa and the Middle East meant that much remained to be done long after 1833; even before that date the antislavery movement had started to broaden its concern to the plight of indigenous peoples, especially in Africa. After the legislative victory of 1833, Thomas Fowell Buxton, successor to William Wilberforce as parliamentary leader of the British abolitionists, established a Select Committee on Aborigines, which he chaired from 1835 to 1837; its work led to the founding, in 1837, of the Aborigines Protection Society (APS) under the leadership of Thomas Hodgkin, with Buxton as its first president. In that same year Buxton organized the African Civilization Society, and in 1839 he helped to launch a new Anti-Slavery Society.

Influenced by the American and French revolutions, secular humanitarians made their case in terms of the universal "rights of man."

Thus, according to English radical Thomas Hardy, those rights "are not confined to this small island but are extended to the whole human race, black or white, high or low, rich or poor" (quoted in Blackburn, 147).[1] Further, the so-called laws of political economy were held to be universally valid, and those laws treated slavery and imperialism as uneconomical if not unethical. Most of the leaders of the antislavery movement were, however, Quakers or evangelicals, influenced by the individualist doctrine of "the inner light" of the Wesleyan revival. Methodism and other versions of evangelicalism tended to be conservative about domestic politics and yet alert to the possible redemption of souls everywhere in the world: all humans were equally worthy (or unworthy) of salvation. Between the 1790s and 1830s the rise and flourishing of missionary societies supported both abolitionism and efforts to protect indigenous peoples throughout the world. Although missionaries viewed savage beliefs and customs as deviltry, they were often astute albeit amateur ethnographic observers, who contributed greatly to knowledge about the cultures they sought to reform or destroy (Stocking, 87–92; Herbert, *Culture*, 150–203).

For a variety of reasons, however, including Buxton's death in 1845, humanitarian idealism began to decline in the 1840s. The APS kept up its efforts on behalf of aboriginals everywhere well into the twentieth century. But the very success of the antislavery movement, at least in the British context, made further efforts on behalf of indigenous peoples abroad seem both anticlimactic and, to many observers, a distraction from social justice issues at home. The Irish Famine of 1845–50, a mass extinction within the boundaries of the supposedly United Kingdom, tragically dramatized this point; humanitarian efforts to alleviate Irish suffering were belated and inadequate. By the end of the 1830s, moreover, the humanitarian attempt to save the last Tasmanian aboriginals had clearly failed. And both missionaries and the general public in Britain and North America were becoming increasingly aware of the difficulties involved in converting and civilizing savages, who often seemed stubbornly resistant to abandoning their beliefs and cultures.

Defenders of slavery saw no connection between it and the extinction of any race. After all, it was in the interest of slave traders and slave owners, no matter how cruel or negligent, to keep their property alive. Even for abolitionists the connections of the slave trade and slavery to the extinction of primitive races were less than clear. Key exceptions, however, were the Bushmen and Hottentots of South Africa, victims of deliberate extermination, forced labor, and enslavement by the Boers (Cape Colony had only recently come under British control, first between 1795 and 1803 and then again in 1806). But there was no way to demonstrate that the slave trade was depopulating central Africa, as abolitionists sometimes claimed.[2] Malthus maintained that the population of Africa outran subsistence despite the slave trade (Higman, 176). The "check" to its population that the trade provided forestalled worse checks, especially famine. Malthus's opinion gestured toward what others—abolitionists themselves, at times—claimed about Africa's great fecundity (and Africans' alleged sexual prowess). From this perspective, Africa was an immense womb of labor, and slaves were a renewable resource.

According to the early economists including Malthus, however, slavery was wasteful in part because it wasted lives. In *The Wealth of Nations* Adam Smith considers "the wear and tear of a slave" versus that "of a free servant" and concludes that "the work done by slaves, though it appears to cost only their maintenance, is in the end the dearest of any" (1:90, 411). Illustrating Smith's economic principles in her abolitionist tale, *Demarara* (1833), Harriet Martineau writes that slavery involves an enormous "waste of labour and capital," including the destruction of the slaves through "the scantiness of their food, and the oppressiveness of their toil" (143). At issue is not the depopulation of Africa but of slave-holding colonies such as Demarara (British Guiana). In debates over the slave trade, the question of whether slave populations would shrink or grow without that trade was crucial; both sides claimed, though from opposite motives, that the number of slaves would decline without continuous importation. Abolitionists were hopeful that, without the trade, slavery would wither away. They were thus unable to view the decline or disappearance of any slave population as a tragedy on a par with the extinction of, say, a few thousand Tasmanians.

Martineau posits a direct correlation or even identity between moral and economic "principles." This is one way in which science and religion often reinforced each other. Alfred Bruce, protagonist of *Demarara*, explains to his slave-owning father how religion and economics work in tandem for the betterment of all: "There is this conspicuous mark of blessing on capital rightly applied, that the more it increases the more it will increase; while precisely the reverse is the fact with . . . unrighteously made capital" (22). And both slaves as a false form of property and what they produce are "unrighteously made capital." Throughout *Demarara*, the didactic young Alfred, "a perfect Quixote," both preaches and demonstrates the superiority of "free" over slave labor to slave owners and to slaves themselves—especially the intelligent, articulate, hard-working Cassius, whose freedom Alfred helps to purchase. In so doing, Alfred also demonstrates that good economic behavior is both profitable and humane (even godly in a liberal way: Martineau in the 1830s was still a Unitarian).

As in *Demarara*, abolitionism often sought to double its persuasiveness by combining religion and economics. Economic laws, human rights, and God's justice and mercy should harmonize; when they did not, as in slavery, then the world was profoundly out of joint. Further, the extinction of an entire race of innocent human beings under the onslaught of European imperialism was almost unthinkable, and yet it was happening and, indeed, had happened. For the world to be put in order again—for Christianity and civilization to be victorious over disorder and evil—both slavery and the extinction of primitive races had to be stopped. At the same time savagery also had to cease, to be converted to Christianity and, insofar as possible, to civilization. But as Hodgkin, Buxton, and the other members of the APS also recognized, extinction as a threatened catastrophe made highly dramatic propaganda. The more the APS and other "friends of the aborigines" talked about preventing the extinction of primitive races, the more they found themselves asserting that extinction was happening and was, indeed, the expected course of events under modern (even British) imperialism.

Needless to say, the APS often found itself in conflict with the Colonial Office in London and with colonizers in South Africa, Australia, and elsewhere. Much of its impetus and information came from missionaries, who were frequently at odds with the forward march of colonization. Of course, missionaries were themselves part of that march; in many places such as Polynesia, New Zealand, and South Africa, they were, though often unintentionally, the vanguard of imperialist expansion. They were also, however, a vanguard with a purpose different from that of other colonizers, whose first aim was, of course, not the salvation of primitive souls or lives.

The contradictions in humanitarian ideology arose in part because those who espoused it did not question the natural historians' insistence on racial inequality. Individuals of all races were entitled to justice and salvation, but that did not make either individuals or races of equal ability or worth in physical, mental, cultural, or even moral terms. Hence humanitarians could be both abolitionists and racists, simultaneously believing that slavery was evil and that members of African and other non-white races were biologically inferior to Europeans. In *Demarara* Martineau, to her credit, insists that slaves and ex-slaves are fully human, as she does also in her antislavery novel, *The Hour and the Man* (1841), based on the life of Toussaint L'Ouverture and the Haitian revolution of the 1790s.

The British abolition of the slave trade in 1807 involved many factors: military, economic, and political, as well as ideological. Eric Williams's *Capitalism and Slavery* (1944) sparked a continuing debate about the relationship between humanitarian ideology and these other factors, especially economic. There is no doubt, however, about Williams's main contention that capitalism and industrialization laid the groundwork for the rise and influence of humanitarian ideology, including abolitionism. Furthermore, abolishing the slave trade was, in several respects, easier than abolishing slavery itself. Slave owners in the United States and the Caribbean sometimes themselves opposed the slave trade. "The suspension of slave imports," writes Robin Blackburn, "could even find support among planters, whose slaveholding thereby became more valuable" (90). This was especially true as abolition of the trade appeared increasingly likely, and as the economies of the older Caribbean colonies weakened under the stress of competition, politics, and slave resistance and rebellions.

During the Napoleonic wars, British politicians found in opposition to the slave trade a popular reform cause that expressed "patriotic conceptions of English liberty and a new sense of global trusteeship" and that did not necessarily entail application of similar ideals at home (Blackburn, 311). Evangelical leader of the abolitionist movement in Britain for many years, and a main force behind the enactments of 1807 and 1833, Wilberforce opposed domestic reform measures that he deemed "Jacobin," and the same was true of Buxton.[3] It was this contradiction—reformist abroad, reactionary at home—as well as its self-righteousness and often religious intolerance that led to frequent condemnations of the "Exeter Hall," evangelical strain of humanitarianism. Thus, in writing about the tragic Niger Expedition of 1841, Charles Dickens lambastes "the heated visions of philanthropists for the railroad Christianisation of Africa, and the abolition of the slave trade" (64), and in *Bleak House* he treats Mrs. Jellyby's

Borrioboola-Gha mission as an absurd distraction from the duties of home and family.[4]

The abolition of slavery in all British territories followed closely on the passage of the first Reform Bill of 1832; in the new climate of reform of the 1830s, humanitarianism came to the fore in governing the expanding British Empire. Presiding over the Colonial Office were James Stephen and Lord Glenelg (Charles Grant), who both had strong ties to the evangelical wing of the abolitionist movement (Knaplund; Mellor, 249). And in 1835 Buxton gained approval for his Aborigines Committee, specifically to examine the causes of the sixth "Caffre War" of 1834–35 but also to investigate "the general treatment of the aboriginal nations bordering on [all] our settlements" (377).[5] By that time Buxton, Hodgkin, and other abolitionists had been in correspondence with the Reverend John Philip, Thomas Pringle, and others in South Africa who supported the antislavery cause. The Boers' practice of slavery, using Indonesians and Malays as well as Africans, made South Africa a crucial focus for the British abolitionists. Like Britain's West Indian colonies, the Cape was slave-holding territory under British control, though the slave owners were not of British origin. And the Caffre War on the eastern frontier, which devastated the already troubled Albany settlement of British immigrants, provided a key motivation for the parliamentary hearings that Buxton conducted.

By the early 1830s Buxton, Hodgkin, Stephen, Glenelg, and other London-based humanitarians had long been aware of the so-called commando system that the Boers used against the Bushmen, the Xhosas, and other indigenous populations. From the time of the "General Commando" of 1774, the Boers had been waging an intermittent war against the Bushmen with the avowed aim of exterminating them (Penn). Together with the fates of the Tasmanian and Newfoundland aboriginals (the Beothuks), the near-extinction of the Bushmen was a clear, troubling case of genocide within British territory. And on the eastern frontier of Cape Colony, patrols and commandos of mixed Boer, British, and Hottentot soldiers had commenced the practice of reprisals against the Xhosas for allegedly stealing cattle. The result on that frontier was a state of constant friction, punctuated by a series of wars. As John Fairbairn, editor of the *South African Commercial Advertiser*, put it in 1835: "We seldom had peace or war for many months together in *a pure state*. There has always been a mixture of both, now the one and now the other pre-dominating" (quoted in Pretorius, 34).

Shortly after the antislavery victory of 1833, Buxton declared that his "attention has been drawn of late to the wickedness of our pro-ceedings as a nation, towards the ignorant and barbarous natives of countries on which we seize." He added that he hated "shooting in-nocent savages worse than slavery itself," and asked: "What have we Christians done for" the savages?

> We have usurped their lands, kidnapped, enslaved, and murdered themselves. The greatest of their crimes is that they sometimes trespass into the lands of their forefathers; and the very greatest of their misfortunes is that they have ever become acquainted with Christians. Shame on such Christianity! (368–69)

In Parliament on July 1, 1834, Buxton spoke on the treatment of abo-riginals, especially in South Africa; he was more exercised about the commando system than about slavery. During the election of January 1835 Buxton reiterated his interest in protecting indigenous peoples, a topic that "formed his principal occupation throughout the year" (376) and that resulted in the formation of the Aborigines Commit-tee. From 1835 to 1837 Buxton and his fellow committee members in-terviewed numerous colonial officials, missionaries, settlers, and sol-diers about the treatment indigenous peoples were receiving at the hands of colonists especially in South Africa, but also more generally throughout the empire.[6]

The humanitarian stance of Buxton's Aborigines Committee is ev-ident from its 1837 summary of its findings:

> The oppression of the natives of barbarous countries is a practice which pleads no claim to indulgence; it is an evil of comparatively recent origin, impercep-tible and unallowed in its growth; it never has had even the colour of sanction from the legislature of this country; no vested rights are associated with it, and we have not the poor excuse that it contributes to any interest of the state. On the contrary, in point of economy, of security, of commerce, of reputation, it is a short-sighted and disastrous policy. As far as it has prevailed, it has been a burthen on the empire. (*Report*, 2:75)

Although this statement is part of its conclusion, throughout its hear-ings there was no doubt about the position of the committee, whose members already believed that the only alternative to the complete extermination of most or all primitive races was their conversion to

Christianity, coupled with free trade and, as far as possible given the capabilities of the non-white races, their elevation to (or toward) civilization.[7]

Perhaps half the hearings of the Aborigines Committee dealt with South Africa, but Hodgkin, who appeared before it as a witness, persuaded Buxton to broaden the inquiry to include Canada, Australia, New Zealand, and Polynesia. Regarding South Africa, the committee learned that the Hottentot population had been reduced from about two hundred thousand (or more) to thirty-two thousand (*Report*, 2:25–26). It also noted that in 1774 the Boer government had ordered "the extirpation of the whole of the Bushmen, and three commandos . . . were sent out to execute it. The massacre at the time was horrible, and the system of persecution [has] continued unremitting" (*Report*, 2:27). In the case of the Boers' "persecution" of the Bushmen, the committee understood that it was confronting an instance of what would today be called genocide.[8]

From the committee's standpoint, the British assumption of the government of the Cape Colony in 1806 should have brought relief and justice to the Bushmen, Hottentots, Xhosas, and other indigenous peoples. There had been, however, various complicating factors leading up to the 1834–35 Caffre War. In its early days the British administration of the Cape tried to reform or at least regularize the forced labor system practiced by the Boers. It did so in part by legislating an employment code for Hottentots and Bushmen. This 1809 "Hottentot code," however, amounted to the first of South Africa's infamous "pass laws": Hottentots and Bushmen could not leave the employment of any white person they were contracted to without permission from that person, and they could not roam freely within the Colony without an official pass. The pass system did nothing to eliminate forced labor, including slavery and the "apprenticeship" of Hottentot and Bushman children to white "employers" for long, fixed terms of service.

Meddlesome though it may have seemed to the Boers, they cannot have been very displeased with the 1809 code. They objected vigorously, however, to what they saw as missionary meddling and its legal consequences.[9] In 1812 missionaries under the auspices of the London Mission Society (LMS) brought the attention of officials in Capetown to the mistreatment and sometimes murder of Hottentots along the eastern frontier. This resulted in the so-called Black Circuit of colonial judges, who put seventeen Boer settlers on trial. Most of the charges were dropped, but, as George Mellor comments, the Black Circuit "had unhappy results. It created a mass of resentment which became focused mainly on the missionaries . . . and to a less degree on the colonial Government" (234). And it led to the Slachter's Nek rebellion of 1815, when forty-seven Boers were arrested by a Hottentot militia and tried on various charges, resulting in five executions. Among the Boers, these events helped to inspire the Great Trek of the late 1830s and 1840s (Walker; Thompson, 87–96).

Recent historians have stressed, however, the complexity of motivations underlying the Trek. They have also noted that it was British settlers and officials as much as the Boers who laid the foundation of racism that contributed to the installation of the apartheid regime starting in 1948. One of the witnesses before the Aborigines Committee, Andries Stockenström, wrote in his *Autobiography*: "The theory which makes the black irreclaimable savages, fit only to be exterminated, like the wolves, was not of Boer origin" (1:79). Perhaps so, although the Boer Voortrekkers viewed all black Africans as nonhuman "creatures" of the devil, much as the Puritans of New England had viewed Native Americans. In any event, quoting Stockenström's remark, Timothy Keegan points out that the "phrase 'irreclaimable savages' was notoriously coined by [British] Governor Sir Benjamin D'Urban in 1835," during the war against the Xhosas (Keegan 36, 303 n. 64).

For the Boers, the Black Circuit and Slachter's Nek rebellion foreshadowed the greater crises of Ordinance 50 in 1828 and the abolition of slavery in 1833. Ordinance 50 canceled the 1809 pass system and other legal restraints on the Hottentots, and the end of slavery meant for the Boers further loss of power over their black labor force as well as a huge financial setback. Meanwhile, the Colonial Office in London had sponsored a group of some four thousand British immigrants, including Thomas Pringle and his family, who in 1820 settled in the Albany territory around Port Elizabeth and Grahamstown. This colonization led in turn to renewed conflict with the Xhosas, who had already seen their territory encroached on by the Boers. The British administration of Cape Colony was now confronted with a triangular struggle between the new British colonists, the Boers, and the Xhosas, just as it was also wrestling with the questions of forced labor and slavery regarding the Hottentots and Bushmen.

The Xhosa "invasion" of what had previously been their own territory led to their defeat in 1835 and the appropriation of territory beyond the original Albany frontier of the Fish River. Governor D'Urban hoped also to evict the Xhosas from the new "Queen Adelaide" territory, which would then, he hoped, serve as an empty buffer zone between them and the Albany settlement. To Lord Glenelg, head of the Colonial Office in London, this looked like more unwarranted territorial expansion and the probable cause of future frontier wars. Glenelg overturned D'Urban's appropriation of the new territory.[10] To most white South Africans, Glenelg's rejection of D'Urban's plan seemed a betrayal of their interests. Yet, for Buxton and the humanitarians, the "retrocession" of Queen Adelaide territory seemed at the time a great victory. Thus, on first hearing of Glenelg's decision, Buxton wrote:

> The hand of the proud oppressor in Africa has been, under Providence, arrested, and a whole nation, doomed to ruin, exile, and death, has been delivered and restored to its rights. On a given day the drum was beat in the front of Tzatzoe's house, and the troops were marched directly back again to the British territory, and the "fertile and beautiful Adelaide" was once more Caffreland. . . . This is, indeed, a noble victory of right over might. (380)

Tzatzoe was a christianized Xhosa chief who had been brought to London to testify before the Aborigines Committee.

In full agreement with Buxton was the Reverend John Philip, superintendent of the LMS missions in South Africa. Instrumental in the enacting of Ordinance 50, Philip was also one of the main movers behind the Aborigines Committee and a key witness before it (A. Ross, 112–15).[11] The exact influence of Philip's 1828 *Researches in South Africa* and of his correspondence with Glenelg, Buxton, Stephen, and other officials and politicians is difficult to assess, though it was certainly considerable. In his own time Philip was both praised by the humanitarians as a savior of aboriginal lives and souls, and condemned by the colonial interests as a meddlesome traitor. A contentious person, he lost a lawsuit against him for libeling one South African official, whom he had accused of maltreating a Hottentot. He was even charged by some of his fellow missionaries with exaggerating and engaging in politics (or engaging in the wrong politics, at any rate) in pursuing his humanitarian aims (Du Plessis, 141–53, 429–32). He was also accused by another witness before the Aborigines Committee, Colonel Thomas Wade, of fomenting the Caffre War of 1834–35 by telling the Xhosas that their territory and their cattle were being taken from them, and that they should appeal for help to King William and the Colonial Office in London (*Report*, 1:284–87). For his part, in his testimony on June 15, 1836, Philip pointed out that the Xhosas "have been represented as bloodthirsty savages," worse even than "the New Zealanders," and blamed for starting the war on the eastern frontier without any provocation from either the Boer or the British colonists. Philip continued:

> It is not my intention to vindicate the atrocities that the Caffres may have actually committed, or to cut off the sympathy due to the colonists who have actually suffered. But the strong language which has been employed is certainly not borne out by facts. The truth is, that before the Caffres returned violence they had been long and greatly provoked. (*Report*, 1:557)

Even if the Xhosas were the aggressors in the 1834–35 conflict, it was, after all, the sixth war they had waged in their effort to stave off the advance of white colonization.

Philip wrote his 1828 *Researches* to bring public attention to "the oppressions of the native tribes, with a view to obtain for them the protection of the British Government" (1:xii). He had earlier appealed to Wilberforce, who, in 1822, had requested, via parliamentary resolution, that the Colonial Office appoint a commission of inquiry to look into "the oppressed state of the natives of South Africa" (2:244). The commission had largely borne out Philip's claims. "What a reproach to civilized nations," Philip writes in the preface to *Researches*, "that their neighbourhood to savage tribes has hitherto proved more fatal to their numbers and their comforts, than famine, pestilence, or the wild beasts of the wilderness" (1:xxxiv). Colonization everywhere has entailed "an unbroken line of crimes and blood" toward aborigines (1:2). Throughout *Researches*, Philip offers a detailed, distressed and distressing account of the history of white South Africa's "system of oppression and extermination" (1:35). The Boer settlers established the system, and early on "formed the project of making the colonial government a party in assisting them to enslave or exterminate . . . the original inhabitants" (1:41). Philip notes, however, that British treatment of those aboriginal inhabitants is often no better—in some instances, worse—than what they received from the Boers: "Whatever may be said, on a comparative view of English and Dutch humanity, it is evident that the mass of evil brought upon the wretched Bushmen is greater under the English government than under the Dutch" (2:46).

The Boers' commando system may at first have been retaliatory, but by the 1770s that hardly mattered, Philip declares, "for we find that in the year 1774, the whole race of Bushmen, or Hottentots, who had not submitted to servitude, was ordered to be seized or extirpated" (1:42). Many authorities acknowledge that this was the case, so Philip is not exaggerating on this point; he continues:

> In the year 1779 the commando system was carried on with great vigour. Most of the reports are lost, but from what remains we learn that one hundred and fifteen Bushmen were killed, while the orders of government for their entire extermination were repeated so peremptorily, that it is matter of surprise that the whole country was not depopulated. (1:48)[12]

Most of those killed were adult males; many women and children were captured and enslaved. Even if enslavement was as frequent as slaughter, the ultimate result, Philip claims, is the same, because slavery itself exterminates. Thus, in the case of the Hottentots, forced labor and enslavement resulted in the "degradation of [their] character":

> A deep and habitual gloom . . . took place of that hilarity which had formerly distinguished them. Their indolence increased to a degree hardly credible, and they became more and more addicted to gluttony and drunkenness. . . . Their numbers began greatly to decline, the very structure of their bodies was said to have shrunk, and to have lost its force and agility, and the whole race seemed rapidly hastening to annihilation. (1:57)

Throughout *Researches*, Philip is careful to cite numerous earlier authorities who bear out most of his claims, so it is hardly the case that he is simply exaggerating or creating a pro-aboriginal case out of whole cloth. Perhaps losing the libel trial made him relatively cautious in his book. Yet exaggeration and outright lying were criticisms often leveled at him, along with the charge of imposing his views on the Colonial Office and on Parliament in London. Certainly Philip's portrayal of the behaviors of Boer and British settlers toward the Bushmen, Hottentots, and Xhosas is almost uniformly negative. But if Philip's exposé was thoroughly anti-colonist, it was also pro-imperialist: a plea for more intervention, at least on the part of the British government. "The Hottentots," writes Philip, "despairing of help from every other quarter, now look to the justice and humanity of England for deliverance" (1:400). This was a troubling message, however, to the authorities in London, most of whom were "reluctant imperialists" (Galbraith).

Though Philip's efforts on behalf of the aborigines of South Africa were well received by most humanitarians and missionaries, he became anathema to Boer and British settlers. According to W. M. Macmillan, Philip is "one of the most hated figures in any national history" (10).[13] Thus, in his multivolume *History of South Africa,* first published in 1892, George McCall Theal accused Philip of fanaticism, lying, and, indeed, along with the more general influence of missionary humanitarianism, of doing great damage to "the progress of the colony in prosperity and of the black races towards civilisation" (5:504). This "progress," Theal claims, "was greatly retarded by the measures which [Philip] devised and his powerful supporters carried out" (5:504). These charges are just as ludicrous as the antithetical claim, often made by abolitionists, missionaries, and their sympathetic historians and biographers, that the humanitarianism of Philip and his allies changed the "racial order" of South Africa significantly for the better (see Keegan).

That humanitarianism in South Africa was not the monopoly of Philip and other missionaries is evident from the testimony before the Aborigines Committee of Andries Stockenström, governor-general of the eastern Cape. Stockenström's father, who had immigrated to South Africa from Sweden, had been killed in a border conflict with the Xhosas. Stockenström himself had organized and led commandos against the Xhosas but had also sought ways to reduce the violence, create a reasonable treaty system, and ensure fair treatment on all sides. It had also been Stockenström's idea to form the Hottentot settlement along the Kat River in 1829 as a buffer between the white colonists and the Xhosas, though this tactic did little to prevent conflict.

In London, after his resignation from his official post, Stockenström appeared before the Aborigines Committee on August 19, 1835, and was asked if commando raids on the Xhosas, supposedly to regain stolen cattle, had "led to a regular war of extermination, and rendered it necessary to take possession of the whole of Caffre land?" Stockenström agreed that that was happening and that the result would be "continual war" until "it arrived at extermination." According to Stockenström:

one party must go to the wall, and that of course would be the weaker. These
people . . . are an agricultural people now, and if you deprive them of the
means of subsistence they become a wandering tribe of huntsmen; in fact they
will become what we have before our eyes, bushmen . . . unless something
can be done now . . . there will be no safety till they are all exterminated. (*Report*, 1:92)

When Stockenström was called to testify again in March 1836, he
was asked: "Your great reliance, then, would be upon cultivation of
trade, and upon justice, in proceedings with the natives?" Stockenström replied:

That is the plan I would act upon with mankind at large, not only with barbarians and savages . . . the main point which I would have in view would be
trade, commerce, peace and civilization. The other alternative is extermination; for you can stop nowhere; you must go on; you may have a short respite
when you have driven panic into the people, but you must come back to the
same thing until you have shot the last man. (*Report*, 1:244)

While Philip and his fellow missionaries were working to end the
slaughter and enslavement of the Bushmen, Hottentots, and Xhosas
by both Boer and British settlers, Thomas Pringle, John Fairbairn,
and other recent British immigrants to the Cape were helping to establish a new, liberal climate, new journals, and a new literature in
English with a critical edge toward both the Boers and the colonial
government of Lord Charles Somerset. Through the influence of Sir
Walter Scott, Pringle, former editor of *The Edinburgh Magazine*,[14]
had received a land grant in South Africa and, with his family, immigrated there as part of the 1820 Albany settlement (Pringle, *Narrative*;
Edwards; Peires, 473–80). Pringle soon moved to Capetown to become head of the Government Library. He also established a school
and invited his Scottish friend, Fairbairn, to join him in journalistic
and literary endeavors. After Fairbairn arrived at Capetown, the two
began editing the *South African Commercial Advertiser*, the first nongovernmental newspaper in the colony. Together with Abraham
Faure and George Greig, Pringle also started the short-lived *South
African Journal*. Its life was short because, after Somerset objected to
an article about "the present state and prospects of the English emigrants in Albany," Pringle stopped publishing it. Reportage of a libel
trial against Somerset in the *Commercial Advertiser* also led to its cen-

sorship. These events, in turn, caused the Colonial Office, though several years after the fact, to rule in favor of freedom of the press at the Cape (Davenport, 315–17).

Pringle returned to Britain in 1826 and published an antislavery article in the *New Monthly Magazine* (October 1826). The article led to his appointment, through Buxton, as secretary of the Anti-Slavery Society (Pringle, *Narrative*, 217). From the time of his appointment until his death from tuberculosis in 1834, Pringle wrote much of the Society's propaganda. Shortly after the passage of the Emancipation Act of 1833, Pringle published *African Sketches* (1834), a volume of poems that has been called "the founding artwork of South African English literature" (S. Gray, 196), and in 1835 he also published his *Narrative of a Residence in South Africa*.

If Pringle's *Sketches* can indeed be viewed as the first important work of South African literature in English, then that literature begins in proleptic elegy.[15] The same can be said of the first novels written in and about South Africa. These include the anonymous *Makanna; or, the Land of the Savage* (1834), which deals with the Caffre War of 1819, and Edward Kendall's *English Boy at the Cape: An Anglo-African Story* (1835).[16] And in one of her first "illustrations of political economy," *Life in the Wilds* (1832), Harriet Martineau writes about the devastating consequences of conflict between a group of British settlers and the "fierce" but inevitably vanishing Bushmen:

> The Bushmen were the original possessors of much of the country about the Cape, which the British and the Dutch have since taken for their own. The natives were hunted down like so many wild beasts. This usage naturally made them fierce and active in their revenge. (4)

For Martineau, hunting down aboriginals to slaughter them is both immoral and uneconomical, especially if—as is the case with the Bushmen—they are able to fight back. In any event, in all these early works of fiction, the Bushmen are depicted as doomed.

Several of Pringle's poems in *African Sketches* feature narrators who are the last survivors of their fallen tribes. Thus Pringle's "Bechuana boy" describes the attack of a Boer commando who set fire to his village, shot all the grown men ("One living man they left us not"), and took him into captivity. The Bechuana boy's lament is addressed specifically to an Englishman who, the boy hopes, will sympathize with his plight, although

> thou ne'er canst know
> The injured bondman's bitter woe,
> When round his breast, like scorpions, cling
> Black thoughts that madden while they sting.
>
> Yet this hard fate I might have borne,
>   And taught in time my soul to bend,
> Had my sad yearning heart forlorn
>   But found a single friend:
> My race extinct or far removed,
> The Boor's rough brood I could have loved;
> But each to whom my bosom turned
> Even like a hound the black boy spurned.
>   (6)

In another poem, the Boers slaughter the tribe of "the captive of Camalú," and enslave its speaker; the grieving captive opines, in standard romantic fashion, that death is preferable to slavery:

> Death the frail body only kills—
> But Thraldom brutifies the mind.
>   (48)

Here and in several of his other poems Pringle identifies the Boers as the villains who are enslaving and exterminating the more primitive races of South Africa. Thus the Boers track down "the Bushman" in "the lone wilderness":

> His secret lair
> Surrounded, echoes to the thundering gun,
> And the wild shriek of anguish and despair!
> He dies—yet, ere life's ebbing sands are run,
> Leaves to his sons a curse, should they be friends
> With the proud "Christian-Men"—for they are fiends!
>   (69)

"Makanna's Gathering," a poem by Pringle about the 1819 frontier war, was even more provocative, at least for one colonialist critic, who thought it had helped to inspire the Xhosas to go to war in 1834–35. This accusation, based on the absurd notion that the Xhosas could somehow have read and been influenced by Pringle's poem, suggests how much animosity and paranoia there was, at least by the time of the 1834–35 war, toward humanitarianism in general. First published in the *Oriental Herald* in 1827 under the title "War Song of Makanna," Pringle's poem represents the prophet-chief of the 1819 rebellion awakening the "Amakósa" (or Xhosas) to "arm yourselves for war . . . To sweep the White Men from the earth, And drive them to the sea" (35, 100). Writing in the *Graham's Town Journal* in 1835, the critic declares:

> Not the most zealous "Makanna," nor the most ferocious Kafir [*sic*] chief . . . could have spirited up his countrymen to the remorseless warfare of revenge and extermination more effectually or more earnestly than has this ungrateful viper, Mr. Thomas Pringle. What!! a Briton! and one who is the conspicuous organ of all the real or apparent philanthropists of the day . . . good God!

The critic goes on to accuse Pringle of "draw[ing] down the horrid vengeance of the unsparing assegai upon our defenceless and, till now, peaceful homes" (quoted in Pretorius, 51).

Pringle received no such hostile response in Britain. On the contrary, his poetry and his *Narrative*, as well as his work for the Antislavery Society, helped to establish him as a perhaps minor but nonetheless representative "philanthropist." Like his poetry, moreover, Pringle's *Narrative* is liberal, romantic, and also sympathetic to the missionaries, including Philip. Pringle again condemns the mistreatment of Bushmen and Hottentots by the Boers, and he speculates that the Bushmen, instead of being the ancient, genuine aboriginals of the subcontinent, are the recent product of Boer violence and enslavement of the Hottentots:

> The Bushmen or *Bosjemen* (as they are termed by the Dutch colonists), appear to be the remains of Hottentot hordes, originally subsisting, like all the aboriginal tribes of Southern Africa, chiefly by rearing sheep and cattle; but who have been driven, either by the gradual encroachments of the European colonists, or by internal wars with other tribes, to seek for refuge among the inaccessible rocks and deserts of the interior. (224)

Pringle adds that it is "doubtful" if "any considerable hordes of these people existed" before the arrival of Europeans. In short, the Bushmen, a branch of the Hottentots in Pringle's account, are South African resistance fighters. They are doomed, but nonetheless noble, savages. In contrast, the tamer Hottentots, who stuck to their domestic ways and minimal property (especially cattle), are not quite doomed, but almost so, and they are less than noble.

> It is certain that numerous tribes, once subsisting in ease and affluence on the produce of their herds and flocks, have by the incessant incroachments of the colonists been either driven to the sterile deserts, and of necessity transformed to Bushmen, or utterly extirpated. This process has been carrying on, as the authentic records of the Colony prove, for at least a hundred and twenty years. (Pringle, *Narrative*, 225)

In his *Narrative*, Pringle praises Philip, "the Las Casas of Southern Africa" (324), and also Stockenström, Buxton, and other humanitarians in part for the passage of Ordinance 50, and he rejects the argument that that law was causing "the *retrogression* of the race [of Hottentots] into *barbarism*."[17] Pringle expresses surprise, however, that "many of the English colonists . . . joined most vociferously in this ungenerous outcry" against Ordinance 50 and then, shortly after, against the abolition of slavery. British settlers also benefited from South Africa's regime of racism and forced labor (albeit not slavery: the 1820 Albany colonists were barred from owning slaves). In any event, Pringle calls Ordinance 50 "the Magna Carta of the Aborigines of South Africa" (249). However, his general conclusion about the future of South Africa's aboriginals under the impact of white colonization is pessimistic. If the "frontier colonists, be they Dutch or British . . . continue to be semi-barbarians" and to employ the "commando system," then the result is predictable:

> The weak will gradually melt away before the strong; tribe after tribe will be extirpated as their brethren have been extirpated; and year after year, while we continue to *talk* of our boundless benevolence and our Christian philanthropy, fresh loads of that guilt which the Almighty has denounced in awful

terms—the bloodstained guilt of *oppression*, will continue to accumulate upon our heads as a nation. (*Narrative*, 231)

Pringle's untimely death prevented his appearing as a witness before the Aborigines Committee and also his participation in the founding and work of the APS. In relation to South African literature and social history, his main significance lies in expressing the new, romantic liberalism and humanitarianism that reinforced the missionary activism of Philip and others. And with John Fairbairn, Pringle as editor and journalist helped to establish freedom of the press at the Cape. As a minor, largely imitative author, Pringle has another significance: both his poetry and his *Narrative* reveal how conventional, even clichéd, proleptic elegy had become by the 1820s and 1830s, even in the multiracial and racist context of South Africa.

Though Buxton served as its first president, the main mover of the APS was Thomas Hodgkin, a Quaker perhaps better known for his medical work.[18] As a teenager, Hodgkin read Alexander von Humboldt's accounts of the destruction of the ancient civilizations of Peru and Mexico by the Spaniards, which led to his penning an "Essay on the Promotion of Civilization" (1819). Therein, Hodgkin offered a comparison "between ancient and modern times, as far as relates to the influence which civilized nations have had upon the uncivilized." The comparison revealed that "in the last five hundred years, those under the name of Christians, have done far more to degrade, corrupt and exterminate their uncivilized fellow creatures than all the heathen world, since the creation of man" (quoted in Kass, 39). Hodgkin advocated civilizing aboriginals but in ways that did not disrupt their cultures; he was critical of the sectarianism of missionaries and condemned their destruction of "idols" and other native artifacts (Kass, 40–41). Perhaps it was his critical stance toward missionary activity that made Hodgkin's partnership with Buxton an uneasy one. In any event, though he served as first president of the APS, Buxton withdrew after several years; the *Memoirs* compiled by his son say nothing at all about that organization or about Hodgkin, who had also been critical of the initial focus of the Aborigines Committee exclusively on South Africa.

Hodgkin had long been active in gathering information about the treatment of "the natives" from correspondents in the colonies; he prompted the Aborigines Committee to examine at least two of those correspondents, Richard King and Saxe Bannister. King had been a medical student under Hodgkin's tutelage at Guy's Hospital in London, and Hodgkin had sponsored his expedition to Canada to collect information about the situation of its first peoples. King testified about the extermination of the Beothuks of Newfoundland and also about the precipitous population declines of other indigenous groups throughout North America. Saxe Bannister had served as a legal administrator in both New South Wales and Natal, and had published, apparently with Hodgkin's help, *Humane Policy; or Justice to the Aborigines of New Settlements* in 1830. While the committee's investigation was still in progress, Hodgkin, Bannister, King, and Philip decided to form the Aborigines Protection Society "for the purpose of gaining information respecting [indigenous populations] . . . and promoting measures for their protection and improvement" (quoted in Kass, 271). For Hodgkin, write his biographers, the founding of the APS "was the culmination of 20 years of effort . . . [and] he had established an organization that carried on the work for 70 years more" (Kass, 271). Hodgkin was, indeed, both the main founder and, until his death in 1866, the main mover of the APS.[19]

When Buxton died in 1845, however, humanitarianism of the evangelical, Exeter Hall variety was already on the wane. Certainly its influence within the Colonial Office was diminishing. Public support for missionary societies declined around mid-century, in part because it was increasingly apparent that missionaries and their supporters tended to exaggerate both the numbers and the lasting effects of their conversions of "the uncivilized" (Galbraith, 77). Moreover, the political weakness of the APS after the 1840s is evident from this 1860s report, drafted by F. W. Chesson, APS secretary from 1856 and Hodgkin's successor as its head from 1866 until the 1880s. The "very existence" of the APS, writes Chesson, "is a protest against oppression":

> It [the APS] may be powerless to arrest the current of war when the tide of angry passion has once set in; but the knowledge that there is a public body having the just and Christian treatment of our aboriginal fellow-subjects as the sole object of its solicitude, must operate as a check upon hasty and oppressive

measures, and stimulate the exertions of those good men in the colonies . . . who share our opinions and cannot fail to be strengthened by the expression of our moral sympathy. (quoted in Bourne, 27)

The tentativeness of Chesson's statement speaks for itself. But the APS carried on well past 1900, although there were many occasions when the good cause of protecting indigenous peoples was not so appreciated by the Colonial Office as it had been from 1837 to 1845 (see, for instance, Hall, 46). In 1909 the APS merged with the Anti-Slavery Society, which continues to work on behalf of the rights of indigenous peoples around the world (for examples of its work, see the books by Julian Burger).

Hodgkin's testimony before the Aborigines Committee in 1836 was that of a general expert, lending a historical, global perspective to the proceedings. As he had done in his youthful "Essay on the Promotion of Civilization," he compared the modern system of colonization to those of the Romans, Greeks, and Egyptians, and opined that "the treatment of the aborigines in modern times has been much more deleterious to them than appears to have been the case formerly" (*Report*, 1:454). The Romans in Britain were not led by their greed "to dispossess the natives, and treat them in the way our people have done" (*Report*, 1:454–55). The difference between ancient and modern colonization lies

in our having, with the exception of the benevolent attempts of missionaries and a few others, a purely selfish motive; our own pecuniary aggrandizement seems to be the principal object, or to found a settlement for our own redundant population, without regarding the welfare of those that have a stronger claim to the country. (*Report*, 1:455)

Hodgkin added that slavery was better than colonization, at least in terms of valuing the lives of aboriginals:

We have been accustomed . . . to draw from Africa a large number of slaves. . . . We have taken those Africans, or our neighbours have taken those Africans, across the Atlantic, and have subjected them to the miseries of slavery, but neither of those have been an exterminating process. . . . If we compare this which has been going on 200 or 300 years with the operations of 50 years in South Africa, I think it will be seen that the colonizing process has done more to reduce these classes in point of numbers, than that other process [slavery], the atrocities of which have been so generally admitted. (*Report*, 1:455)

Hodgkin had not been to South Africa, but he based this view on "the accounts of travellers who have visited the southern extremity of Africa at a remote period, [and who] speak of it as highly populous, and at the present day it is quite the reverse. . . . A few days ago I had a letter from Sir John Herschel [the astronomer], who stated that a Hottentot or a Caffre was quite a rarity in the neighbourhood of the Cape" (*Report*, 1:456).

Hodgkin also corresponded with James Cowles Prichard, who did as much as anyone to establish ethnology as a new social science in Britain (Kass, 259–60; Stocking, 47–53). In *Victorian Anthropology* George Stocking writes that the APS "may be regarded as the oldest lineal ancestor of modern British anthropological institutions" (240–41). As early as 1839, however, a fault line emerged between the humanitarian and the scientific emphases within the APS. "By 1842," writes Stocking, "there was clearly a feeling that the opportunity provided by the [Aborigines] Committee had been lost, and that some reorientation was necessary" (244). Buxton's evangelical humanitarianism took a blow from the disaster of the 1841–42 Niger Expedition, pet project of his African Civilization Society, when most of the Europeans on that journey died from disease shortly after arriving in Africa. The "increasing pessimism" within the APS and "the gradual disengagement of the scientific impulse seem clearly related to this more general ebbing of the humanitarian tide," Stocking indicates; "in this context, the printed statement of the Society's object was changed in 1842: rather than 'protecting the defenceless,' it would 'record the[ir] history,' and a resolution was passed to the effect that the best way to help aboriginals was to study them" (244). In July 1842 Richard King, then secretary of the APS, started the Ethnological Society as a separate endeavor (which Hodgkin, however, joined). This is not to say that humanitarianism disappeared altogether or was in some sense displaced by the new science of anthropology; as noted, the APS continued down to 1909 and beyond. But as Douglas Lorimer points out, "After the death of . . . Hodgkin in 1866, no leading member of the Aborigines Protection Society played a significant role in anthropological studies or in the Anthropological Institute" (217). Certainly by the time *The Origin of Species* was published in

1859, the heyday of humanitarian and missionary optimism, fueled by the energizing crusade against slavery, was over.

From the perspective of most white colonists in South Africa, whether Boer or British, the humanitarianism of the missionaries, of the Aborigines Committee, and of the APS was wrong-headed, hyperbolic, and dangerous, even treasonous. Anthony Trollope was close to the mark when he wrote that the Boer republics created after the abolition of slavery in 1833—Natal, the Transvaal, the Orange Free State—"were . . . in the first instance, peopled by sturdy Dutchmen running away from the to them [sic] disgusting savour of Exeter Hall. They would encounter anything, go anywhere, rather than submit to British philanthropy" (South Africa, 2:331). Humanitarianism was also unable to prevent continued attempts to exterminate the Bushmen, whose destruction "was almost complete by 1910" (Skotnes, 17).[20] Even in regard to pacifying relations between white settlers and the Xhosas on the eastern frontier, a major goal of Buxton's Aborigines Committee, little was accomplished.

The 1834–35 frontier war was devastating to both sides but especially to the Xhosas, who once again were defeated mainly because of the superior weaponry of their adversaries. The Xhosas lost thousands of warriors and much of their wealth in cattle, which they had to surrender as reparations. During the peace negotiations, one of the Xhosa chiefs, Hintsa, was shot and mutilated by British soldiers (his ears were cut off and some of his teeth extracted, presumably for souvenirs), an atrocity that both the Xhosas and the Aborigines Committee found deeply disturbing (Mostert, 724–26; Pretorius, 178–258).[21] In 1847 Sir Harry Smith, who had been "responsible for killing Hintsa" (Thompson, 76), was named governor of Cape Colony and proceeded to re-annex much of the Queen Adelaide territory as "British Kaffraria." The so-called Voortrekkers under Piet Retief fought their first major battle against the Zulus at Blood River in 1838 (Walker, 185–90). And conflict with the Xhosas, who were being pressured by the Zulus as well as by the Europeans, flared up into two more wars prior to the ultimate tragedy of the mass cattle-killing of 1857 (Mostert; Wilson, "Co-Operation and Conflict," 256–60).

As more than one witness before the Aborigines Committee testified, the Xhosas were being driven into "wars of extermination" by both the whites and the Zulus, though they were the ones being exterminated. The war of 1834–35 was followed by the War of the Axe of 1846 and Mlanjeni's War in 1850–53. Defeat in these wars, the appropriation of most of their territory by the white colonizers, severe drought, and cattle sickness led to the final catastrophe. In 1857, after a lung ailment had already killed thousands of their cattle, a revelation from the gods came to a sixteen-year-old Xhosa girl, Nongqawuse. According to the revelation, the ancestors would return to restore ancient ways, wealth, and power if the Xhosas killed all their remaining cattle and destroyed their crops and other property. Many of the Xhosas believed and acted on this prophecy. "At least 150,000 to 200,000 cattle were killed," writes Monica Wilson, a massive sacrifice that resulted in widespread famine ("Co-Operation and Conflict," 258).[22] From the European perspective, the "mass suicide" of the Xhosas was the fantasy of self-exterminating savages come true.[23]

Robert Ross calls the Xhosa cattle-killing and famine "the end of the beginning of [modern] South African history," because "for the first time" an African society other than the Hottentots "had been broken" (53). By the 1850s humanitarian response to the fate of the Xhosas was muted. According to its official history, the APS, still under Hodgkin's leadership, seems to have been more concerned with defending the Zulus from the encroachments and "cruelties perpetrated by the Boers" in the Transvaal and elsewhere than with what was happening under British auspices to the Xhosas (Bourne, 17).[24] Further, by the end of the nineteenth century, the idea that the Xhosas, the Zulus, and other Bantu peoples were the first invaders of South African territory and therefore the first exterminators of the Bushmen and Hottentots was firmly engrained in white South African culture. Europeans—first the Dutch, then the British—were only repeating what had been done through eons of so-called prehistory, but with the difference that they (the British, at least) were bringing civilization, Christianity, and history to the Dark Continent (see, for instance, Theal, *The Yellow and Dark-Skinned People*). However, even as late as the 1960s the extermination of the supposedly truly aboriginal inhabitants of all of Africa was still incomplete, and their supposed original exterminators—the Bantu "hordes" from the north—were not about to disappear (not even the Xhosas).

The invading and exterminating Bantu "horde" myth in white South African discourse goes back at least to the 1830s and such works as Godlonton's *Narrative of the Irruption of the Kafir [sic] Hordes into the Eastern Province of the Cape of Good Hope, A.D. 1834–35*. With the Anglo-Zulu War of 1879, the myth reached a climax. Numerous writers both in South Africa and Britain depicted the Zulus as the savage opposites of the perishing Bushmen and Hottentots. Thus, in his first book, *Cetywayo and His White Neighbours* (1882), H. Rider Haggard writes that when Chaka became "king" around 1813,

> the Zulu people consisted of a small tribe; when his throne became vacant in 1828, their name had become a living terror, and they were the greatest Black power in South Africa. The invincible armies of this African Attila had swept north and south, east and west, had slaughtered more than a million human beings, and added vast tracts of country to his dominions. Wherever his warriors went, the blood of men, women, and children was poured out without stay or stint; indeed, he reigned like a visible Death, the presiding genius of a saturnalia of slaughter. (2–3)

Both in *Cetawayo* and in his Zulu romances such as *Nada the Lily*, Haggard, though able to create Zulu characters who are more complex and interesting than mere killing machines, produced a mythical history of that "nation" or "kingdom" as one long, extremely violent atrocity story (see Wylie). According to Haggard, the Zulus may not be self-exterminating, but they are nevertheless the epitome of the extermination process that was African prehistory. Now the arrival of "white civilization," though attended by some setbacks and discomforts to black Africans, is reversing the process and, especially through the forward march of British imperialism, turning extermination into progress and salvation.[25]

The myth of extreme savagery regarding Chaka and the rise of the Zulus in which one savage "horde" threatens to exterminate all the other savage "hordes" around it suggests that the only cure for savagery is conquest and government by the white, civilized, ruling race. This influential interpretation of the rise and fall of the Zulus is, needless to say, different from that of the APS, which was highly critical of "the ruthless persecution of Cetewayo and his Zulu followers" (Bourne, 44). But by its own admission, the APS was "tardy" and ineffective in its criticism of the events that led to the Anglo-Zulu War of 1879. Nevertheless, its historian credits the APS with preventing worse "wrong-doing." Through its work, "though the mischief caused in Zululand is lasting, and but a small fragment of its once numerous population remains to be cared for, the survivors have been rescued

from the complete ruin that threatened the whole community"
(Bourne, 45).

None of the major, modern histories of South Africa have given
the APS even that much credit in relation to "Zululand." Furthermore, one function of the APS throughout its history was, according
to its historian, "to urge on 'the British Crown and nation' the duties
and responsibilities of empire-making in South Africa [and] elsewhere" (Bourne, 36). This is true also of the general results of Buxton's Aborigines Committee. Its final *Report* reinforced the general
notion of imperial trusteeship that had been developing since the
time of the Warren Hastings trial of the 1790s (Mellor).[26]

After the late 1830s humanitarianism at the Cape declined. "Disil-
lusioned humanitarians formed the core of a new conservatism in the
1850s," writes Andrew Bank, "and articulated a racial discourse that
was stridently imperialist and often strikingly anti-humanitarian"
(380). The greatest achievements of nineteenth-century humanitarianism in regard to the non-white races of the world were the abolition
of the slave trade and of slavery. Missionary intervention on colonial
frontiers in South Africa and elsewhere may have done much to prevent violence and to promote fair treatment of indigenous peoples,
but it also contributed to official imperial expansion. Whether religious or secular, moreover, humanitarian ideology was almost always
a variant of white supremacism that insisted on transforming savage
customs and cultures into Christianity and white civilization. Humanitarianism did cause governments, at least intermittently, to pay
attention to the effects of white settlement and exploitation on aboriginal populations throughout the world, but it did not alter the basic
terms of extinction discourse: unless they could be civilized, which
usually also meant Christianized, primitive races everywhere were
doomed. How much greater the decimation of those races might
have been without humanitarian and missionary activity is a matter
of speculation, though no doubt it would have been greater.

5. The Irish Famine

In South Africa and elsewhere, accusations of cannibalism were usually reserved for the indigenous groups who were most warlike and resistant to colonization. Within Britain itself, the "wild Irish" had, from the 1500s on, been tarred with that and virtually every other stereotypic accusation about savages that their English adversaries could think of. The bloody, frustrating attempts of sixteenth-century Englishmen to subdue the Irish paralleled, and in some measure influenced, the earliest encounters between the English and Native Americans. "The doctrine that the only good Indian is a dead Indian," writes Howard Mumford Jones, "first took shape . . . in the doctrine that the only good wild Irishman is a dead wild Irishman" (172–73).[1] Jones cites a number of sixteenth- and seventeenth-century writers who compared the Indians of the New World with the Irish in terms of their lawlessness, their nomadism, their treachery, their cruelty, and their cannibalism—in short, in terms of their savagery. In these accounts, however, the Irish appear to have two characteristics not shared by Native Americans: overpopulation and starvation. Writing to Queen Elizabeth in 1567, Sir Henry Sidney declared "there was never people that lived in more misery than" do the Irish and that "matrimony among them is no more regarded in effect than conjunction between unreasonable beasts" (quoted in H. M. Jones, 169). And in 1617 Fynes Moryson described "a most horrible spectacle of three [Irish] children . . . all eating and gnawing with their teeth the entrails of their dead mother" (quoted in H. M. Jones, 169). If Moryson was telling the truth, then that "horrible spectacle" was cannibalism for survival and not for ritual or any other purpose, such as sating bloodthirstiness. There is no hint of noble savagery in accounts of Irish cannibalism, which is almost always associated with starvation (cf. Canny, 587).

Edmund Spenser's *View of the Present State of Ireland*, written in the late 1500s but not published until 1633, is the best known early example of the centuries-old English tradition of depicting the wild Irish as hard-core, perhaps irreclaimable, even cannibalistic savages. Given that accounts of Irish cannibalism associated that savage activity with famine, the Irish were apparently less than savage—far more miserable than South Sea islanders, for instance, who were not starving but who were rumored to practice cannibalism in relation to war or as a sort of sadistic luxury.[2] In any event, Spenser depicts a race of miserable savages in a state of constant rebellion, anarchy, and warfare. Writing about Irish soldiers, Spenser declares:

> Marrie those bee the most barbarous and loathly conditions of any people (I thinke) under heaven; for . . . they doe use all the beastly behaviour that may be; they oppresse all men, they spoile aswell the subject, as the enemy; they steale, they are cruell and bloodie . . . licentious, swearers, and blasphemers, common ravishers of woemen, and murtherers of children. (74)

Even in the rare condition of peace, Spenser's Irish live in a "savage condition," in "swyne-stycs [instead of] houses . . . or rather a foul dunghill" (84). To curb their lawless, rebellious ways, Spenser recommends "the sword" and enforced starvation (100). If the English cannot starve the Irish into sweet reasonableness, then they can just starve them.

From what he witnessed during the Desmond rebellion or "war" of 1579–83, Spenser understood the effectiveness of famine as a weapon. Through his persona, Irenaeus, Spenser opines that enforced starvation will defeat or kill off the rebellious Irish more swiftly and with less cost of English lives than "the sword" alone. Indeed, famine will cause the rebels to "consume themselves, and devour one another":

> The proofe whereof, I saw sufficiently exampled in these late [Desmond] warres of Mounster [Munster] . . . for not withstanding that the same was a most rich and plentifull countrey, full of corne and cattle . . . yet ere one yeare and a

halfe they were brought to such wretchednesse, as that any stony heart would have rued the same. Out of every corner of the woods and glynnes they came creeping forth upon their hands, for their legges could not beare them; they looked like anatomies of death, they spake like ghosts crying out of their graves; they did eate the dead carrions. (101)

Today Spenser's account seems less a commentary on the wretchedness of the Irish than on the violence of imperialism at its genocidal worst: enforced famine leads to survival cannibalism.

That the Elizabethan armies included deliberate starving-out or famine in their arsenal against the wild Irish was a presage of worse to come. The Cromwellian conquest of Ireland was not carried out with the intention of exterminating the entire population, but its effects were genocidal. In what amounted to the first attempt at an accurate census, economist William Petty estimated that Ireland's population in 1641 had been 1,448,000. More than 600,000 had died during the fighting and another 140,000 had emigrated to the continent or the Americas (Johnson, 56). If Petty's figures are at all close to the mark, in percentage terms the decimation of the Irish in the 1640s was far greater than two hundred years later during the Great Famine of 1845–50.

The 1652 Act for the Settling of Ireland aimed at "a total reducement and settlement of that nation" by the English, although, it declared, "it is not the intention of parliament to extirpate that whole nation" (quoted in Johnson, 55). Among other results, the Act led to the execution of some 100,000 rebels. It also led to the redistribution of the land, partly as a means of paying Cromwell's soldiers. "By 1700 Catholics held only one-eighth of the land in Ireland," writes Paul Johnson; "this proportion fell further over the next half-century" (62). And as Catholics were losing their land, they were also being debarred from business and the professions, the main processes leading to the modern immiserization of Ireland.

From Spenser on, the tradition of anti-Irish stereotyping by the English relies on an equally stereotypic notion of savagery, merging Native Americans, Africans, and the Irish into a single category that Jonathan Swift, in *Gulliver's Travels*, calls "the Yahoos." A celebrity in Ireland after the publication of his satiric masterpiece in 1726, Swift was, according to Paul Johnson, "haunted by the notion that the real object of English policy towards Ireland was depopulation" (68).

Mass emigration from Ireland had already begun among Protestants, and "Irish Catholics were leaving all the time" (Johnson, 68). In the previous four decades perhaps as many as 120,000 "wild geese" had fled, mainly to enlist in foreign armies. In his 1730 pamphlet, *Answer to the Craftsmen*, Swift ironically urged that the Irish should sign up for the French army, which would aid the English cause of depopulating Ireland (Johnson, 68).

Throughout his career Swift expressed opposition to English and European imperialist violence and exploitation. In *Gulliver's Travels* Swift has Gulliver describe the general process of conquest and colonization. First, pirates discover a new land, which they set out "to rob and plunder." Encountering "an harmless People" who entertain them "with Kindness, they give the Country a new Name, they take formal Possession of it for the King . . . they murder two or three Dozen of the Natives, bring away a Couple more by Force for a Sample, return home, and get their Pardon." Their actions create "a new Dominion acquitted with a Title by *Divine Right*," says Gulliver:

> Ships are sent with the first Opportunity; the Natives driven out or destroyed, their Princes tortured to discover Gold; a free Licence given to all Acts of Inhumanity and Lust; the Earth reeking with the Blood of its Inhabitants: And this execrable Crew of Butchers employed in so pious an Expedition, as a *modern Colony* sent to convert and civilize an idolatrous and barbarous People. (Swift, 258)

This was the very colonizing and civilizing process, Swift implies, that the English had been applying to the Irish for the past two centuries. All the same, Swift could wax just as indignant about the abject wildness or barbarism of the Irish peasantry. The Yahoos may represent the English, or all mankind, but they also more pointedly "resemble both Indians and Irish": small wonder, then, that the Houyhnhnms contemplate exterminating them (Rawson, 84, 231). However, in *God, Gulliver, and Genocide* Claude Rawson notes that Swift's "explosions of ethnic resentment do not pretend to be other than they are, but they include contempt for ethnic resentment and the inhumanities that flow from it" (11). Also, just as Swift's portrayal of the Yahoos extends beyond the wild Irish and the wild Indians to encompass all humanity, so he includes himself in his satire: Lemuel Gulliver is Swift's skewed, barbed self-portrait.

In *A Modest Proposal* Swift revisits Sir Henry Sidney's, Fynes

Moryson's, and Spenser's portrayals of starving, abject Irish savages, grass eaters, and cannibals. To solve at once Ireland's overpopulation, lack of economic production, endemic poverty, disease, ignorance, begging, and starvation, the Modest Proposer recommends having the Irish butcher, market, and eat their own children. According to Rawson, while A Modest Proposal exploits "the old myth that the Irish (like Indians) are cannibals," it applies that myth satirically "to the ruling group of Anglo-Irish landlords, merchants, and bankers," as well as "to the street riff-raff of thieving and wife-beating native vagabonds" (10). Swift's satire, Rawson argues, is only tangentially concerned with "what the English do or might do to the Irish"; it is much more concerned "with what the Irish do or might do to themselves"—another version, in other words, of self-exterminating savagery. In any event, the act or threat of cannibalism "extends to all levels of Irish society" (84). Elsewhere Swift could recommend, perhaps only half-ironically, solving the problem of Irish mendicancy by letting the beggars starve (Rawson, 186). Rawson demonstrates that Swift's satires are part of a much broader "Anglo-Irish"—or British, and one could add American—discourse about exterminating the poor, from the 1500s to the present.

Well established as aspects of English and Anglo-Irish stereotyping of the Irish peasantry, wildness, "unreasonable" coupling, starvation, and even cannibalism as a result of that starvation show up in many later accounts of the Irish, most notably in English discourse about the Irish Famine of 1845–50 and its often violent political aftermath. The idea of the Irish as "the niggers of Europe," perhaps most familiar from Roddy Doyle's 1987 novel, The Commitments (O'Toole, 121), goes back at least to the 1830s. In that decade the contrast between the success of the antislavery crusade and the mounting problems of Ireland elicited numerous comparisons between the slaves or former slaves and the Irish peasantry. During and after the Famine, Punch often portrayed the Irish as not just slave-like but simian, "the missing link between the gorilla and the Negro" (Punch; quoted in Lebow, 67; see also Curtis, Apes; Foster). But Daniel O'Connell and other Irish leaders also made the comparison between the peasantry and the slaves or ex-slaves in Jamaica and elsewhere: it was hypocritical, went their complaint, to worry about slavery and not worry about Irish poverty and starvation.

O'Connell tried to forge an alliance between his movement to repeal the Act of Union of 1800 and abolitionism. He could not support the more extreme American abolitionists such as William Lloyd Garrison, but he repeatedly insisted that liberating the slaves and liberating Ireland were related causes. And he was a signatory to an 1842 abolitionist address to Irish Americans to "treat the colored people as your equals, as brethren" and to support "liberty for all" (quoted in Ignatiev, 10). Nevertheless, as Noel Ignatiev argues in *How the Irish Became White*, the slaveholding bloc wooed Irish Americans, many of whom soon found it expedient not to support abolition but instead to purchase their citizenship, their respect from other white Americans, and their political influence partly by distancing themselves from African Americans in social, legal, and economic ways. Especially in the southern United States, supporters of repeal were often pro-slavery (Ignatiev, 16–23).

Between 1800 and the time of the Great Famine of 1845–50, though little was done to alleviate it, the poverty of the Irish peasantry received much official attention (O'Gráda, 30–31). Anglo-Irish writers and intellectuals such as Maria Edgeworth, in her novels *Castle Rackrent* and *The Absentee*, also publicized Irish distress. From the end of the Napoleonic wars in 1815 into the Chartist era of the 1840s, the plight of the Irish was a key theme of political radicals such as William Cobbett, who, in his *Political Register*, published some of the results of his 1834 tour of Ireland. "Of all the wonders of the world," Cobbett declared, "Ireland is the greatest, for here we see a country teeming with food; we see that food sent . . . to other nations . . . and we see at home the people starving and in rags" (67). Cobbett blamed Ireland's misery partly on the economics of "the Scotch *feelosofer* vagabonds," the "monsters of the school of . . . Parson MALTHUS," who he believed were scheming, through the New Poor Law of 1834, to reduce England's peasantry to the level of Irish starvation and rags (60, 64). And in 1839 Thomas Carlyle, who also detested Malthusian economics, spoke of the "perennial starvation" and "squalid apehood" that English misgovernment had produced in Ireland, and sarcastically declared that the time had come "when the Irish population must either be improved a little, or else exterminated" ("Chartism," 183). From an official standpoint, moreover, the Devon Commission of 1843–45 was only the last in a series of investigations into the causes of Irish misery prior to the Famine. According to its report, the main cause was "the bad relations between landlord and tenant," writes Cecil Woodham-Smith; "Ireland was a conquered country, the Irish peasant a dispossessed man, his landlord an alien conqueror" (21).

Cobbett, Carlyle, the Devon Commission, and many others anticipated the greatest misery of the aptly named Hungry Forties, the Famine of 1845–50, in which approximately one-eighth of Ireland's population did, in fact, starve. That disaster brought home an example of the mass extinction of a "race" that seemed to many English observers unpreventable, mainly because of the wildness, ignorance, or evolutionary unfitness of the Irish. In much English writing about the Famine, the chief cause of it was not the potato fungus that nobody knew how to deal with but rather the savage or worse than savage traits of the Irish "race." Viewed through the cloudy lens of age-old stereotyping of the wild Irish, the Famine appeared to be an obvious instance of self-liquidating savagery or its more squalid European counterpart.

Most accounts of the Famine raise the question of whether the relief measures of the British government were effective or the reverse, failures that did not prevent and may even have promoted the starvation of more than one million people and the emigration of many more. Though charges of deliberate genocide are today usually dismissed, most historians accept some version of the thesis that "the ideological blindness shown by British ministers," as Graham Davis puts it, exacerbated instead of helping to minimize the deadly outcome (17). This is to charge the politically dominant liberalism of the 1840s and 1850s that sought to deal with the Famine with a sort of myopia produced by the limitations of that liberalism. There were at least six limitations: first, the belief that political economy was a science that had discovered "laws" that both governments and individuals had to obey; second, the belief, often also viewed as scientific, that the English and Irish were separate races, and that the racial inferiority of the Irish was the cause of their ignorance, poverty, and starvation; third, coupled with race, the insistent feminization of Ireland and of the victims of the Famine; fourth, the belief in the inevitability of progress, at least for those obedient to the "laws" of economics; fifth, the presumption that, despite the democratic implications of liberalism, its proponents were empowered to represent the scientific truth about women, the working class, and the non-English races of the world, including the starving Irish. The sixth limitation was Protestant anti-Catholicism. But typically expressions of anti-Catholicism were based on or framed by one or more of the other five items. Thus, for example, it was frequently claimed that the Irish peasantry was mired in superstition and Catholicism because it was inherently irrational, and irrationality, in turn, was seen as both a feminine and a bestial (racialized) trait. Catholicism, according to many Protestants, was an antiprogressive religion. Although certain liberals and radicals—John Stuart Mill, for instance—rejected one or more of them, these six ideological factors were hegemonic in the English press and underwrote the famine relief policies of both the Tory and the Whigliberal governments of the late 1840s.

Everything about the Great Famine was extreme, and so have been its interpretations. Though the revisionist school in Irish historiography claims to be objective, it has also been charged with ideological culpability or at least blindness by the two major critical perspectives—Marxism and Irish nationalism—that were developing during the 1840s and that remain influential today.[3] From either perspective, the revisionists, far from being impartial, are in the lineage of the liberalism that, struggling to cope with the Famine, perhaps only compounded the disaster. According to both nationalists and Marxists, official liberalism failed to understand the causes of the Famine; failed to see the Irish, whether peasants or landlords, as anything other than threats to English prosperity and progress; failed to recognize the powers and responsibilities of government; failed to fulfill the terms of the Act of Union of 1801; failed also to encourage Christian charity; and thus failed to prevent "the Irish holocaust."

At its most extreme, nationalism charges official liberalism not just with failing to prevent the Famine but with pursuing a deliberate policy of racial extermination. So Young Irelanders such as John Mitchel and Gavin Duffy declared that the Famine was "a fearful murder committed on the mass of the people" (Duffy; quoted in Gray, "Ideology," 86). For his part, Mitchel believed that although "the Almighty . . . sent the potato blight . . . the English created the Famine." According to Mitchel, English officials discovered in the blight a tool to effect the purpose they had long entertained:

> the potato blight and consequent famine, placed in the hands of the British government an engine of state by which they were eventually enabled to clear off not a million, but two millions and a half of the "surplus population"—to "preserve law and order" in Ireland (what they call law and order) and to maintain the integrity of the Empire. (Quoted in Davis, 17)

The nationalist belief that the British government was trying either to exterminate the Irish or force them into exile was one cause of the rise of Fenianism in the 1860s (Sigerson, 1–10).

Instead of cold-blooded genocide, Marxists charge the English with ideological myopia, mainly in the form of "free trade" economic orthodoxy and capitalist cupidity. Marx himself argued that the pressure to modernize agriculture caused Irish landlords, "most [of them] deep in debt, [to] try to get rid of the people and clear their estates" and that this pressure increased during the Famine, especially after passage of the 1847 New Poor Law Extension Act, which forced landowners either to "support their own paupers" or to evict them, leaving them to starve (Marx and Engels, *Ireland*, 134).

Marx rightly identifies the 1847 Poor Law with the doctrine or dogma of free trade, which resisted state intervention in any aspect of the economy. Though that Law was itself an instance of state intervention, its framers—as in the case of the New Poor Law of 1834—sought to make its provisions so punitive that only paupers in the direst straits would avail themselves of the "relief" it offered. Marx was correct that the 1847 Law, with its so-called Gregory or Quarter-Acre Clause, increased "ejectments" (evictions): under that clause, peasants who rented more than a quarter-acre were not entitled to relief; to receive it, they had to leave their holdings—except through taxes, the landlords had no legal responsibility for them.

At least two aspects of capitalist economics, Malthusianism and laissez-faire, shaped the famine relief policies both of Sir Robert Peel's Tory administration in the first year of distress, from autumn 1845 to June 1846, and of Lord John Russell's Whig-liberal regime from that date on. For both nationalists and Marxists, starvation by political economy remains a key accusation especially against Russell's government. John Mitchel had leveled this charge against English officialdom, and it was not far from the truth. Agreeing with Mitchel, the Irish socialist leader James Connolly later declared: "England made the Famine by a rigid application of the economic principles that lie at the base of capitalist society" (quoted in O'Gráda, 57). As early as May 1847, the Catholic priests of Derry blamed "the Murders of the Irish Peasantry . . . [in] the name of economy [on] the administration of [Russell's] professedly Liberal . . . government" (quoted in Kinealy, 102). Given the extent to which capitalist economics shaped the official response to the Famine, the Derry priests had a point.

"In the Famine's darkest hours," writes Lawrence J. McCaffrey,

"Nassau Senior, a distinguished economist prominent in Whig circles, lamented that . . . only a million Irish would die, an insufficient number to solve the population problem" (McCaffrey, 57). It cannot be proven that Senior was hoping for the extermination of the entire Irish race, but such genocidal wishes on the part of English observers and officials were not rare. Commenting in 1850 on the Encumbered Estates Act that was passed in the wake of the Famine, Robert Knox declared that it "aims simply at the quiet and gradual extinction of the Celtic race in Ireland" (27). "Even as sober a commentator as George Sigerson," Eagleton notes (17), writes "as late as 1868 of a 'policy of extermination' for Ireland in which men and women will give way to cattle" (see Sigerson, 4). And Wilfred Scawen Blunt reported that in 1892 the Irish chief secretary Gerald Balfour, brother of Arthur Balfour and an anti–Home Rule conservative, cited Darwin's "survival of the fittest" as a "law" that meant the Irish "ought to have been exterminated long ago" as an unfit race, "but it is too late now" (quoted in Gailey, 30). So, too, G. K. Chesterton declares that the repression of the 1798 United Irishmen's rebellion was a "Massacre of the Innocents" (50), and adds:

> The conduct of the English towards the Irish after the Rebellion was quite simply the conduct of one man who traps and binds another, and then calmly cuts him about with a knife. The conduct during the Famine was quite simply the conduct of the first man if he entertained the later moments of the second man, by remarking in a chatty manner on the very hopeful chances of his bleeding to death. The British Prime Minister publicly refused to stop the Famine by the use of English ships. The British Prime Minister positively spread the Famine, by making the half-starved population of Ireland pay for the starved ones. The common verdict of a coroner's jury upon some emaciated wretch was "Wilful murder by Lord John Russell": and that . . . is the verdict of history. (58)

Chesterton concludes: "We, as a matter of fact, have not even failed to save Ireland. We have simply failed to destroy her" (60).

For his part, Senior opined that famine was "a calamity which cannot befall a civilised nation; for a civilised nation . . . never confines itself to a single sort of food" such as the potato. "When such a calamity does befall an uncivilised community . . . things take their course; it produces great misery, great mortality, and in a year or two the wound is closed, and scarcely a scar remains" (1:208). Meanwhile, according to Senior, the English did everything that their natural benevolence prompted them to do, although this only prevented the Irish from dying more quickly. Senior agreed with the Irish land agent William Trench, who said that the "interference" of the English government was "beneficial" only insofar as "it relieved the feelings of the English people":

> But I doubt whether it really saved much life. It spread the destruction over a longer period. Instead of dying of the absence of food, people died of diseases produced by insufficient food. . . . Many too remained to die, who, if they had not relied on the Government, would have fled from the country. (Trench; quoted in Senior, 2:3)

So much for the misspent generosity of the English toward their "uncivilised" neighbor.[4]

Likening Ireland to a "rabbit warren" (quoted in O'Gráda, 12), Senior expressed the Malthusian doctrine that the only way to overcome poverty and starvation was for the poor to control their birth rate, thereby enlarging their per capita shares of the "wages fund." The economists viewed both government relief and private charity as backfiring: both were only inducements for the poor to continue to overpopulate. This was the most significant limitation of Victorian liberalism as it tried to cope with the Famine: it shaped all its actions in terms of the "laws" of economics. In the case of Malthusianism, this meant uncritical acceptance of a pseudo-scientific dogma that identified impoverished masses as "surplus" populations.[5]

From the Malthusian perspective, the poor are always an overpopulation, a cancerous growth on the body politic. In the Reverend Sidney Godolphin Osborne's memorable phrase, they are "immortal sewerage." In his 1853 essay of that title, Osborne, with the Famine in mind, advocated "the draining of civilization." The equation between excrement and the "superfluous masses" of the poor, especially the Irish poor, is hardly unique to Osborne. In 1826, the economist J. R. McCulloch, urging Parliament to transport one-seventh of the population of Ireland to the colonies, warned that a "tide" of Irish paupers was "inundating" England. "Half-famished hordes . . . are daily pouring in from the great *officina pauperum*" or sewer of Ireland (54). Pauperism "will find its level. It cannot be heaped up in Leinster and Ulster without overflowing upon England" (54). And Malthus himself asserted that "Ireland is infinitely more peopled than . . . England, and to give full effect to the natural resources of the country, a great part of the population should be swept from the soil" (quoted in Kinealy, 16). But in his *Principles of Political Economy*, Malthus also defended the Irish peasantry against the racist charge that they were "naturally" indolent and improvident. In a fertile country where the easy cultivation of potatoes had led to a rapid expansion of the population at subsistence level, there was little employment and little demand for that employment to stimulate industry (345–51).

Underwriting Malthusianism was, moreover, a gender stereotype that said, in effect, women were more to blame for overpopulation than men. The English and Scottish economists viewed the Irish "race" in general as "improvident" and out of control, but it was women's lack of education, and of sexual restraint in particular, that produced excess population. In the English press the iconography of the Famine was dominated by images and stories of helpless, starving Madonnas—or, perhaps, anti-Madonnas—with their dead or dying children in their arms. Mothers who could not care for their offspring were featured even in the most sympathetic accounts, such as the articles that appeared in *The Illustrated London News*, accompanied by John Mahoney's dreary pictures of starvation. Mahoney's starving Madonnas and children were at once an appeal to English benevolence and an indication that Ireland itself was being figured, at least subliminally, as a so-called fallen woman.[6]

From the perspective of capitalist economics, the Irish were one large, clearly identifiable aspect of the bigger problem of population "redundancy" and hence of chronic poverty. But the idea that any "population" is "surplus" or "redundant" is a basic ideological prop for the commission of genocide, in part because it underwrites what Zygmunt Bauman calls the gardening model of social progress.[7] The consensus among historians today seems to be that, by the 1840s, though its pre-Famine population had grown to more than eight million, Ireland's birth rate was beginning to decline. Contrary to the English stereotype, the Irish were not prone to the Malthusian vice of marrying early. Given a reasonable system of land distribution and agricultural production, moreover, Ireland would not have seemed overpopulated (O'Gráda, 12–19; Davis, 21). Nevertheless, English officials saw Ireland as a sort of accidental experiment that proved Malthus right. For both officials and economists, poverty meant too many mouths to feed, and the government had a scientific responsibility *not* to give food to the overpopulating hungry. Government intervention only undermined the "natural" workings of the market-place and the chance for prosperity. Thus the Famine was nature's or God's way to rectify the conditions that had caused the Famine in the first place: overpopulated Ireland would be depopulated, to its future benefit.[8]

Even in 1798, the date both of the first edition of *Essay on Population* and of the abortive United Irishmen's Rebellion, Malthus's treatment of famine as the worst of all checks against population reflects the general Irish tragedy. Though the Irish laborer, Malthus thinks, has plenty of potatoes to eat, he does not have even the dubious benefit of savage customs such as infanticide and cannibalism to check his improvidence. The Irish "are in so degraded a state as to propagate their species without regard to consequences" (537), and Malthus knows what the worst of those consequences will be: "Famine . . . the last . . . most dreadful resource of nature" (52). If war, disease, and other violent "checks" to population do not "succeed," then "gigantic inevitable famine stalks in the rear, and with one mighty blow levels the population with the food of the world" (52). No wonder Thomas Carlyle called economics "the dismal science."

For Malthus, however, the deadly workings of famine and the other checks to population were the outcome of divine wisdom as expressed through "nature's laws." "Providence" was the ultimate regulator both of population and of the food supply (132). And for those who agreed with him, the starvation in Ireland was an indication that the Irish were out of touch with divine wisdom—indeed, they were more so than many savage tribes and races, who, after all, did not starve but, Malthus claimed, kept their populations under control through their savage customs. In any event, from the Malthusian perspective, mass starvation was just nature's—and Providence's—way of righting the balance in a society reeling from its own misbehavior and lack of foresight and restraint.

Supervising famine relief under both Peel and Russell, Charles Trevelyan was an evangelical liberal of the Clapham sect, antislavery variety, and as fundamentalist in economics as in religion. He believed that "perfect Free Trade is the right course" in dealing with all economic matters (quoted Woodham-Smith, 123), and he strove mightily to cut costs and to minimize the government's role.[9] Nothing should be given as a handout, because "if the Irish once find out there are any circumstances in which they can get" any form of assistance for free, "we shall have a system of mendicancy such as the world never saw" (quoted in Woodham-Smith, 171). That Ireland had become a "nation of beggars" seemed self-evident (Lebow, 67); moreover, Trevelyan believed that the only cure was to make the beggars work for their livings.

While Peel is often credited with a more generous relief policy than that of the liberals under Russell, that view is simplistic if only because Trevelyan served in both administrations. The chief aim from the outset was to get the Irish upper classes to pay for as much of the relief as possible. Under neither regime was food or money delivered straight to the starving peasants. Leaders within Ireland demanded that the export of the grain harvests of 1846 and 1847 be halted and the grain used to feed the starving, but economic "laws" overruled this obvious expedient.[10] Trevelyan believed that preventing Irish merchants from exporting grain would leave those merchants without money to put into circulation in Ireland or to help pay for famine relief.

Trevelyan pursued the same logic under both Peel and Russell, though official policy did become more economical, both stricter and stingier, as the Famine grew worse. According to Cormac O'Gráda, "The decision, taken in the summer of 1847 [at the height of the Famine], to throw the burden of relief on the Irish Poor Law and the Irish taxpayer . . . amounted to a declaration that, as far as Whitehall was concerned, the Famine was over" (46). O'Gráda calls this decision "the most cynical move of all," and adds: "This callous act, born of ideology and frustration, prolonged the crisis" (46). James Donnelly writes of "the workhouse horrors of the early months of 1847" ("Administration," 318), and no wonder: the Poor Law workhouses were overflowing with the diseased and dying, mostly women and children, and "roadside deaths were still commonplace in the winter of 1848–9" (O'Gráda, 46).

Though Peel did not rely on the Poor Law to deal with the emergency, he had the advantage over Russell of being in power only when the Famine was in its early stages—indeed before it had become a famine. When the potato blight appeared in Ireland in the fall of 1845, it destroyed only a third of that year's crop. That no one died of starvation before Peel resigned has less to do with his emergency measures than with the fact that the full crisis was yet to come. In the fall of 1846 the blight destroyed nearly the entire potato crop, and by then the poor who had been affected earlier were in desperate shape, with thousands more added every day to the roster of the starving. Further, Peel resigned partly under the pressure of the Famine, because he had converted from protectionism to the free-trade ideology of the Anti-Corn Law League. His conversion had begun much earlier than 1845, however, so that from the start of the Famine, on economic matters Peel was almost as liberal as Russell (cf. Woodham-Smith, 49).

When, against Trevelyan's advice, Peel authorized the first purchase of Indian maize from abroad, he was only doing what had been done to alleviate earlier food shortages, and in any event the maize was not doled out for free. The plan was to put the corn on the market in order to keep down all food prices. The distressed peasantry could purchase the ground corn—"Peel's brimstone"—from official depots at cost. And they could acquire the money to pay for it through their own labor on the public works, mostly road building, that the government funded both to provide employment and to bring them into the money economy. Further, funding for the public works consisted mostly of loans that the Irish were expected to repay once the Famine was over.

In *The Irish Crisis*, which he published in 1848 to defend the relief efforts he directed, and to declare—prematurely—that those efforts had helped to end the Famine, Trevelyan asserted that government action was insignificant compared to the long-range benefits of the Famine itself, the very handiwork of Providence: "posterity will trace . . . to [the] famine . . . a salutary revolution in the habits of a nation long . . . unfortunate, and will acknowledge that . . . Supreme Wisdom has educed permanent good out of transient evil" (1). This is Trevelyan's version of the Malthusian theodicy. As Peter Quinn notes, in the discourse of Trevelyan and other supporters of the government's relief policies, "Providence and economics [were] mashed together in the mortar of politics" (14). Providentialism often also went hand in hand with "rabid anti-Catholicism" (Donnelly, "Construction," 50–51), though this is less evident in official discourse than in the press and evangelical sermonizing about the Famine as God's punishment of the Irish both for Catholicism and for general bad behavior (at times, the two are synonymous).

In any event, for Trevelyan, and from the hegemonic perspective of English public opinion, it was the bad national "habits" of the Irish—poverty, idleness, sex, potatoes, whisky—that had produced the Famine. "The great evil with which we have to contend," Trevelyan claimed, is "not the physical evil of famine, but the moral evil of the selfish, perverse and turbulent character of the [Irish] people" (quoted in Woodham-Smith, 156). In asserting that the bad "habits" of the Irish caused the Famine, Trevelyan invokes race rather than economics or politics. Despite the Act of Union and despite the centuries-long intermingling of English and Celtic peoples that made any claim of racial difference between them untenable, English commentators usually treat the Irish as a race apart, as in Senior's distinction between civilized and uncivilized. Indeed, to Senior, Trevelyan, and other English observers, the bad national habits of the Irish make even savages seem superior.[11]

Trevelyan declares that the "domestic habits" of the Irish are "of the lowest and most degrading kind" (7). He quotes Sir John Burgoyne's claim that their standard of living is "on the lowest scale of human existence" and yet that they are "perfectly content" with this "lowest grade" of poverty and ignorance (4–5). And he likens the Irish to "South Sea" savages, lowest of the low, he implies, on the human totem pole. If anything, the Irish are even lower and worse than savages, because, as white Europeans, they ought to know better: they should be, but aren't, civilized.

Both in official discourse and in the English press, there are two main lines of explanation for how the Irish had caused the Famine and should therefore pay for relieving it. The first stresses how land in Ireland had been subdivided and rack-rented into ever smaller units, leaving the poor at the mercy both of the potato and of the tenant farmers and middlemen above them, with the landowners often absent, as in Maria Edgeworth's novels. Besides Marx, John Stuart Mill makes this argument with passionate eloquence in his letters to the *Examiner* and the *Morning Chronicle*.[12]

But the second, very prevalent explanation was race, although, as in Trevelyan's *Irish Crisis*, the two explanations often merge. According to the racial explanation, the Irish are inherently lazy, ignorant, and brutishly contented with their poverty and potatoes. The London *Times* often compared the slothful, "potatophagous" Irish with the energetic, bread- and meat-eating English. It claimed that "the potato blight [is] a blessing" that will teach the Irish the virtues of sexual restraint, hard work, and being carnivorous. And it looked forward to when, "in a few more years, a Celtic Irishman will be as rare in Connemara as the Red Indian on the shores of the Manhattan" (quoted in Donnelly, "Construction," 45). Nor was the *Times* alone in stereotyping the Irish as a vanishing primitive race. Especially after the abortive Young Ireland rebellion of 1848, racist stereotyping, as in innumerable *Punch* cartoons, makes the Irishman out to be not only

brutish and apelike but also dangerously violent, "the Irish Frankenstein" (Donnelly, "Construction," 52; Foster, 178–80). Such stereotyping is common also in the discourse of liberal intellectuals such as
the Reverend Charles Kingsley, who, in recalling his 1860 trip to Ireland, wrote: "I am haunted by the human chimpanzees I saw . . . to
see white chimpanzees is dreadful; if they were black, one would not
feel it so much, but their skins . . . are as white as ours" (Kingsley,
236). The writings of many Victorian ethnologists such as John Bed-
doe, with his "index of [Irish] nigrescence," gave quasi-scientific status to this view of the Irish as a separate, apelike, or "Africanoid" race
(Curtis, *Anglo-Saxons*, 66–73; Jahoda, 227). In *The Races of Men*,
Robert Knox declared that those who blame Roman Catholicism for
the Famine were mistaken; the real cause was race, with the usual list
of negative attributes attached.

Racist stereotyping made it easy either to ignore the Act of Union
altogether or to believe that, within the terms of the Union, England
was doing everything possible to help her retrograde neighbor (see
Corbett). In Famine discourse, Ireland is usually referred to as a "nation" or even "state" quite separate from England, though England
has to pay for this separate, bankrupt state. In an 1844 leader, the London *Times* asserted: "It is by industry, toil, perseverance, economy,
prudence, . . . self-denial, and self-dependence that a state becomes
mighty and its people happy. . . . It is because the people of Ireland
generally do not *labour* either physically or mentally, in anything like
the proportion that the people of England do, that they are not generally near so wealthy" (quoted in Lebow, 65). The *Times* apparently
did not recognize that, after the Act of Union of 1800, Ireland was not
a separate "state" but rather, along with England, part of the single
"state" known as Great Britain or the United Kingdom. As Peter
Quinn notes, "The Great Famine exposed this promise [of Union] as
a lie" (14). Yet most English officials were adamantly opposed to the
repeal of the Union. In any event, the *Times* "repeatedly drew a comparison between the ungrateful and feckless poor of Ireland and the
'respectable' poor of England" (Kinealy, 103). "What is given to the
Irish," it declared, "is so much filched from English distress. . . . The
English labourer pays taxes from which the Irish one is free—nay, he
pays taxes by which the Irishman is enriched" (quoted in Kinealy,
104). Trevelyan and other officials, of course, knew that the starving
Irish were not being "enriched" by taxes "filched" from the poor of
England, but they did believe that Irish landlords were not doing

their duty, that those landlords, even small farmers who were themselves often "tumbled" into the starving masses, should pay for relief. And therefore they shaped a policy that, whenever possible, made famine relief a local responsibility.

When Osborne, author of "Immortal Sewerage," published a series of letters in the London *Times* criticizing the famine relief policies of Russell's liberal administration, Anthony Trollope responded with letters to *The Examiner*, a liberal journal edited by John Forster, Dickens's friend and biographer. At the time Trollope was working for the Post Office in southwestern Ireland; he had just commenced his career as a novelist, publishing *The Macdermots of Ballycloran* and *The Kellys and O'Kellys* in the late 1840s. These were the first of his half-dozen novels that deal with Ireland. Though neither depicts the Famine, both portray Irish poverty and economic backwardness using the conventions of fictional realism. Set in the 1830s *The Macdermots* offers the tragic theme of "the fall of a house" or family estate, one "prevalent in Irish literature from Maria Edgeworth onward" (Wittig, 99). In contrast, *The Kellys* deals with Irish politics—specifically the trial of Daniel O'Connell in 1844—but there is little connection between the trial and the main, comic plot. For Trollope, the trial is merely symptomatic of the irrationality of all Irish politics.

In his *Examiner* letters, Trollope views the Irish people as incapable of self-government: "I find it impossible to believe," he writes, "that the Irish are gifted with those qualities, which are required to support a stern struggle for constitutional liberty" (104). Those Irish leaders like O'Connell who do "struggle for constitutional liberty" are mere demagogues. This is the negative view of Irish politics that Trollope offers in his last, unfinished novel, *The Landleaguers* (1882), a "melodrama" in which Michael Davitt's Land League "is condemned outright," while the good English landlord, Philip Jones, is treated as" 'Ireland's best friend'" (Wittig, 112).[13]

Far from always presenting them as benevolent overseers of the peasantry, however, in his *Examiner* letters Trollope adopts the widespread English tactic of blaming the Famine on the landlords of Ireland.[14] "The country is afflicted by a race of landlords," he writes, "who [because of their indebtedness] have no longer any property in the land, and who will not, nay too often cannot, escape from their position. This is the fertile cause of full poor-houses, high rates [taxes], low markets, and impoverished tenants" (94). During the

Famine, moreover, these same bankrupt landlords failed to shoulder the responsibility for alleviating it:

> At a time when English families afflicted with no want, with no debts, were abstaining from their usual comforts that they might pour into Ireland the funds thus paid, in Ireland itself no carriages were abandoned, no hounds . . . destroyed, no retinues reduced—the effort . . . made by landlords was to secure as large a proportion as possible of the funds provided by Government. (81)

Besides blaming the landlords for the sorry condition of Ireland and for stealing the English funds meant for the starving peasants, Trollope, like Trevelyan, views "the measures adopted by the Government" as "the best" possible "to effect the immediate preservation of life" (81). Because of those measures, most observers, Trollope thinks, "are beginning to . . . agree . . . that the deaths from absolute famine were, comparatively speaking, few" (82).

When a decade later Trollope again tackled the subject of the Famine in *Castle Richmond* (1860), it was perhaps to give fictional form to the opinions he had expressed in *The Examiner* (see Knelman). But there is at least one major difference between the novel and the letters, and that involves his treatment of Irish landlords. While Trollope still claims that "the scourge of Ireland was the existence of a class who looked to be gentlemen living on their property, but who should have earned their bread by the work of their brain, or . . . by the sweat of their brow" (67), and while he also claims that one benefit of the Famine has been to "cut up root and branch" "the idle, genteel class," "punish[ing them] with the penalty of extermination" (68), nevertheless the main characters of *Castle Richmond* are landowning aristocrats who are treated as blameless in regard to the Famine and even as bending over backward to prevent starvation.

The main connection between the Famine and Trollope's landowning characters comes through the charitable efforts of young Herbert Fitzgerald, his sisters, and his future wife, Clara Desmond. Herbert attends meetings of the local relief committee, and he and the young women help out at a soup kitchen. Herbert also gives money to beggars, although he knows that this violates the "laws" of political economy (192). Trollope's attitude toward those "laws," which teach that indiscriminate benevolence encourages the poor to beg and to overpopulate, is ambivalent. Trollope evidently thinks that political economy is scientific but also hard-hearted. For Herbert and his sisters to adhere to the dictates of economics, they would have "required frames of iron and hearts of adamant," says the narrator; "It was impossible [for them] not to *waste* money in almsgiving" (192; my emphasis).[15] Thus Trollope figures benevolence as feminine irrationality, in contrast to the manly, rational science of economics.

In *Castle Richmond*, the Famine serves only as a bleak backdrop to the main plot, though one that allows the Fitzgeralds and Clara to exhibit their benevolence. Their story centers on the rivalry between Herbert and his cousin, Owen Fitzgerald, for the hand of Clara.[16] Apart from the charitable work of the upper-class characters, what happens to them and what happens to the starving peasants have nothing to do with each other. There is no causal link between the behaviors and fortunes of the Fitzgeralds and Desmonds and the misbehaviors and misfortunes of the peasantry. Only in one episode, featuring the Protestant clergyman Townsend and his wife, does Trollope treat a scene of good dining among upper-class characters as an ironic contrast to the main activities of the peasants, which are begging and starving. None of Trollope's upper-class characters cause anyone to starve. Instead, he treats the begging and starving of the peasants as self-induced—just the sort of misbehaviors one expects from begging, starving peasants who have not learned the values of work, prudence, and self-help. And the figure of the pauperized mother who cannot feed her children is central to his depiction.

Trollope's version of fictional realism divides along conventional social class lines. On the one hand, there is the main story of the Fitzgeralds and Desmonds, which takes the form of a comic novel of manners, with the untangling of the inheritance plot and marriage as the resolution. The histories and futures of the upper-class characters are mapped as individual and familial progress; the comic fullness and continuity of their plot mirrors the fullness and continuity of their identities. The parallel but antithetical story of the Famine is punctuated by the stereotypic identities and discontinuous lives of begging and starving peasants. Though there are episodes in which peasants speak at some length (in dialect) to Herbert, his sisters, and Clara, there is only one—a beggar named Martha—who shows up more than once, and she makes only two brief appearances. The begging and starving are mostly nameless, ungrateful objects of the young Fitzgeralds' benevolence. The starving peasants usually also appear in chapters distinctly marked off from the main narrative, melancholy interruptions to the upper-class story of comic progress.

The sections in which the starving peasants appear are narrated both journalistically and reluctantly. The narrator even asks, "Why describe [the Famine] at all?" (375). Trollope does not rely on the melodramatic rhetoric of extremity according to which no language is adequate to describe the Famine.[17] But in the perfunctory language of documentary realism or reportage of mere fact, Trollope treats the starving as doomed, despite the benevolence of the good upper-class characters and despite the wisest imaginable government policy. Of the starving woman with dead and dying children whose cabin Herbert enters, and to whom he gives some useless coins while promising to "send someone" to help her, the narrator indicates that Herbert's charity will do no good: "Her doom had been spoken before Herbert had entered the cabin" (374).

From the start of *Castle Richmond*, Trollope emphasizes the normality of his Irish upper-class characters and presumably therefore of Ireland. "Irish acquaintances I have by dozens, and Irish friends, also, by twos and threes, whom I can love and cherish — almost as well, perhaps, as though they had been born in Middlesex" (1). Castle Richmond "might have been in Hampshire or Essex; and . . . Sir Thomas Fitzgerald might have been a Leicestershire baronet" (3). But, of course, all the main characters are no different from the English because they are English, or at any rate Anglo-Irish. But the English normality of the central characters makes the starving Irish seem all the more distant and different, a race apart. When Trollope speaks of his Irish friends and acquaintances, he is obviously not referring to the pauperized mothers and children who show up en masse at the soup kitchens and the public works. These have no role to play in the main narrative of progress either of the novel or of Ireland. For that matter, they have no role to play in God's narrative of progress either, which, for Trollope, is just a larger version of the progressive history of Great Britain. Like the Bushmen and the Australian aborigines whom he declares in his imperial travelogues to be inevitably doomed, the starving Irish are, for Trollope, a surplus or refuse population needing to be swept away to make room for a tidier, more English world.[18]

As in his letters to *The Examiner*, so in *Castle Richmond* Trollope says that the Famine was the work of God: not God punishing Ireland for her sins but God in His infinite mercy helping Ireland to depopulate, to reform her ways, and to achieve prosperity for the remainder of her population. Between God's merciful visitation of mass starvation and the benevolent but scientific expertise of Lord John Russell's liberal government, Trollope thinks that the future of Ireland has been secured. "And now again the fields in Ireland are green, and the markets are busy, and money is chucked to and fro like a weathercock" (347). Here one can see how the two disconnected plots of Trollope's novel—the aristocratic inheritance plot and the plot of mass starvation—reflect each other. For Trollope, they are *both* ultimately comic plots in which dire misfortunes are suddenly reversed, turned into their opposites, as if by divine intervention. As Margaret Kelleher notes, "when the Fitzgerald patrimony is most in danger, the famine is at its worst" (43). And when the fortunes of the Fitzgeralds and of Clara Desmond are set straight again, then the narrator tells us that the future prosperity of Ireland is at hand.

At just this point in the novel, one sees the fourth major limitation of Victorian liberalism, or at least of that commonsense, "advanced conservative" version of it that Trollope exemplifies.[19] He can only think of the trajectory of social history as a narrative of progress (cf. Eagleton, 13). In Trollope's liberal imagination, whoever or whatever does not fit into the story of progress falls out of the parade, blurs into the nameless, starving masses, or otherwise fails to achieve narrative coherence and continuity, like the already doomed starving woman and children whom Herbert encounters en route to his future fortune and happiness.

Trollope refuses to think that the narrative of history may not add up to progress. Like Trevelyan and other liberal defenders of the government's famine relief measures, he even refuses to see the Famine as a major calamity and setback for Ireland. On the contrary, the death of more than one million paupers is just the medicine Ireland needed to cure its endemic poverty and put it on the road of progress and prosperity. In the conclusion to *Castle Richmond*, Trollope writes that, with mass suffering and starvation all around, the future looked bleak. "But in truth the Irish cakes were only then a-baking, and the Irish ale was being brewed" (488). Having conjured cakes and ale out of a famished landscape, Trollope can do no better than to continue with loaves and fishes—that is, with biblical allusions to bring God once again into the benign, comic picture that serves as the novel's ending:

> But if one did in truth write a tale of the famine, [says the narrator,] after that
> it would behove the author to write a tale of the pestilence; and then another,
> a tale of the exodus.

This biblical triptych represents the Famine, the diseases spawned by it, and mass emigration from Ireland.

> These three wonderful events, [the narrator continues,] . . . were the blessings
> coming from Omniscience . . . by which the black clouds were driven from
> the Irish firmament. If one . . . could . . . have had from the first that wisdom
> which has learned to acknowledge that His mercy endureth for ever! And then
> the same author going on with his series would give in his last [chapter], —Ire-
> land in her prosperity. (489)

"Ireland in *her* prosperity"—once again, Ireland is figured as a woman, learning her lesson mainly through the unfortunate deaths of her surplus children. Here, as in Trevelyan's *Irish Crisis*, God in His merciful wisdom, by dispatching more than a million "doomed" Irish paupers, proves to be a devout believer in the science of political economy and no doubt also in the good work of the Post Office—a solid, commonsensical, beef-eating, and not too imaginative "ad-vanced conservative liberal" very much like Anthony Trollope.

6. The Dusk of the Dreamtime

In *The Road to Botany Bay* Paul Carter declares that Australian aboriginals and convicts "enter white history in much the same role . . . fused into the figure of unreason" (320).[1] The convicts viewed the aboriginals as beneath them, mere beasts of the field or the outback. But what did the first Australians think of the convicts? Robert Hughes notes that, when offered leftover "convict slops," the aboriginals rejected them as "'No good—all same like croppy,' [their] disdainful term for an Irish convict" (279). And the missionary James Günther reported that when presented with clothes the aboriginals removed the stitches to turn them into blankets, because they identified the clothes as Irish. According to Günther, "our natives commonly attach some idea of inferiority to what is Irish and Ireland" (quoted in Hughes, 279).

To most white (even Irish) observers, however, the aboriginals were the absolute antithesis of progress and civilization. In his 1827 memoir, *Two Years in New South Wales*, the naval surgeon Peter Cunningham remarked that the aboriginals were "at the very zero of civilisation" and seemed therefore to constitute "the connecting link between man and the monkey tribe" (quoted in McGregor, 6). So, too, in his 1834 *Excursions*, Lt. W. H. Breton declared: "Speaking of them collectively . . . I entertain very little more respect for the aborigines of New Holland, than for the ourang-outang; in fact, I can discover no difference" (173). It was even frequently claimed that the aboriginals were without language or, at any rate, without any coherent, rational means of communication.[2]

It was not simply that the first Australians seemed devoid of customs, beliefs, values, reason, and even language, it was also as if, to many of the early commentators, they were already nonexistent. They did not live in villages, they did not farm or garden, and they possessed little or nothing of economic value except the land, which they were deemed not to possess. Further, they did not pose the threat of organized warfare that colonists encountered in North America, South Africa, and New Zealand. From the First Fleet in 1788 until the 1970s, white appropriation of Australian territory was legitimized by the doctrine of *terra nullius*, a phrase that, as Henry Reynolds notes, carries a double meaning: "both a country without a sovereign recognized by European authorities and a territory where nobody owns any land at all, where no tenure of any sort existed" (*Law*, 12). This was almost tantamount to the convenient notion that the aboriginals were not there, an idea often expressed in colonial legal decisions. Thus the Crown Law Officers declared, in 1819, that New South Wales had been "desert and uninhabited" in 1788, and three decades later the Chief Justice of that colony spoke of "newly discovered and unpeopled territories" (quoted in Reynolds, *Dispossession*, 67; *Law*, 32).[3]

Despite the imagined nonexistence of the aboriginals, the literature of white Australia, like those of North America and South Africa, begins in the mode of proleptic elegy.[4] The consoling belief that savages are self-exterminating is quite explicitly rendered in what has been called Australia's first children's book, *A Mother's Offering to Her Children* (1841). The anonymous author includes a section of "Anecdotes of the Aborigines of New South Wales," which J. J. Healy describes as "a list of Gothic horrors." Healy quotes an exchange between the white mother and her daughters:

> Mrs. S: — "Little Sally, the black child has been accidentally killed."
> Clara: — "Oh! Mamma, do you know how?"
> Mrs. S: — "She was playing in the barn, which is only a temporary one; and pulled down a heavy prop of wood upon herself. It fell on her temple; and killed her immediately."

Emma: — "Do you not think her mother will be very sorry, when she hears of
   it?"

Mrs. S: — "Alas! my dear children, her mother also met with an untimely
   death. These poor uncivilized people, most frequently meet with some deplorable end, through giving away to unrestrained passions." (Quoted in
   Healy, 32)

But while "unrestrained passions" is a stereotypic allegation frequently applied to savages in general, it was not always applied to the
first Australians. Many accounts have trouble identifying what the
aboriginals were unrestrainedly passionate about—they were said to
be lethargic, they wandered, they cared little about material values or
bettering themselves, and so on—though they did seem to care about
defending their lives and land. In any event, W. E. H. Stanner notes
that between the 1820s and the 1850s white Australians produced
"scores of sorrowful expressions of regard for 'the real welfare of that
helpless and unfortunate race'; tenfold the number of condemnations of them as debased, worthless and beyond grace; and, one-
hundredfold, acceptances of their inevitable extinction" (147).

Before the 1960s even sympathetic observers portray the aboriginals in negatives, that is, in terms of what they do not possess. Thus in
The Aborigines of Australia, first published in 1853–54 as a series of articles in the Sydney *Empire*, Roderick J. Flanagan contends that they
have lost many of the skills that enabled their ancestors, thousands of
years ago, to migrate across the South Pacific. They have no recorded
history, moreover, so confronting any investigator "is the extreme dif-
ficulty . . . [of] dispelling . . . the thick cloud which hangs around
[their] primeval origin":

   No monumental ruin, however obscure, or however feebly defined, has ever
   been discovered, throughout the length and breadth of the country, which
   might afford a clue to the civilization or barbarism of the people from whom
   they have descended. No form of worship, or well-defined religious belief,
   such as is found amongst almost all other barbarians, suggests the particular
   class of worshippers to which they originally belonged. No arts, however
   rude—none, however, in any way worthy of the name . . . [and so on]. (2)

Lists of what savages do not possess or know, as in Montaigne's "Of
Cannibals," can betoken utopian innocence, but that is not Flana-

gan's point. Whether in terms of depopulation or not, the aboriginals have, he claims, been declining throughout their (pre)history. The advent of the white race may hasten that decline—will certainly not prevent it—but is not its main cause.

Contrary to Flanagan, in the journals of his treks through western Australia, George Grey insists that the aboriginals could not have degenerated from an earlier, higher level of social organization (2:222). This is because of the rigidity of their "laws and customs," which have frozen them in time, making it "impossible" for them to emerge from their "state of barbarism" (2:223). Nevertheless, Grey is both a careful and a sympathetic observer of those laws and customs. To Thomas Hodgkin and the APS he writes that the Australians have a definite conception of land ownership and that they have been systematically denied their rights (2:233–37):

> It is true, the European intruders pay no respect to these Aboriginal divisions of the territory, the black native being often hunted off his own ground, or destroyed by European violence, dissipation, or disease, just as his kangaroos are driven off that ground by the European's black cattle; but this surely does not alter the case as to the right of the Aborigines. (2:234)

Grey also corresponded with Lord John Russell, advising the then head of the Colonial Office, in some thirty-seven points, on "the best means of promoting civilization" among the aboriginals (2:373–87).

To Russell, Grey declares that the aboriginals are "as apt and intelligent as any other race of men I am acquainted with; they are subject to the same affections, appetites and passions as other men" (2:374). Yet only gradual, patient educational and missionary work may wean them from their tyrannical culture and lead them eventually to civilization. By that time, Grey believes, it will probably be too late. Either their "ancient system" of laws and customs has to "expire or be swept away" (2:223), or else the aboriginals themselves will expire. However, Grey detects Providence in the thought that "this people should until a certain period remain in their present condition," but also that "the progress of civilization over the earth has been directed, set bounds to, and regulated by certain laws, framed by Infinite wisdom" (2:223–24). The extinction of the aboriginals is part of God's plan, and, for Grey, the chief worldly agents of that plan are white traders and capitalists:

> With the wizard wand of commerce, [the businessman] touches a lone and trackless forest, and at his bidding, cities arise, and the hum and dust of trade collect—away are swept ancient races; antique laws and customs moulder into oblivion. The strong-holds of murder and superstition are cleansed, and the Gospel is preached among ignorant and savage men. The ruder languages disappear successively, and the tongue of England alone is heard around. (2:201)

Such a passage suggests why Grey, for all his sympathy toward primitive peoples, could go on to become an influential colonial administrator in South Australia, New Zealand, and South Africa.

In contrast to the view that the aboriginals barely exist, flitting lightly over a landscape they do not possess, there is the long and bloody record of conflict with white explorers and colonizers. Their resistance, however, was sporadic and, because of the technology gap, rarely successful; it was not even always understood as resistance. "Only in 1967," writes Steve Hemming, "through an Australia wide Referendum, were Aboriginal people recognized as 'equal' citizens and included in the Census" (31). The counterdemonstrations and ceremonies staged by aboriginal activists in 1988, bicentenary of the First Fleet, marked a further turning point in the recognition of the rights and history of Australia's first people. In that year the Mackay Report and the conclusions of the Royal Commission on Aboriginal Deaths in Custody were indications of changing attitudes. These reports were followed by the Eddie Mabo and Wik Peoples High Court decisions of 1992 and 1996, which restored to the first Australians the right to possess land and corrected in legal terms *terra nullius,* or the notion that they had not been in possession of the continent in 1788.[5]

Not only was Australia inhabited in 1788 but the number of aboriginals may have been far greater than most estimates well into the twentieth century. Getting an accurate tally of a nomadic population spread over a vast territory, much of it unexplored well past 1850, was not possible, but the estimates were made anyway. As in other contexts such as North America, the ideological utility of unverifiable but low numbers is obvious. As recently as 1966, official estimates placed the indigenous population of Australia in 1788 at only 251,000 and at 67,000 in 1901; by 1911 "it was speculated that the Aboriginal and [Torres Strait] Islander population had fallen to about 31,000" (E. Bourke, 45, 38). In *Our Original Aggression* (1983), however, Ned Butlin argues that the figures both for the early aboriginal population and thus for the genocidal depopulation of the continent were much higher. Though working with circumstantial and comparative evidence that, he acknowledges, is itself far from certain, Butlin believes that the indigenous population of Australia in 1788 may have been more than one million.[6]

At least since World War II, the aboriginal population has begun to recover. In just a five-year period (1991–96), it increased by an apparently miraculous 33 percent, from 265,371 to 352,970. One of the factors in this remarkable growth, Eleanor Bourke points out, is an "increased identification rate," which means both more accurate counting on the part of census takers and, on the part of aboriginals, more willingness to be counted, including many who are of mixed racial descent (46–47). Before the 1930s, however, the aboriginals were deemed by virtually all white commentators to be slated for total, rapid extinction, a view often expressed by missionaries, secular humanitarians, and anthropologists as well as by those who clearly wished them to vanish.

In his study of "the doomed race theory" in the Australian context, Russell McGregor claims that the earliest observers of the colonization process "made no reference to the possibility of extinction, despite the fact that they witnessed the terrible decimation of the Port Jackson tribes in the first smallpox epidemic of 1789" (13). The "expectation of extinction" developed in correlation to white settlement and also to "declining faith" in attempts to civilize the aboriginals (13). Not until the period between the two world wars, McGregor notes, did "the doomed race idea" begin to weaken, "although it persisted, albeit with declining vigour, until at least the 1950s" (ix). McGregor thinks that the belief in inevitable extinction was "neither a sop for disturbed consciences nor an empirical demographic prediction":

> More than anything else, it was a manifestation of ultimate pessimism in Aboriginal abilities. As . . . attempts to civilise and convert failed, and as racial attitudes hardened, it came to be considered that the best that could be done for

the Aboriginals was to protect them from overt injustice and brutality—for the short time they had left upon this earth. (18)

As in other colonial contexts, moreover, there was plenty of empirical evidence that the aboriginals were rapidly depopulating as well as fleeing into the interior where, according to C. D. Rowley, "possibly more people died from the direct and indirect effects of starvation than from . . . newly introduced diseases or the use of the gun" (7).

From about the 1820s on, the view became widespread, at least among the white colonists, that the chief causes of the demise of the aboriginals were such savage customs as interminable warfare, cannibalism, and infanticide. In his 1846 *Report on the Condition . . . and Prospects of the Australian Aborigines* William Westgarth summarizes a number of early government reports, as well as books and essays by such authorities as Flanagan, Edward Eyre, and the Polish traveler Count Strzelecki, all insisting that nothing can be done to prevent the ultimate, total extinction of the aboriginals throughout Australia. Among the causes of extinction, Westgarth lists "their own mutual wars; their hostile encounters with the whites; the diseases and vices of European society . . . ; the common practice of infanticide; and . . . the gradual disappearance of various animals used as food, and of other sources of their support" (6). As Westgarth must have known, however, "their own mutual wars" were not a major cause of the depopulation of the first Australians; many accounts stress the ritualized character of their "warfare"—typically spear-throwing confrontations in which, as soon as one of the combatants was wounded or (less often) killed, the conflict was over.

Westgarth adopts the common practice of exaggerating the role of savage customs in exterminating savages. "The general prevalence of infanticide is established beyond any reasonable doubt," he notes; "the half caste infants appear to be the most exposed to this fate" (12). So, too, uninvited strangers chancing upon an aboriginal encampment "incur the penalty of death. This sanguinary custom is traceable to a superstitious belief that the death of any member of a tribe is occasioned by the hand of some enemy. . . . This . . . superstition has originated [or caused] the practice, on the occasion of a death in the tribe, of sacrificing some individual of a neighbouring tribe, who is supposed to be the murderer" (20). On this account, it is wonderful that there were any aboriginals left to murder. It is also difficult to understand how and why white strangers who did not themselves threaten violence to the aboriginals often received a friendly welcome. And it is even more difficult to understand how there could be any "half caste infants." Nevertheless, other white observers express a similar notion. Thus, on his travels around Australia and Tasmania in the 1830s, Lieutenant Breton heard that "whenever one of their own tribe" died, the aborigines "invariably destroy an individual of a neighbouring tribe" (167).[7]

As in North America, South Africa, Ireland, and elsewhere, extinction discourse in Australia was fueled by multiple, conflicting motives and forms of evidence, including the desire to ease "disturbed consciences." For the first white Australians, the long-distance news—both disturbing and consoling—about what was happening to other indigenous populations throughout the world helped make their own bad news seem natural and inevitable. There was also the vivid, at-home example of Tasmania, where the aboriginals—who were thought to be both culturally and racially distinct from those on the mainland—were totally exterminated (supposedly) by 1876. With Darwin's treatment of racial extinction in *Descent of Man*, the story of the first—and last—Tasmanians became a key instance of the inevitable vanishing of perhaps all primitive races everywhere.

For many observers, Tasmania offered a moral and political lesson in how the progress of empire and civilization could be badly botched. In 1803, the date of the first white settlement—a penal colony—of what was then called Van Diemen's Land, the number of aboriginals was perhaps between four thousand and seven thousand (Ryan, 14). Disease began immediately to work its depopulating effects. In 1805 the government of the infant colony, threatened by famine, gave the convicts "license to forage"—that is, to occupy the island as they chose; there was no way to prevent them from taking whatever liberties they chose with its primitive inhabitants (West, 263; Bonwick, *Last*, 30).

Before 1824, notes Henry Reynolds, "the common view among the colonists was that the Tasmanians were a mild and peaceful people" (*Fate*, 29).[8] From the late 1820s, however, the Tasmanians began to fight back in fairly concerted ways. Between 1824 and 1830, approximately 170 whites were killed, some 200 wounded, and another 200 or so harassed or threatened (Reynolds, *Fate*, 28–29). In response, in 1830 Gov. George Arthur organized the "Black Line," a dragnet com-

posed of all soldiers, free settlers, and convicts, to sweep across the island and corral the resistant natives on the Tasman Peninsula. But
the roundup was a fiasco: groups of aboriginals slipped through the
line and attacked from the rear or speared the occasional settler who
remained behind. Some were shot, but only two natives, an old man
and a boy, were captured.

Through the rest of the 1830s the story of the surviving Tasmanian
aboriginals merges with that of the so-called Friendly Mission of
George Augustus Robinson. A methodist bricklayer who had immigrated to Tasmania in 1824, Robinson had served as overseer of a
small aboriginal settlement on Bruni Island. Between 1830 and 1834,
with the governor's blessing, he made six treks into the wilderness to
"conciliate" and "bring in" the remaining natives—a sorry total of
203. These last Tasmanians were then transported to a reservation on
Flinders Island in Bass Straits, which one recent historian has called
the world's first "concentration camp" (Robson, 220).

Robinson had high hopes for resurrecting the Tasmanian race at
least in a spiritual sense. He wanted to be their earthly savior but, bar-
ring that, he would at least be their religious savior. True, a population of several thousand had been reduced to a few dozen, who themselves were rapidly dying. By 1835, when Robinson took charge of the
Flinders Island reservation, there were only 130 Tasmanians. Nevertheless, his reports glow with a before-and-after rhetoric typical of
early Victorian conversion narratives.[9] "In their native forests [the
aboriginals] were without the knowledge of a God," he writes, and so
in a "deplorable state of mental degradation . . . but little removed
from the brute. . . . Such is not now the case" (Robinson, 397). The
good news on the religious front, moreover, is matched by the news
on the civilizing front:

> I have much satisfaction in reporting that the aborigines are daily progressing
> in civilization. Their diurnal employments are now regularly and willingly
> performed, information is eagerly sought after, examples immediately fol-
> lowed, and industry among them is becoming habitual. (398)

"Industry" in Robinson's 1839 "Report" deserves emphasis. For the
colonists, the chief vice of both the Tasmanian and the mainland
aboriginals was not ferocity, cannibalism, polygamy, or the like, but
"indolence." Try to make a "blackfellow" work, and chances are he
would walk away into the bush (especially if you could not give him

anything he wanted in exchange for his labor). In his apparently humane, Christian concentration camp, Robinson saw to it that his Tasmanian subjects learned the value of work by turning them into proletarians and even penny capitalists. He proudly reported that he had established:

1. An aboriginal fund.
2. A circulating medium.
3. An aboriginal police.
4. A weekly market, and
5. A weekly periodical. (399)

Of these measures "put in force for the civilisation of the aborigines," Robinson declared, "the circulating medium is paramount" (399). He could imagine no better means than the profit motive to get savages to practice the virtue of industry. "With a circulation of coin not exceeding . . . fifteen pounds," he wrote, "labour in the value of upwards of one hundred pounds has been created" (399). The aboriginals were beginning to construct, purchase, and own property; the men were building roads and houses and tilling the soil for potatoes; the women were gathering grass for thatch, cooking, bird-snaring, and also learning the more "refined" arts of needlework and "French net" from the wife of the resident "catechist," Robert Clark.[10]

Despite his claims to Christianizing and civilizing the last Tasmanians, Robinson could not avoid the fact that they continued to die out at an alarming rate. Medical and humanitarian critics in Hobart and London began to accuse him of contributing to the bad health of his subjects by dressing them up, smothering them with blankets, and making them lead sedentary lives. The site of the Flinders Island settlement was cold and barren, and the drinking water "brackish." Apparently oblivious to these criticisms, Robinson declared that "the only drawback on the establishment [at Flinders Island] was the great mortality among them" (quoted in Bonwick, Last, 255). He compounded this tautological sentiment by adding: "Had the poor creatures survived to have become a numerous people, I am convinced they would have formed a contented and useful community" (258). Of course this is like saying, had the poor creatures survived they would not have expired.

James Bonwick, author of The Last of the Tasmanians (1870), recognized that what Robinson meant by civilizing the aboriginals involved the eradication of their beliefs, customs, and even identities.[11]

"Even the ... Aborigines' [Protection] Society were at last sensible of the folly of [Robinson's] over-legislation," Bonwick declares; "for, in their Report for 1839, they regretted that 'from the first a system had not been applied more suitable to the habits of a roving people'" (*Last*, 255–56). In short, Bonwick believed that civilization in the guise of Robinson's conversion tactics killed the final Tasmanians, almost as surely as disease and violence had earlier killed the majority of that tragic race.[12]

Robinson did not pursue his good works on Flinders Island for long. In 1838 he accepted an offer to become chief Protector of Aborigines at Port Phillip in New South Wales. He left his son in charge of the Flinders Island reservation; in his report of 29 March 1839, after eight aboriginals died in five days, G. A. Robinson Jr. wrote: "It would be impossible to describe the gloom which prevails ... from the bereavement of so large a portion of their kindred and friends, and the anxiety they evince to leave a spot which occasions such painful reminiscences is hourly increasing ... the island has been a charnel house for them" (quoted in Rowley, 53).

The Protector of Aborigines at Port Phillip was a position that Buxton's Aborigines Committee and the APS had been instrumental in establishing. From the outset, however, Robinson's new venture was attended by tragedy. He apparently allowed the Tasmanians he brought with him to wander away begging; in October 1841, with what provocation is unclear, they killed two white men (Turnbull, 213; Rae-Ellis, *Black Robinson*, 211–16). The trial and executions of the two Tasmanians alleged to be the aggressors caused a great sensation, in part because theirs were the first public executions in Melbourne—one more way to hasten the inevitable doom of a dying race.

What Robinson thought of this tragedy is unclear. At the trial he testified that he had "endeavored to instruct them" (quoted in Turnbull, 219) and that he had "never found these persons wanting in humanity" (quoted in Bonwick, *Last*, 331). Perhaps by this time he had come to believe that once a savage, always a savage. Maybe he had even concluded, with Bonwick, that his rescue work on Flinders Island had been a failure, though he would probably not have agreed with some of his modern critics that it had also been a fraud. In any event, by the early 1840s, when a number of the Australian missions were declared failures and closed, the Port Phillip protectorate was also declared a failure and was ended in 1842 (Rowley, 58).

By 1843 the number of Tasmanian aborigines on Flinders Island had dwindled to fifty-four. In 1846, this shrinking remnant was shipped back to Tasmania and placed in a reserve at Oyster Cove, not far from Hobart. There these depressed, docile bodies "guzzled rum," writes Robert Hughes, "which was thoughtfully provided by their keepers; they posed impassively for photographers in front of their filthy slab huts; and they waited to die" (423). By 1855 there were just sixteen survivors, including Truganini and William Lanney, the last man of his race.

Lanney had received a bit of education at the Hobart Orphans School; as a young man he was a familiar figure in Tasmanian ports and on whaling vessels as a deckhand. Ashore, he was often drunk: alcoholism was probably one of the causes of his death in 1869. But Lanney still had his moment of glory; along with Truganini, he became famous as the last of his race. In 1868, during the visit of Queen Victoria's son, Prince Alfred, he was paraded as "King Billy" at the Hobart regatta.[13] According to Bonwick, "Clad in a blue suit, with a gold-lace band around his cap, he walked proudly with the Prince on the Hobart Town regatta ground, conscious that they alone [in Tasmania] were in possession of royal blood" (Last, 395).

It is not clear that the usually sympathetic Bonwick captures "King Billy's" thoughts on this regal occasion. It is clear that William Lanney died a year later and that his death caused great agitation among both the scientific community and the general public. For some inexplicable reason, although European race scientists had been collecting and measuring the bones of extinct, primitive, and, for that matter, civilized peoples for decades, apparently no one had had the foresight to collect male specimens of this perhaps first human race which was breathing its last.[14] So with the death of the last Tasmanian man, members of the Royal Society of Tasmania and other race scientists woke up to the inestimable significance of King Billy's bones.

There followed a series of grave robberies and mutilations worthy of Victor Frankenstein.[15] The official inquiry into these crimes, in fact, revealed that two rival Dr. Frankensteins had been at work; both physicians at the Hobart hospital, one had hoped to secure Lanney's remains for the Royal College of Surgeons in London, while the other was working for the Royal Society of Tasmania. The first, who took Lanney's skull, was dismissed from the hospital; the second— who had removed the hands and feet and then the rest of the corpse, presumably to protect it from further mutilation and theft—was exonerated. Lanney's skull wound up in possession of the College of

Surgeons in London; what happened to the rest of his corpse is un-clear, although one authority declares that the exonerated surgeon "had a tobacco pouch made out of a portion of the skin, and other worthy scientists had possession of the ears, the nose, and a piece of Lanney's arm. The hands and feet were later found in the [Tasmanian] Royal Society's rooms in Argyle Street" (Ryan, 217). No advance in scientific knowledge came from this grisly fiasco (Cove, 146–47).[16]

What did the last Tasmanian man think during his last days? Perhaps more to the point, since she survived Lanney by seven years, what did Truganini think about the extinction of her race? Neither left memoirs. Truganini's dying words are known, however, and these express her terror that her remains would be scientifically dealt with just as Lanney's had. According to those at her deathbed, Truganini awoke briefly from the coma into which she had fallen and cried out, "Don't let them cut me, but bury me behind the mountains" (quoted in Rae-Ellis, *Trucanini*, 148).

This last wish of the last Tasmanian was not granted. Once again, the Royal Society of Tasmania hovered ghoulishly over the bones. Once again, extraordinary precautions were supposedly taken to prevent the mutilation or disappearance of the corpse. Once again, the precautions were ineffective: Truganini's grave was opened and her corpse removed. At least the grave robbers were tidier this time; no one but they were the wiser until an official exhumation two and a half years later. The skeleton had by then come into the possession of the Tasmanian Museum in Hobart. Its curator had packed the bones away in an apple crate labeled "Trucanini's skeleton." There these objects of supposedly inestimable scientific value remained, unstudied and unmeasured, until, in the 1890s, a new curator almost threw them away by accident. Then they were resurrected, so to speak; Truganini's skeleton was put on display in the museum, until aboriginal protests led to its removal and cremation in 1976. As one aboriginal activist noted in 1970, "it must surely be a fact that all scientific data possible has been gathered" from her bones (quoted in Cove, 146)—though apparently no such data were ever gathered.[17]

With Truganini's death, some observers believed that, for the first time in modern history, an entire primitive race had totally vanished from the planet.[18] According to the 1975 census, however, there were approximately two thousand mixed-race people, mostly on the Bass Straits Islands, who claimed Tasmanian aboriginal status (Cove, 115). Lyndall Ryan notes that the myth of the complete extinction of the

Tasmanian race has been ideologically useful in at least two ways (2–3). First, it meant that the government could ignore the claims to recognition, land rights, schools, and so forth, of the mixed-race Tasmanians—officially they did not exist as a separate or unique population and culture. Second, the claim that the Tasmanians had been completely wiped off the face of the earth, despite the heroic efforts of humanitarians like Robinson, reinforced the belief that primitive peoples elsewhere in the world, including mainland Australia, were doomed to extinction and that there was nothing even the most vig-orously humane intervention could do to save them. There is still another myth to dispel: that the Tasmanians were a separate "race," so distinct from other races of humans that the demise of their tiny number was almost equivalent to the extinction of a separate species, like the dinosaurs.[19]

The failure of George Augustus Robinson's humanitarian efforts seems symptomatic of a more general disillusionment with both secular and religious rescue work that paralleled the emergence of scientific racism in the 1840s and 1850s. Also symptomatic is the career of the Reverend Lancelot Threlkeld, missionary to the aboriginals of New South Wales from the late 1820s to the early 1840s. After seven years with the Reverend John Williams in Raiatea, and following his first wife's death in 1824 on that island, Threlkeld went to Sydney where he remarried and received permission, both from the London Missionary Society and from the government of New South Wales, to establish a new mission. He began his missionary labors near Lake Macquarie north of Sydney in 1826, and also started his pioneering work of learning and codifying aboriginal languages. He hoped to instruct "the natives" in religion and to civilize them in their own tongues. He used his linguistic studies to combat the stereotype of the aboriginals as both apelike and without intelligible speech: "What has hitherto been considered as the mere chatter of baboons, is found to possess a completeness and extent . . . that must eventually . . . defeat the bold yet groundless assertions of many who maintain, 'that the blacks of New South Wales are incapable of receiving instruction' " (1:42). Threlkeld believed that the aboriginals' incapacity for civilization was a "convenient assumption" (1:46), especially for "the murderers of the blacks [who] boldly maintained that [they] were only a specie [sic] of the baboon, that might be shot down with impunity, like an Ourang Outang" (1:69).

After Threlkeld ran afoul of the LMS executive committee in 1828 over expenditures, he set up his Ebenezer Mission on the other side of Lake Macquarie with the approval and support of the government of New South Wales. Through the 1830s he was also frequently called to Sydney to serve as a courtroom interpreter in trials involving aboriginals, and so was as well positioned as any colonist to report on "the deadly extirpating warfare which has so long been carried on against" the aboriginals (1:145):

> If Government were to institute an enquiry into the conduct of some Europeans in the interior towards the blacks, a War of extirpation would be found to have long existed, in which the ripping open of the bellies of the Blacks alive; — the roasting them in that state in triangularly made log fires . . . ; — the dashing of infants upon the stones . . . together with many other atrocious acts of cruelty, which are but the sports of monsters boasting of superior intellect to that possessed by the wretched Blacks! (1:139)

For all their years in the wilderness, Threlkeld and his family encountered little hostility or danger from aboriginals; they were much more threatened, as were the aboriginals, by white "monsters," especially bushrangers (2:275–85).

The rapidity with which violence, disease, and other factors were decimating the aboriginals in New South Wales gave an urgency to missionary and humanitarian efforts to save at least the remnants of the perishing race. By 1841, however, Threlkeld was prepared to acknowledge failure, his mission going the way of the Port Phillip Protectorate. As he said in his final official report, "This Mission to the Aborigines has ceased to exist, not for want of support from the British Government, nor from the inclination of the agent, but purely from the Aborigines themselves becoming extinct in these parts" (1:170).

Prior to this mournful result, Threlkeld's annual reports had been growing increasingly pessimistic. Nevertheless, as late as 1838 he continued to believe that, with adequate support from the LMS and from the government, he might have been the savior of the aboriginals at least within his district. He interpreted the LMS retraction of its support in 1828 as a betrayal of his good works, and ten years later he was ready to blame both the LMS and the government for aiding and abetting the extinction of the aboriginals:

> No Mission in the annals of modern missionary history, ever had a more pleasing prospect of success than this had for the first two years, in which many of

the Blacks were employed at labor, sometimes to the amount of sixty daily; several lads were learning to read and write, in their own language.

However, Threlkeld goes on to say that the LMS decided the "expenses necessary for . . . supporting . . . so large an establishment" were "encroaching on the claims of other heathens, much more numerous than these," and the government also failed to provide adequate "pecuniary aid." The result was a reduced missionary establishment—"an alteration, under false principles of Economy, which could never be overcome" (1:147). Because of this false economizing, Threlkeld adds, "death in various shapes carried off the tribes, until there is barely the name of a few tribes left in existence in these parts; thus rendering the present mission the most unpromising in the world" (1:147). This is, perhaps, the first and only time that the stinginess of a missionary society was cited as a cause of the extinction of a primitive race.

But in regard to Threlkeld's potential converts, "extinction" is probably a less accurate term for what became of them, at least in the short run, than vanishing into the outback. Besides lack of support and the mostly white violence and cruelty he witnessed all around him, Threlkeld had other reasons for his increasing pessimism. One was the intractability of his aboriginal charges. Even John M'Gill, the Christianized "black" from whom Threlkeld took most of his language lessons, was prone to long absences in the bush and to drunkenness. Aboriginals preferred not to stay in one place for long and, no matter how deferential they might at first seem, they preferred not to relinquish their own beliefs and customs in favor of ones that made little or no sense to them. Like other missionaries, moreover, Threlkeld believed that all humans were doomed anyway and that the Bible proved God had often willed that entire races should perish. He even cited geological evidence of the perishing of "certain races of animals" as evidence that "nations and tribes of the human race," including the Australians, were doomed by God's will to extinction, "because the cup of their iniquity was full" (1:65).

Though at first he rejected the pessimism of the Reverend Samuel Marsden, the New South Wales agent for the LMS who held that the Australian aboriginals were probably hopelessly beyond redemption (even though Marsden advocated trying to redeem them anyway), Threlkeld came close to sharing the opinion, "founded on a literal acceptance of everything in the Old Testament, that some tribes lay outside the scheme of salvation" (Gunson, Introduction, 9; Yarwood, 241). Thus Threlkeld also came close to blaming the aboriginals themselves for their inevitable extinction and damnation: "Let a nation reject the light of the Gospel, and how gradually would it sink deeper and deeper into the darkness of the most wretched ignorance, until like the aborigines of New South Wales, it would ultimately become extinct" (1:52). Just when the aboriginals had first rejected "the light of the Gospel," if they had ever received it, is uncertain, though the likely date, given Threlkeld's evangelical perspective, was the Flood. From that Old Testament event, evangelicals dated the dispersal of the sons of Noah over the globe, with the dark or darkening sons of Ham occupying the darkest places of the earth.

Although condemning white cruelty and violence in no uncertain terms, Threlkeld also condemned the aboriginals for their heathenish, sinful ways: "They appear most likely to be annihilated through their own wicked dispositions urging them to Rob and Murder," he wrote in 1827, "which in many instances bring upon themselves a just retribution, whilst drunkenness and disease mark them a prey for total destruction" (1:97). Yet, in his *Reminiscences*, Threlkeld cites many more robberies and murders committed by whites, whereas his most frequent complaint about aboriginal behavior is nomadism: the blacks will not stay in one place for long but seem compelled by an irrational urge to wander off into the bush.

Petroglyphs were proof to Threlkeld both of "the capabilities of the aborigines" and, because they no longer seemed to be making them, that they "have degenerated, and will continue so to do, until the few remaining individuals shall have become extinct, like many other portions of the human race" (1:59). He also thought it possible that "some future traveller" would discover the "ruins of very ancient buildings lying hid in Australia" (1:60).[20] As in the case of Native America and white speculation about the mound builders, there was the possibility at least that aboriginal Australia had been on the wane long before the arrival of the First Fleet in 1788. Once again, from this perspective, the advent of white civilization was only hastening the aboriginals toward their inevitable vanishing point.

Threlkeld thought that "Providence" was "being manifested toward the Aborigines," even though there were only two possible outcomes: "either . . . their total extinction, or, a very small remnant will be called to the acknowledgment of the truth as it is in Jesus" (1:148). Though he continued to claim that, had he been properly supported by the LMS and the government, he could have saved and civilized "a very small remnant," more often than not Threlkeld also asserted that it was God's will that the "race" as such would soon disappear. It was easier for him to believe that the aboriginals around Lake Macquarie had perished than that they had deserted him. In any event, Threlkeld often expresses a religious variant of proleptic elegy:

> But the blacks where are they, and the aborigines do they live for ever? No, like the Hittites and the Jebusites, and the Aboriginal Canaanites, they have been left to the natural consequences of the effects of not retaining the knowledge of God. The Aborigines of New South Wales will soon all have passed away, like the tribes [near Lake Macquarie] I have outlived, and their remembrance will be no more; but, "blessed is that nation whose God is THE LORD." (1:54)

Although most of Australia remained to be explored and colonized, by the early 1840s Threlkeld was prepared to declare his mission finished because of the "extinction" of the aboriginals: "In 1841 it was clearly ascertained that I had outlived the majority of the Aborigines in the vicinity where I was located, and that universally the diminution of the Aboriginal race was found to be similar throughout the colony [of New South Wales]. My mission, therefore, terminated from natural causes, and not from defective means employed to remedy the evil" (2:303)—an apparent retraction of his earlier accusation that lack of support by the LMS and the government had doomed both his mission and his aboriginal charges.

Though frustrated by their nomadism and ready to declare them "extinct" in the area of his responsibility, Threlkeld does not often cite savage customs as the cause of the demise of the aboriginals. In 1856, however, he wrote to Richard Cull, the former secretary of the Ethnological Society in London:

> The Aborigines of this part of the world, not only of Australia, but of all the Islands in Australasia also are becoming extinct without exception, whether Christianized or heathen. In the former state the females amalgamate with the Europeans, and the customs of the latter [heathen] are so abominably cruel that they destroy themselves by their wicked practices, and in a genera-

tion or two more the pure aborigines of these parts will be numbered amongst the numerous extinct nations of which we read in sacred scripture. (2:299)

Here Threlkeld expresses the thoroughgoing pessimism of Westgarth and many other white observers; he had, however, started his missionary career in a far more positive state of mind.[21]

Perhaps because their numbers were so small and their extinction so rapid and apparently total, the Tasmanians were not often depicted as self-exterminating because of their savage customs. That was not so with the mainland aboriginals, who, from about the 1820s on, were tarred with every stereotypical brush imaginable. In 1814, Governor Lachlan Macquarie declared: "The Natives of New South Wales have never been Cannibals" (quoted in Reece, 109). So, too, Lieutenant Breton writes that accounts of the cannibalism of the aboriginals "are greatly exaggerated, probably utterly false" (213). Other careful, fair-minded observers such as Threlkeld and George Grey avoid treating the first Australians as irredeemably ferocious. In contrast, even the Quaker missionary James Backhouse writes that although the aboriginals of New South Wales do not "openly make feasts upon human subjects, like the natives of New Zealand, and of some other islands of the Pacific; [yet] there are pretty well authenticated instances of cannibalism among them" (317).[22]

In *Savage Life and Scenes in Australia and New Zealand* (1847), George French Angas offers no firsthand evidence about the savageness of the South Australian aboriginals among whom he traveled with George Grey. But he has little hesitation retelling other people's atrocity stories, including those told by one aboriginal group at the expense of others. Thus, as to the Tattayarras "being cannibals occasionally, there appears to be but little doubt." This is so because "the people of the Murray" say that the Tattayarras "devour their children in times of scarcity." And the Murray group is no better, according to Angas, because they "themselves kill boys for the sake of their fat, with which to bait their fish-hooks" (1:72–73)—or so Angas was told. It follows from such behavior that the South Australians are self-exterminating:

> Constant wars and quarrels between the tribes, polygamy, and infanticide are amongst the causes of this. Their mode of life, too—not cultivating the ground, but seeking a scanty and precarious subsistence by wandering over

large tracts of country in search of food, when the soil naturally produces but
little comparatively for the support of the human race—necessarily causes
their numbers to be limited. (1:81)

Angas cites disease as still another factor, but regarding white violence against the aborigines, he says little—or, rather, he says it the
other way around. If blacks die in confrontations with whites, it is because the whites are defending themselves and their property.

The first atrocity story Angas retells concerns what supposedly be-
fell the shipwrecked crew and passengers from the *Maria*, gruesomely
murdered and mutilated by the Milmendura tribe. In apparently just
retribution, the search party who tried to rescue them "burnt the native huts to the ground, and succeeded in capturing" and hanging
"two of the murderers" (1:66–67). For Angas, aboriginal savagery of
the most bloodthirsty sort is a constant: "the Tattayarra tribes had
come down to the lake and taken away several black children for the
purpose of devouring them" (1:123), for instance. If the Tattayarras can
behave so savagely toward other aboriginals, it is no surprise that they
behave the same way toward both whites and themselves.

In her study of the Eliza Fraser captivity stories, Kay Schaffer notes
that during the first two or three decades of colonization, "it is difficult to find even one reference to native cannibalism in the local Australian press." But as white settlement expanded and met with increasing aboriginal resistance, starting in "the late 1820s . . . the
Sydney Gazette began to publish letters from settlers attesting to
scenes of native cannibalism." Such stories "helped to justify colonial
practices of extermination" (Schaffer, 118). As late as 1889 Norwegian
Carl Lumholtz could give his travel narrative the title *Among Cannibals,* just as in the African context travelers such as Henry Morton
Stanley and Winwood Reade were eager to play the cannibalism card
in order to accentuate the dangers they confronted.[23]

Even later, in her 1938 *Passing of the Aborigines: A Lifetime Spent
among the Natives of Australia,* the redoubtable Daisy Bates treated
cannibalism as a central feature of aboriginal culture. Bates saw herself—according to Arthur Mee, who introduces the 1967 edition of
her book—as "the last friend of the last remnant of this dying race"
(xiv). Yet neither Bates nor Mee hesitate to offer stories about cannibalism. "I shall never forget her writing to me," declares Mee, "that a
woman she had had for tea at her tent had eaten her own child. Dramatic and terrible as such a thing is to us, it was no new experience

for Daisy Bates, for cannibalism has never died out among these wandering tribes. They will kill and eat from revenge, or from primeval motives beyond our understanding" (xiv)—this, again, asserted as recently as 1967.

"Baby cannibalism," according to Bates, was so frequent among some groups that they did not "preserve a single living child for . . . years" (107), which certainly helps to explain why she regarded the aboriginals as a dying race. On the other hand, cannibalism "had been rife for centuries in these regions" (121), and yet before the advent of Europeans the aboriginals had managed to maintain and perhaps increase their population. Whatever Bates's motives, she herself provides no evidence about cannibalism except stories she accepts at face value from both aboriginals and whites. This is not to say that Australian aboriginals never practiced cannibalism, but the evidence is slim or nonexistent (Salter, 87, 190–94; Pickering).

As in other contexts around the world, emphasis on cannibalism, infanticide, and other savage customs bolstered the arguments of those who claimed that the aboriginals had no future and who wished to explain their inevitable vanishing as the result of causes other than white conquest and colonization. In summarizing the views of many observers, both official and private, down to 1846, Westgarth expressed an already prevailing pessimism about doing anything at all to help save the aboriginals from their doom: "All plans that have been hitherto adopted for the civilization of the Australian Aborigines appear to have proved almost uniformly unavailing for the accomplishment of any permanent good" (27). And that pessimism encompassed both religion and science. To turn Westgarth's statement around, neither aspect of Western "civilization" had been able to accomplish the salvation—earthly or spiritual—of the aboriginals. So perhaps civilization was not the force for "permanent good" that it believed itself to be.

Despite his failure as a missionary, Threlkeld succeeded as a linguist and, to some extent, as an amateur ethnographer. As in New Zealand and Polynesia, missionaries were often able to provide detailed accounts of primitive cultures, even while laboring to extinguish those cultures. According to D. J. Mulvaney, however, the first major attempt "at the systematic co-ordination of data with the object of the better understanding of Aboriginal life," conducted by the Select Committee on Aborigines in the colony of Victoria in 1859, "failed" (23). Not till the turn of the century did anthropological works about the first Australians appear that had any claim to scientific validity. These include H. Ling Roth's *Aborigines of Tasmania* (1890), Baldwin Spencer and Francis Gillen's *Native Tribes of Central Australia* (1899), and A. W. Howitt's *Native Tribes of South East Australia* (1904).

It is questionable, however, just how scientifically valid even these works are: informed by social Darwinism, they do not challenge the prevailing doctrine that the aboriginals are doomed to total extinction. Further, as L. R. Hiatt demonstrates in *Arguments about Aborigines*, the evolutionists seldom reach agreement over such basic questions as conceptions of land ownership and methods of government. Because Roth never had any contact with the Tasmanians, moreover, his study is an obvious instance of anthropology as a science of mourning. The preface to Roth's book, by Edward Burnett Tylor, the leading British exponent of cultural anthropology, declares the Tasmanians to have been "representative of the rudest type of man" (Tylor, Preface, vii). From the "workmanship" exhibited by their stone implements, Tylor claims, "the Tasmanians may be generally taken as below that of the Palaeolithic Drift and Cave men" (vii). Tylor adds that "anthropologists must join with philanthropists in regretting their unhappy fate, which fills a dismal page of our colonial history" (vii).

Compiled long after Truganini's death in 1876, Roth's tome is basically an anthology of other people's observations—apparently every scrap of information that he believed helpful in constructing a scientific portrait of the vanished aboriginals. Roth was also unable to observe at first hand Fanny Cochrane Smith, who, in 1889, had been identified by another anthropologist as "the last living aboriginal of Tasmania." Mrs. Smith was perhaps the last person who could speak a Tasmanian tongue. In any event, Roth had photographs taken of Mrs. Smith and sent to him in London, which he reproduces in an appendix, along with photographs of Truganini. He compares their facial features and hair to demonstrate, at least to his satisfaction, that Mrs. Smith is only of "mixed blood. Hence we cannot consider her a true Tasmanian aboriginal, and must conclude that with the death of Truganini we have lost for ever a living representative of the Tasmanian race" (lxxxvii). Mrs. Smith did not count; Truganini did but was no longer available for testimony or evidentiary purposes.

Roth (perhaps needless to say) does not show up in recent histories of anthropology, but Tylor and also Spencer and Gillen do. Even as late as 1927, however, in *The Arunta: A Study of a Stone Age People*, Spencer and Gillen treat their subjects as "creatures" locked in an evolutionary past who are about to disappear from their habitat:

> Australia is the present home and refuge of creatures, often crude and quaint, that have elsewhere passed away and given place to higher forms. This applies equally to the aboriginal as to the platypus and kangaroo. Just as the platypus, laying its eggs and feebly suckling its young, reveals a mammal in the making, so does the Aboriginal show us, at least in broad outline, what early man must have been like before he learned to read and write, domesticate animals, cultivate crops and use a metal tool. It has been possible to study in Australia human beings that still remain on the culture level of men of the Stone Age. (1:vii)

Because their subjects are almost at the vanishing point, moreover, for Spencer and Gillen anthropology is of necessity elegiac, mourning the last vestiges of "the Stone Age."

As evolutionary anthropologists, Spencer and Gillen do not believe that history can take divergent paths. The trajectory of evolution is universal, upward from the apes, even though it is one that supposedly unfit races are unable to travel. And the Australian aboriginals, despite clear evidence of having survived for millennia, are perhaps the most unfit: only their isolation has preserved them, until very recently, from the doom that, Spencer and Gillen believe, now awaits them. As McGregor notes, Spencer, Gillen, and the other evolutionary anthropologists also depict human history "as a series of collisions between discrete racial entities, from each of which one race emerged victorious both physically and culturally" (53). In the late 1930s A. P. Elkin, for instance, speculated that the Tasmanians had been the original inhabitants of all of Australia but were driven off the mainland or else "extinguished" by "the Australoid invasion" (Elkin, 10). In this regard, not much had changed since the days of the early Victorian race scientists such as Charles Hamilton Smith and Robert Knox.[24]

The anthropologists' supposedly scientific views informed white Australian discourse and policy toward the aboriginals down to at least the 1960s. By World War II, however, the Australian version of the "doomed race theory" was beginning to come under scrutiny, in part because the aboriginal population was starting to rebound (McGregor, 122–23). The increase in the "half-caste" population was also evident and gave rise to much anxiety about the future racial purity of an all-white Australia—an anxiety Daisy Bates, for one, expressed in no uncertain terms (243).

The first, 1938 edition of Elkin's *Australian Aborigines* contained little that was optimistic about the future of that ancient race. But by the early 1950s Elkin wrote an epilogue noting that, in part because of "improved official policies and administration," the approximately fifty thousand "full-bloods . . . seem likely to increase, rather than decrease." Moreover, according to Elkin: "In addition the mixed-blood Aborigines, a continuing core of about 30,000 apart from those who become 'lost' or assimilated in the general Australian community, are becoming more and more a positive factor in the relations between the full-bloods and ourselves" (339). Yet for a century and a half, Elkin adds, most white Australians believed "that the cry of the Aborigine was, *or should be*: 'I must decrease; you [the white man] must increase,' and that, therefore, the problem of the Aborigines would disappear with them" (339; my emphasis). Needless to say, "the problem" has not disappeared; Australia's first inhabitants have been both resilient and unpredictable, contradicting the countless forecasts of their inevitable, total demise. Today, as Hiatt notes, the aboriginals of Australia "attract more attention as leaders in the struggle for a better future than as models of an ancient past" (183).

7. Islands of Death and the Devil

From the time of Captain James Cook's momentous voyages between 1768 and 1779, the advent of Europeans spelled the transformation of South Pacific island paradises—as Diderot, Rousseau, and Cook himself at first viewed them—into tropical mortuaries. On his second voyage Cook perceived the inroads that venereal and other diseases had made on several populations, and opined that the natives of those places would have been much better off if Europeans had never discovered them. About the Maoris of New Zealand, he wrote:

> We debauch their Morals already too prone to vice and we interduce [sic] among them wants and perhaps diseases which they never before knew and which serves only to disturb that happy tranquillity they and their fore Fathers had injoy'd. If anyone denies the truth of this assertion let him tell what the Natives of the whole extent of America have gained by the commerce they have had with Europeans. (Cook, 2:175)

Celebrated today as a founding father of the modern nation-states of Australia and New Zealand, Cook was also, as this statement shows, an early mourner of island societies and cultures that he saw as perishing under the "fatal impact" of white immorality and imported disease (Moorehead, 78).

Although the spread of firearms among the Maori, Fijians, and other South Seas populations exacerbated the depopulating effects of warfare, the violence inflicted by Europeans was slight compared to what happened in Australia or the Americas. Disease was the most evident factor, and, among the imported diseases, those that received the most attention from Cook through Robert Louis Stevenson were the effects of "licentiousness," or of savage but also European promiscuity. Thus, in his 1866 history of Hawaii, Manley Hopkins, while making the by then standard claim that "the decay of native races when in contact with white-skinned settlers or invaders" was "universal" (367), added that "the prevailing vices" of the Hawaiians "were indolence, deceit, lewdness, and intemperance" (372). Although "lewdness" was a "sin" endemic to South Seas cultures before the arrival of Europeans, Hopkins and many other commentators including Cook had to acknowledge that both "the sin" and the death rate were "greatly increased" by the arrival of ships' crews infected with venereal disease. Hopkins writes that the "blood of the nation was affected by it; energy and procreative power were withered up, and the probability of a healthy progeny was cut off" (372). Add leprosy to the fatal mix, and, by the end of the 1800s, places that had often been portrayed as paradisal had become the morbid, diseased South Pacific of Stevenson, Mark Twain, and Jack London (Edmond, 160–222).

"Licentiousness" was one reason why the first British missionaries to the South Seas, sponsored by the London Missionary Society in the 1790s, believed they were intervening, not in tropical edens but in some of the darkest, most diabolical places in the world. Polynesian islanders, the Maori of New Zealand, and the Australian aboriginals were all perishing by God's will, a process begun long before the arrival of Europeans, because these savages had been, ever since the Flood, in Satan's thrall. Like the Puritans of New England in the 1600s, the evangelical missionaries of the 1790s and early 1800s interpreted savage customs as sins or, at any rate, as the outcomes of sin and superstition, and also as the main cause of the steep declines in native populations.

The missionaries came to Polynesia and New Zealand to save the otherwise damned souls of the already dying races they encountered. In common with secular humanitarians, however, missionaries opposed violence on colonial frontiers and often also opposed further incursions by white settlers into territories populated by indigenous peoples (they were themselves white settlers of a special type, of course). Yet missionary discourse expressed a version of proleptic elegy that both exaggerated the speed with which savages were dying and savagery itself as the main cause of their extinction. The fatality clock sped up, because island populations (including the Maori) were small and fragile; because the customs of several of those populations seemed especially, diabolically savage; and because the missionaries believed they were dealing with an either/or situation: conversion had to happen quickly, because the natives were perishing quickly.

The missionaries represented themselves as the natives' best and sometimes only European friends but also as white authority figures who insisted categorically that all savages must abandon their sinful customs and cultures in order to be saved. As in the case of Threlkeld's work in New South Wales, missionaries in Polynesia and New Zealand had to study native languages, beliefs, and customs in order to make any headway, and, like Threlkeld, many of them became careful albeit amateur ethnographers. But the cultures they studied and in some ways admired they were nevertheless committed to destroy.[1]

British missionaries in the first half of the nineteenth century had their greatest successes and also tragedies—or, at any rate, their greatest publicity successes and tragedies—in the South Pacific. The Reverend Thomas Haweis and other officials of the LMS were influenced by Cook's *Journals* and similar accounts of Polynesian societies as near-paradises, both welcoming and yet dangerous to Europeans, to select Polynesia as the site of their first proselytizing endeavors. According to Haweis, referring in 1795 to Tahiti:

> No other part of the heathen world affords so promising a field for a Christian mission: Where the temper of the people, the climate, the abundance of food, and early collection of a number together for instruction, bespeak the fields ripe for harvest. No-where are the prospects of success more flattering, or the dangers and difficulties of the Missionaries less to be apprehended, except, as the worthy Admiral Bligh informed me, such as may arise from the fascination of beauty, and the seduction of appetite. (Quoted in Newbury, xxix)

In Haweis's estimation, the main danger facing missionaries in Polynesia would be sexual temptation rather than violence. His edenic description of Tahiti, stressing the hazardous "fascination of beauty," is repeated in the Reverend John Davies's *History of the Tahitian Mission, 1799–1830*. Davies quotes James Wilson, captain of the *Duff* which transported the first group of missionaries to Polynesia, writing to the LMS directors: "[Tahiti's] inhabitants are more mild generous and hospitable, and have fewer horrid customs" perhaps than other Polynesians but certainly fewer such customs than "the New Hollanders," sunk in "deplorable wretchedness," and also than the ferocious "New Zealanders," with their "furious temper, and horrid customs" (Davies, 31). The LMS and its agents were at least aware, despite general condemnation of savagery, that there were important distinctions to be made among the Polynesian islanders, the New Zealanders, and the Australians, if only in terms of moral and spiritual degradation.

In later missionary discourse, and in stark contrast to the romantic strain of island-paradise sentiment, the "horrid customs" of the Maori and the various Polynesian islanders compete for something like the record or nadir of devilish degradation among all the primitive races and cultures of the world. The schizophrenic split between the edenic and the infernal, and between attraction and repulsion, towed missionary authors into hyperbole, especially where—as they saw it— evil was concerned, and especially where evil was also tempting.

South Seas customs and cultures, particularly sexual attitudes and behaviors, were stark opposites to the attitudes and behaviors of the missionaries who were far less tolerant toward difference than were the natives. Most missionaries received curious but friendly welcomes. Some missionaries, however, responded badly to sexual temptation and "went native" (or, from the missionary perspective, surrendered their souls to the devil), while a few others fled from scenes and environments that they found either too tempting or too horrific and dangerous to endure.[2] The instances of missionaries being killed and eaten by cannibals are rare or perhaps nonexistent, in part because wherever the missionaries came—so they claimed—savage customs such as cannibalism vanished.[3]

Missionary proselytizing in Tahiti, Hawaii, New Zealand, and in some of the other Pacific islands was more effective than in Australia. When in 1812 "King" Pomare II of Tahiti declared himself a convert to Christianity, the missionaries thought they had won a providential victory and that many more such victories would soon follow (Davies, 153). For a time, though Pomare continued to misbehave (or sin) in various troubling ways (Edmond, 100–101, 121), LMS missionaries and their home supporters believed that their godly work had achieved great triumphs in Polynesia (Lovett, 1:194–237). This triumphalist strain in missionary discourse reached a climax in the Reverend John Williams's 1837 *Narrative of Missionary Enterprises in the South Sea Islands;* two years later, climax became apotheosis, at least for the evangelical British reading public, when Williams and another missionary, James Harris, were slain and supposedly eaten by the natives of Erromanga. According to Vanessa Smith, the natives' reasons for killing Williams are "as complex, though less subsequently theorized, as those that motivated the death of Cook" (Lamb, Smith, and Thomas, 220). In any event, Williams became an evangelical martyr-saint, eulogized by, among other authors, Samuel Smiles in his 1859 bestseller, *Self-Help*, under the rubric of "energy and courage":

> The islands of the Pacific Ocean were the principal scene of his labors—more particularly Huahine in Tahiti, Raiatea, and Rarotonga. Like the Apostles, he worked with his hands—at blacksmith work, gardening, ship-building; and he endeavored to teach the islanders the arts of civilized life, at the same time that he instructed them in the truths of religion. It was in the course of his indefatigable labors that he was massacred by savages on the shore of Erromanga—none worthier than he to wear the martyr's crown. (272)

Williams and the other South Seas missionaries were also eulogized in Victorian fiction. In Robert M. Ballantyne's 1858 bestseller, *The Coral Island*, Ralph Rover learns from the pirate Bloody Bill that the captain of the pirate ship "favours" missionaries not because he is religious but because "they are useful to him" (214). According to Bloody Bill, "The South Sea Islanders are such incarnate fiends that they are the better of being tamed, and the missionaries are the only men who can do it" (215). The thought that missionaries make the bloody job of piracy easier is jolting but does not seem to bother Ballantyne. After all, the pirates are wiped out both by the savages and by their own violence, while the missionaries go right on with their godly conversion work.

The final third of *The Coral Island* offers a series of episodes illustrating the diabolical savagery of the islanders before conversion and their domestic peace and harmony afterward. As J. S. Bratton notes, much of what Ballantyne has to say about "the savages" is taken directly from missionary sources. Bratton cites the Reverend Michael Russell's *Polynesia: A History of the South Sea Islands, Including New Zealand* (1852), but Ballantyne could have borrowed from a dozen other sources such as William Ellis's *Polynesian Researches* (1833),

David Darling's *Remarks about the Marquesas* (1835), John Williams's *Narrative* (1837), and William Wyatt Gill's *Gems from the Coral Islands; or, Incidents of Contrast between Savage and Christian Life of the South Sea Islanders* (1856). The journals of the major missionary societies also carried reports of the benighted, "fiendish" customs of the South Sea islanders, and, at least before the 1850s, of their almost instantaneous conversions to Christianity (Gunson, *Messengers,* 217–36). A passage like this one from Ballantyne, on infanticide and "the Aréoi," could have come from Ellis's *Polynesian Researches* as well as from Russell's *Polynesia* (cf. Edmond, 147). After Ralph asks why Polynesian mothers allow their newborn babies to be murdered, Bloody Bill turns piratical ethnographer:

> Allow it? The mothers *do* it! It seems to me that there's nothing too fiendish or diabolical for these people to do. Why, in some of the islands they have an institution called the *Aréoi,* and the persons connected with that body are ready for any wickedness that mortal man can devise. In fact they stick at nothing; and one o' their customs is to murder their infants the moment they are born. The mothers agree to it, and the fathers do it. (231)

Bill lists some of the diabolical ways that infanticide is performed, including strangulation, live burial, and piercing "with sharp splinters of bamboo," and continues: "But it's a curious fact . . . that wherever the missionaries get a footin' all these things come to an end at once, an' the savages take to doin' each other good and singin' psalms, just like Methodists" (231). Ralph adds the predictable peroration: "God bless and prosper the missionaries till they get a footing in every island of the sea!" (231).[4]

In *Polynesian Researches,* Ellis says that infanticide "was practised [to an] awful extent . . . [and] was one of the first of the many horrid cruelties filling these 'dark places' of paganism that deeply affected" the missionaries and that they worked hard to prevent, though often with little or no success (3:23). Besides infanticide, the missionaries stress cannibalism, usually as the outcome of savage warfare. When Ballantyne's boy-heroes first realize that "canoes" are approaching their island, Jack serves as ethnographer: "Whether war-canoes or not I cannot tell; but this I know, that all the natives of the South Sea Islands are fierce cannibals, and they have little respect for strangers" (171). Cook had declared of Fiji that it "is said to be" populated by

"Canibals, brave, Savage and Cruel. That they are Canibals, they themselves do not deny" (3:163).[5] So, too, Ellis has no hesitation in describing the Marquesans, even though he spent little time among them, as "feeding on each other," a behavior which "does not appear to be confined to seasons of famine, or the feast of triumph, but to be practised from motives more repulsive and criminal" (3:236). And in *Fiji and the Fijians* (1858), Thomas Williams includes such episodes as this one, although he does not claim to have witnessed it:

> After having kissed his relative, Tanoa cut off his arm at the elbow, and drank the blood as it flowed warm from the severed veins. The arm, still quivering with life, he threw upon a fire, and, when sufficiently cooked, ate it in presence of its proper owner, who was then dismembered, limb by limb, while the savage murderer looked with pitiless brutality on the dying agonies of his victim. (20)

Williams later writes: "Murder is not an occasional thing in Fiji; but habitual, systematic, and classed among ordinary transactions" (134). He is no doubt thinking partly about infanticide, but many of his examples involve adults treacherously killing adults on such an everyday basis that it is remarkable that any Fijians survive the murderous onslaught of their own "horrid customs."

Despite what appears to be sensationalism, Thomas Williams is credited, by both George Stocking and Christopher Herbert, as being one of the better, more sympathetic missionary ethnographers (Stocking, 87–92; Herbert, 175–77). According to Herbert, of all the "early Polynesianists," Williams was the one "who explored most daringly the issue of the possible transformation of the 'civilized' Christian through contact with barbarous heathens" (175). However that may be, in common with other missionary authors, Williams also engages in a rhetoric of "unspeakability": "Atrocities of the most fearful kind have come to my knowledge, which I *dare* not record here" (Williams, 133). The reader is asked to fill in the blank with imagined customs even more horrible than cannibalism and infanticide.

When Ralph, Jack, and Peterkin later meet a "native" missionary in the service of "that excellent body the London Missionary Society," they hear as well of the difference between "the Christian village" which the missionary serves and the unconverted "savages." This difference is Manichaean, absolute: light versus darkness. The missionary adjures his young friends:

> "There are hundreds of islands here the natives of which have never heard of Jesus . . . and thousands are living and dying in the practice of those terrible sins and bloody murders of which you have already heard. I trust . . . that if you ever return to England, you will tell your Christian friends that the horrors which they hear of in regard to these islands are *literally true*, and that when they have heard the worst, the *'half has not been told them;'* for there are perpetrated here foul deeds of darkness of which man may not speak." (Ballantyne, 297)

Ballantyne echoes the trope of "unspeakable" horror that ran through missionary discourse before it became endlessly recycled in imperialist adventure fiction, from *Coral Island* down to Joseph Conrad's *Heart of Darkness* (1899) and beyond. Given the graphic accounts of savage warfare, cannibalism, torture of captives, infanticide, strangling of widows, burial alive of the infirm and aged, and treacherous murder of political rivals both in Ballantyne and in missionary journals and letters, one wonders what exactly remained "unspeakable"?

The answer, at least for the missionaries, probably lies in the realm of sexual behavior (or, from their standpoint, hellish misbehavior). What is most "unspeakable" to a missionary author such as Thomas Williams or William Ellis is patterns of sexual promiscuity and homosexuality or bisexuality that Polynesians carried on without shame or any notion that they should be concealing or closeting their behaviors. "The sexual difficulties of missionaries form the forbidden subject of most missionary literature," writes Herbert (179).[6] According to the missionary J. M. Orsmond, even after conversion "Tahiti [was] a vortex of iniquity, the Sodom of the Pacific. . . . All licentiousness and obsequiousness. Even now we dare not suffer our children to assemble with the native tribes. Virtue is not in Tahiti; chastity is unknown save in the presence of some only of the Missionaries" (quoted in J. Davies, 358).

So, too, Ellis, whose four-volume *Polynesian Researches* provides the most detailed and, in some ways, most sympathetic account of Pacific island customs and beliefs by any missionary author, says of the feasting and "general amusements" of the Areoi that they engaged in activities which were "abominable, unutterable":

In some of their meetings, they appear to have placed their invention on the rack, to discover the worst pollutions of which it was possible for man to be guilty, and to have striven to outdo each other in the most revolting practices. The mysteries of iniquity, and acts of more than bestial degradation, to which they were at times addicted, must remain in the darkness in which even they felt it sometimes expedient to conceal them. I will not do violence to my own feelings, or offend those of my readers, by details of conduct which the mind cannot contemplate without pollution and pain. (1:192)

And so forth (like other missionary authors, Ellis speaks volumes about "the unspeakable"). This chapter of *Polynesian Researches* ends with a condemnation of the god Oro, belief in whom contributes to "the indolent habits and depraved uncontrolled passions of the people," a belief supported by the diabolical activities of members of the Areoi. This "institution [is] a masterpiece of satanic delusion and deadly infatuation, exerting an influence over the minds of an ignorant, indolent, and demoralized people which no human power, and nothing less than Divine agency, could counteract or destroy" (1:195).[7]

Ellis writes that Cook, Bougainville, and other early explorers of the South Seas found evidence that the "race has evidently, at no very remote period, been much more numerous" (1:90). The evidence included various "monuments of former generations," among them ruins of stone buildings and pavements. Further, Polynesians themselves testified that their "race" was vanishing:

The present generations, deeply sensible of the depopulation that has taken place even within the recollection of those most advanced in years, have felt acutely in prospect of the annihilation that appeared inevitable. Their priests . . . denounced the destruction of the nation, as the greatest punishment the gods could inflict. (1:91)

On this score at least, if no other, the missionaries were in full agreement with the idolatrous "priests" of the South Seas. Ellis quotes the prediction of these "priests"—one that serves as a refrain in much nineteenth-century European discourse about the edenic yet infernal savages of Polynesia and New Zealand: "'The *fau* (*hibiscus*) shall grow, the *farero* (coral) shall spread . . . but man shall cease'" (1:91). Ellis continues: "At the time when [Tahiti] renounced idolatry, the population was so much reduced, that many of the more observant

natives thought the denunciation of the prophet was about to be literally fulfilled." And he then quotes the chief Tati, who, in 1815, told
John Davies that "'if God had not sent his Word at the time he did,
wars, infant-murder, human sacrifices, &c. would have made an end
of the small remnant of the nation,'" a sentiment also expressed by
"King" Pomare (1:91–92). Ellis continues:

> I have often heard the chiefs speak of themselves and of the natives as only a
> small *toea*, remainder, left after the extermination of Satani, or the evil spirit;
> comparing themselves to a firebrand unconsumed among the mouldering
> embers of a recent conflagration. . . . Under the depopulating influence of vi-
> cious habits—the dreadful devastation of diseases that followed, and the early
> destruction of health—the prevalence of infanticide—the frequency of war—
> the barbarous principles upon which it was prosecuted, and the increase of
> human sacrifices, it does not appear possible that they could have existed as a
> nation for many generations longer. (1:92)

Given such diabolically depopulating customs, just how the societies
of the South Pacific arose and flourished at all is a question Ellis does
not try to answer. According to this version of Polynesian history, the
missionaries, to their own eternal glory, arrived just in the nick of time
to prevent the total depopulation of the South Pacific. "The philanthropist . . . will rejoice to know," writes Ellis, specifically of Tahiti,
"that although sixteen years ago the nation appeared on the verge of
extinction, it is now, under the renovating and genial principles of
true religion . . . rapidly increasing" (1:94).[8] On Tahiti, as in New
Zealand and elsewhere, the chief remedy the missionaries offer for
the auto-genocide of the natives is their own godly conversion work.

In his first novel, *Typee* (1846), Herman Melville is highly critical of
the endeavors of Ellis and other missionaries to bring so-called civilization and Christianity to the South Seas (Anderson, 86–116). He—
or "Tommo," as he winds up being called by the Marquesans—cites
Ellis's account in *Polynesian Researches* "of the abortive attempts
made by the Tahiti Mission to establish a branch Mission upon certain islands" including the Marquesas (39), and he offers the perhaps
apocryphal story of a missionary who landed there with his wife.
Eager to ascertain her gender, the Marquesans stripped her of her
clothing and gave her "to understand that she could no longer carry

on her deceits with impunity. The gentle dame was not sufficiently evangelical to endure this, and, fearful of further improprieties, she forced her husband to relinquish his undertaking, and together they returned to Tahiti" (39). Melville also criticizes the missionaries as propagandists who exaggerate both the success of their proselytizing efforts and the savagery (cannibalism, infanticide, etc.) of Polynesians. Are the South Sea islanders "happier," he asks, now that missionaries, traders, and beachcombers have invaded their territories, bringing new diseases and forms of violence along with so-called civilization and religion?

> Let the once smiling and populous Hawiian [*sic*] islands, with their now diseased, starving, and dying natives, answer the question. The missionaries may seek to disguise the matter as they will, but the facts are incontrovertible; and the devoutest Christian who visits that group . . . must go away mournfully asking—"Are these, alas! the fruits of twenty-five years of enlightening?" (179–80)

As to cannibalism and other savage customs, Melville plays a double game (T. W. Herbert, 149–91; Edmond, 86–87). He accuses missionary authors of hyperbole and falsification, although he also makes the fear of being eaten, along with the fear of being tattooed (Otter), central to his own presumably autobiographical narrative. About cannibalism, he declares that "it is a singular fact, that in all our accounts of cannibal tribes we have seldom received the testimony of an eye-witness to the revolting practice. The horrible conclusion has almost always been derived either from the second-hand evidence of Europeans, or else from the admissions of the savages themselves, after they have in some degree become civilized" (310). Nevertheless, Melville has much to say about the Typee "Feast of Calabashes," although he insists it is not the outcome of mere bloodthirstiness but is instead "a religious solemnity" and hence on a par with Christian observances. This comparison obviously corresponds to "the horrible descriptions of Polynesian worship . . . with which the missionaries have favoured us." Melville writes: "Did not the sacred character of these persons render the purity of their intentions unquestionable, I should certainly be led to suppose that they had exaggerated the evils of Paganism, in order to enhance the merit of their own disinterested labours" (234).

Like Captain Cook, Melville treats the Marquesas, Tahiti, and

Hawaii in terms almost entirely opposite to those used in missionary discourse. Instead of infernal islands under the dominion of Satan, these are tropical paradises characterized, in part at least, by leisure and sexual freedom. Indeed, as Cook had also indicated, the latter especially is an aspect of paradise that leads to its downfall. In his description of the "riot and debauchery" the sailors on his ship indulge in with "voluptuous" Marquesan women, Melville's language of "contaminating contact with the white man" (50) has nothing to do with sin but everything to do with sexual license and venereal disease. The "fatal embrace" of white sailors (sometimes also missionaries) and Polynesian women introduces a new, highly ironic item to the list of causes in extinction discourse. Although smallpox, measles, and other Western diseases were factors in Polynesia, the ravages of gonorrhea and syphilis were, of course, the outcome of sexual activity—that is, of reproductive activity which, instead of increasing populations, did just the reverse.

On the subjects of population and depopulation, Melville is somewhat contradictory. One aspect of missionary discourse he does not disagree with is the idea that the Marquesans were once more advanced than they are in the nineteenth century. When Tommo comes across stone ruins, he "can scarcely believe they were built by the ancestors of the present inhabitants. If indeed they were, the race has sadly deteriorated in their knowledge of the mechanic arts" (218). Later, and with a good deal of irony, he applies the notion of "deterioration" or degeneration to religion: "I regard the Typees as a backslidden generation. They are sunk in religious sloth, and require a spiritual revival" (246). The revival Tommo has in mind, however, would be a pagan rather than Christian one.

Unlike the missionaries, Melville (Tommo) does not connect depopulation to the degeneration he suspects the Marquesans to have undergone even before the European invasion. On the contrary, Melville, like Malthus, speculates that indigenous populations throughout the South Seas had been stable for centuries, or perhaps were slightly increasing, before the advent of Europeans. Here is Melville as Malthusian demographer:

> The ratio of increase among all the Polynesian nations is very small; and in
> some places as yet uncorrupted by intercourse with Europeans, the births
> would appear not very little to outnumber the deaths; the population in such

instances remaining nearly the same for several successive generations, even upon those islands seldom or never desolated by wars, and among people with whom the crime of infanticide is altogether unknown. This would seem expressively [sic] ordained by Providence to prevent the overstocking of the islands with a race too indolent to cultivate the ground, and who, for that reason alone, would, by any considerable increase in their numbers, be exposed to the most deplorable misery. (262)

Melville adds that, while in Typee, he saw very few babies and was aware of only two births. He goes on, however, to blame promiscuity and "the looseness of the marriage tie" for "the late rapid decrease of the population of the Sandwich Islands and of Tahiti":

The vices and diseases introduced among these unhappy people annually swell the ordinary mortality of the islands, while, from the same cause, the originally small number of births is proportionally decreased. Thus the progress of the Hawiians [sic] and Tahitians to utter extinction is accelerated in a sort of compound ratio. (263)[9]

Melville contends that the missionary effort to eliminate "paganism" from the world has resulted in nothing less than the extermination of the pagans:

Let the savages be civilized, but civilize them with benefits, and not with evils; and let heathenism be destroyed, but not by destroying the heathen. The Anglo-Saxon hive extirpated Paganism from the greater part of the North American continent; but with it they have likewise extirpated the greater portion of the Red race. Civilization is gradually sweeping from the earth the lingering vestiges of Paganism, and at the same time the shrinking forms of its unhappy worshippers. (266)

Melville also compares cannibalism (whether real or imaginary) with the "barbarity" of forms of capital punishment "practised in enlightened England" until just recently, and he imagines a scenario in which, rather than having supposedly civilized missionaries corrupting the previously happy Marquesans, a mission of islanders sent to America might benefit so-called civilization:

The term "Savage" is, I conceive, often misapplied, and indeed, when I consider the vices, cruelties, and enormities of every kind that spring up in the
tainted atmosphere of a feverish civilization, I am inclined to think that so far
as the relative wickedness of the parties is concerned, four or five Marquesan
Islanders sent to the United States as Missionaries might be quite as useful as
an equal number of Americans despatched to the Islands in a similar capacity.
(181)

Several later authors—Robert Louis Stevenson, Mark Twain,
Louis Becke, Jack London—echo aspects of Melville's primitivism,
while seconding the urgency of his message regarding the depopulation of the South Seas. Sailing the Pacific in search of health, Stevenson, in the late 1880s, writes that "the thought of death . . . is upper-
most in the mind of the Marquesan" islanders (26). The effects of
disease and depopulation have been so drastic since Cook's time,
Stevenson declares, that, from depression, the remaining Marquesans
have waxed suicidal, hastening their ultimate demise: "Hanging is
now in fashion" (30).

Wracked by consumption, the dying Stevenson found a bond of
sympathy between himself and the dying Polynesians on all the islands he visited (Edmond, 161). But in strict Malthusian and Darwinian fashion, he asserts that the islanders were once victorious over
their circumstances of scarcity—so much so, that they overpopulated.
And as Malthus contended, overpopulation produced its opposite:
depopulation. So "the teeming people" of the Marquesas and Hawaii
found themselves confronting the no-win choice between "famine"
and the practice of such savage customs as cannibalism, abortion,
and infanticide (35–36). Curiously Stevenson does not include warfare among the savage customs causing depopulation but instead insists that warfare was, until the introduction of guns made it far dead-
lier than it ever had been before, "one of the elements of health" (42):
warfare equals welfare. In any event, in the chapter of *In the South
Seas* entitled "Depopulation," Stevenson writes:

Man-eating among kindly men, child-murder among child-lovers, industry in
a race most idle, invention in a race the least progressive . . . the report of early
voyagers, the widespread vestiges of former habitation, and the universal tradition of the islands, all point to the same fact of crowding and alarm. And today
we are face to face with the reverse. To-day in the Marquesas, in the Eight Is-

lands of Hawaii, in Mangareva, in Easter Island, we find the same race perishing like flies. (38)

In contrast to many observers, however, Stevenson does not think
that "depopulation" is inevitably leading to total extinction. Despite
"the coming of the whites, the change of habits, and the introduction
of new maladies and vices," the populations of Tahiti, the Paumotus,
Samoa, and New Zealand seem to have stabilized or are perhaps
even slightly increasing. Nevertheless, instead of celebrating the resurrection, as it were, of native Polynesia, Stevenson offers a standard
version of proleptic elegy; he even quotes "the sad Tahitian proverb"
offered by Ellis in *Researches* and Harriet Martineau in *Dawn Island*
(Stevenson, 14; and see Edmond, 164). And Stevenson's portrayals of
Tari Coffin, Tari's grandchild, and his daughter-in-law underscore
the Marquesans' passive acceptance of their racial doom. "Tari's
grandchild becomes an image of the impending extinction of the
Marquesans and their tranquil despair," writes Rod Edmond, "the
proleptic image of a doomed culture" (164).

A similar backward-looking, nostalgic, mournful view is evident in
Paul Gauguin's Tahitian paintings, as well as in his journals: "Many
things that are strange and picturesque existed here once, but there
are no traces of them left today; everything has vanished. Day by day
the race vanishes, decimated by the European diseases." Quoting this
passage in his study of the European invasion of the South Pacific,
The Fatal Impact, Alan Moorehead writes: "In Gauguin's Tahitian
paintings no man or woman ever smiles; supine, defeated, despairing
and beautiful, his people gaze in a reverie into the lost past. They
have no hope at all" (95). Moorehead notes that one of Gauguin's
paintings, of a beautiful Tahitian girl lying "inert and naked on her
bed . . . waiting for nothing, hoping for nothing," has its English title
painted on it: "Nevermore."

Prior to the Treaty of Waitangi in 1840, which made New Zealand a
British colony, the Maori appeared to have better prospects than did
the Australian aboriginals and many smaller South Seas populations.
Thus, in his 1807 *Account of New Zealand*, John Savage expressed
surprise that the natives, reputed to be cannibals, displayed "no symptom of savage ferocity" and were "of a very superior order, both in . . .
personal appearance and intellectual endowments" (quoted in Mc-
Cormick, 11). So, too, the Reverend Samuel Marsden, who estab-

lished the first mission in New Zealand in 1814, declared: "I do not believe that there is in any part of the world, or ever was, a native in a state of nature superior to the inhabitants of New Zealand . . . nor anywhere people who would in a shorter period render themselves worthy of being numbered with civilized nations, provided they were favoured with the ordinary means of instruction" (Marsden, 122). And in his 1832 *Narrative of a Residence in New Zealand*, Augustus Earle wrote of a "splendid race" who were superior physically, intellectually, and morally to the "Indians" of both North and South America (57–58). In short, in the early 1800s whites generally viewed the Maori as Noble Savages, amenable both to civilization and to survival.

In *The New Zealanders*, published anonymously in 1830 by the Society for the Diffusion of Useful Knowledge (SDUK), George Lillie Craik also claimed that the Maori "present a striking contrast to the timid and luxurious Otaheitans [Tahitians], and the miserable outcasts of Australia" (14). According to Craik, along with their "savage propensities," the Maori possess "many high qualities, both moral and intellectual" (401). Nevertheless, he warns, their "barbarism" may be their undoing: "Their passion is war; and they carry on that excitement in the most terrific way that the fierceness of man has ever devised; —they devour their slaughtered enemies" (15). So warlike and cannibalistic are the Maori that it is a wonder they have not already exterminated themselves, which is what Malthus believed they were doing. The "constant state of warfare" among the Maori, Malthus declared, would lead to race-suicide if the Maori could manage it (174).

As Melville would do in *Typee*, Craik goes on to compare various "savage" customs, born of "the spirit of war"—beheading, scalping, and eating one's slain enemies—to modern European practices, including death by guillotine and hangings. The "New Zealanders," however, preserve and display the heads of their enemies as status symbols, and they eat the rest of their corpses, "for it is understood that when any one eats of the person he has killed, the dead man becomes a part of himself" (221–23). In contrast to many accounts in which cannibalism is treated as completely irrational and atrocious, Craik at least insists that there is a reason for it, and so once again presents the Maori as both savage and noble.[10]

Craik and the SDUK may have produced *The New Zealanders* to promote immigration, along the lines of Edward Gibbon Wakefield's "systematic colonization" schemes. At any rate, Craik believes that the Maori are not only a good match against Europeans in war but

that they are fully civilizable and will one day take their place along-
side Europeans in a global utopia of peaceful free trade. Through
commerce, he writes, "will New Zealand be ultimately civilized"
(424). Partly because of the Noble Savage qualities of the Maori, New
Zealand certainly evoked utopian prospects in European imagina-
tions, as Samuel Butler's *Erewhon* (1872) suggests.[11] Craik offers a vision of the pacification and civilization of the South Seas that
matches the free-trade utopianism in Wakefield's writings and also in
Harriet Martineau's *Dawn Island* (1845).[12] For all three authors, "useful knowledge" partly means that which will enable savages to enter
into the free exchange of commodities, whereupon both they and
their partners in peaceful commerce—that is, the British—will
progress in material harmony.

In the 1830s the Colonial Office and the APS hoped that relations
between the Maori and the colonists would not be destructive but the
reverse. There was the possibility, at least, that New Zealand could
become an ideal colony in racial as well as other ways.[13] Yet starting
in that decade the Maori were added to the growing list of primitive
races doomed to extinction through contact with white civilization.
In part, the thesis of "fatal impact" bolstered the case of the missionaries and humanitarians to bring official, military protection to New
Zealand. In 1837 the British Resident James Busby "first laid major
stress on the decline in the Maori population," writes Peter Adams
(88). Busby's report to the Colonial Office in that year was a plea for
protection especially of the Maori; without it, he claimed, New
Zealand would soon be "destitute of a single aboriginal inhabitant"
(quoted in Adams, 88). So, too, in 1839 the secretary of state Lord
Normanby instructed Captain William Hobson, newly appointed the
first governor of New Zealand, that one of his main responsibilities
would be saving the Maori from the fate of other indigenous populations. Hobson was to check cannibalism and infanticide among the
Maori, but he was also to check "the same process of war and spolia-
tion under which uncivilised tribes have almost invariably disappeared, as often as they have been brought into the immediate vicinity of emigrants from the nations of Christendom" (quoted in
McNab, 731).[14]

At the time of the signing of the Treaty of Waitangi in 1840, estimates of the numbers of Maori ranged from 90,000 to 200,000; the
European population then amounted to only about 2,000 in both islands (Orange, 6–7; cf. Pool, 194–95). By the early 1870s, notes Clau-

dia Orange, there were more than 256,000 white colonists, whereas "the Maori totalled only some 45,470 in 1874 and were declining steadily" (185). Coupled with their defeat in the wars against the British, declining numbers apparently reinforced the belief among the Maori themselves that "their mana was passing away or had already been lost" (Orange, 189). By the 1840s, moreover, Maori were becoming aware of what was happening to indigenous populations elsewhere in the British Empire and the United States. They were unhappy about New Zealand's status as a dependency of New South Wales, itself a British colony with an already bad record of mistreating its natives. And by that decade, the near-total extinction of the Tasmanian aboriginals had become well publicized, in part through the missionary press in the Bay of Islands (Orange, 95).

Official colonization even under humanitarian auspices did nothing to change the bad news about the pending, supposedly inevitable demise of the Maori. From the late 1830s well into the 1900s the thesis that the Maori were yet another doomed primitive race turned into a dogma both in Britain and in increasingly white New Zealand. In *Making Peoples*, James Belich notes that the "fatal impact" thesis "persisted to 1930, a generation after census evidence showed conclusively that Maori were on the increase" (174). The Maori have certainly been subjected to "crippling impact," he writes—devastated and demoralized but not exterminated (174). Among the many explanations of the predicted extinction of the Maori were, besides God's will or the work of the Devil, a variety of less sublime causes, which Belich lists in no particular order:

> the disuse of traditional foods, clothing and customs; the misuse of new foods, clothing and customs; living in cold draughty houses; living in hot airless houses; working too hard, and not working enough. While disease predominated, other alleged causes of death and low birth rates included mass suicide, deaths from sulking, colds, excessive excitement, fatness, too much sex, horse riding and the ravening katipo spider. (*Making Peoples*, 174)

Warfare with the colonists in the 1840s and again from 1860 to 1872 perhaps killed 2,000 Maori but was less devastating than warfare among themselves and not nearly so significant a factor as disease (Sorrenson, 184). After many Maori groups had acquired guns, the so-called Musket Wars from 1818 into the 1830s "killed more New

Zealanders than World War One—perhaps about 20,000," writes Belich. Further, some missionaries "were so influenced by fatal impact
that they used the Musket Wars to explain the depopulation of communities that had been at peace," Belich notes. "They bequeathed estimates of up to 80,000 killed, which would have left few Maori alive"
(*Making Peoples*, 157).

In *Te Ika A Maui, or New Zealand and Its Inhabitants* (1855), however, the missionary Richard Taylor contests the view that the Maori
were another vanishing race; he cites census returns from 1843 and
1853, which, for a few specific areas, show slight increases among the
Maori. He also disputes the notion that the Maori were, through warfare, cannibalism, and other savage customs, exterminating themselves (254–58). Taylor's optimistic account, contradicting the "fatal
impact" thesis, foreshadows the conclusions of such recent historians
as Belich and J. M. R. Owens, both of whom contend that Maori savagery, depopulation, and the disease factor have all been exaggerated.[15]

In *The Story of New Zealand: Past and Present—Savage and Civilized* (1859), the physician Arthur S. Thomson also expresses cautious
optimism about the future of the Maori. Certainly in terms of health
factors, his account is the most authoritative and detailed to appear in
the 1800s. Thomson accepts that the number of Maori is declining
but treats that decline as reversible. Though formerly ferocious cannibals, the Maori are apt candidates for full civilization. "The last au-
thentic instance of cannibalism occurred in 1843," Thomson writes
(1:148). Especially after the acquisition of guns, warfare was a major
cause of depopulation, but not cannibalism: the Maori only ate the
corpses of their enemies slain in battle. Infanticide, however, is a
probable cause of decline, even though, Thomson notes, "the evidence of the existence of this horrid custom is chiefly circumstantial"
(2:286).[16] Both cannibalism and infanticide, however, have ceased
since the introduction of Christianity; Thomson claims that nearly
half the Maori have been converted (2:297). And they are making
rapid strides toward civilization in many other ways. A key cause of
their decline, however, has been inbreeding, which Thomson believes has led to their susceptibility to various diseases. The physical
salvation of the Maori, therefore, lies in the "amalgamation" of the
races, or the creation of a mixed race. New Zealand is one of the few
places in which the recommendation of miscegenation as a solution

to racial decline seems to have become fairly common.[17] The end point of Thomson's version of "amalgamation," however, will still be the eventual disappearance of "the Maori race" (2:306). But compared to the standard view of the Maori as doomed, Thomson's version of the possible future for both the Maori and the Pakeha is distinctly utopian: "It may savour of romance, but it is every day becoming more probable that the once visionary hope of the illustrious Gibbon will be realised, and the Hume of the Southern Hemisphere [will] spring from among the cannibal races of New Zealand" (2:307).[18]

Even though some observers saw cause for optimism, white missionaries, travelers, and officials frequently offer laments by Maori, or anyway by fictional Maori, about their inevitable demise. To take just one of many instances, in his 1847 *Savage Life and Scenes in Australia and New Zealand*, George French Angas writes:

> The Maori has now his eyes open . . . and in the perspective of a dark and gloomy future, he sees his children's land no longer their own, and his proud and swarthy race disappearing before the encroaching European. He broods over this; for he loves his country and the rights of his ancestors, and he will fight for his children's land. He reasons thus:—as the red Indian has been driven back into the far west, and the *mungo mungo*, or black man of New South Wales, has dwindled away before the civilization of the white man, so his nation . . . must pass into oblivion. It is this that rouses his feelings into jealousy and mistrust; and this feeling it is, which among *ourselves* would be called patriotism, that kindles in him the seeds of so-called rebellion. (339)

Whether this is an accurate rendition of Maori "feelings" is today, of course, a moot point.

In *Greater Britain*, Charles Dilke serves up the self-lament of the dying Maori race twice, with a twist of Darwinism.[19] Dilke insists on "the superiority in virtue, intelligence, and nobility of mind" of the Maori "over the Red Indian or the Australian Black" (1:386). The Maori, after all, are able to hold their own in their wars against the British and occasionally to defeat them. Like the English, moreover, the Maori are a seafaring as well as a martial race, and, according to Dilke:

> All races that delight in sea are equally certain to prosper, empirical philosophers will tell us. The Maories own ships by the score, and serve as sailors

wherever they get a chance: as deep-sea fishermen they have no equals. . . .
They are shrewd, thrifty; devoted friends, brave men. With all this, they die.
(1:389)

And they know "they die"; Dilke cites Maori themselves testifying to
this tragic future: "'Can you stay the surf which beats on Wanganui
shore?' say the Maories of our progress; and, of themselves: 'We are
gone—like the *moa*'" (1:389). So ends chapter 5; chapter 6, entitled
"The Two Flies," begins with these "mournful words of a well-known
Maori song":

> As the Pakéha fly has driven out the Maori fly;
> As the Pakéha grass has killed the Maori grass;
> As the Pakéha rat has slain the Maori rat;
> As the Pakéha clover has starved the Maori fern,
> So will the Pakéha destroy the Maori.
> (1:390)

Dilke proceeds to translate this alleged Maori song into the Darwinian terminology of survival of the fittest: "The English fly is the
best possible fly of the whole world, and will naturally beat down
and exterminate, or else starve out, the merely provincial Maori fly"
(1:391).

It does not matter that, just two pages earlier, Dilke has said the
Maori are similar to the Anglo-Saxons and that "all races that delight
in sea are certain to prosper." On the contrary, "The English fly,
grass, and man" all are superior to the New Zealand varieties:

> Natural selection is being conducted by nature in New Zealand on a grander
> scale than any we have contemplated, for the object of it here is man. In
> America, in Australia, the white man shoots or poisons his red or black fellow,
> and exterminates him through the workings of superior knowledge; but in
> New Zealand it is peacefully, and without extraordinary advantages, that the
> Pakéha beats his Maori brother. (1:392)

No matter that "the workings of superior knowledge" might be an instrument of "natural selection." No matter, too, that Dilke overlooks
Anglo-Maori warfare. For some obscure reasons having to do with

competition and the sturdiness that comes from living in a northern climate, everything English is, according to Dilke, superior to everything comparable in New Zealand, where nature seems to have spawned a number of weak, vanishing plants and animals as well as people.[20]

Despite his invocation of natural selection, it is not "the struggle for existence" with Europeans that Dilke blames for the demise of the Maori. Once upon a time they had been naturally selected, apparently, to survive in New Zealand. But the Maori and all other native animals and plants were, for some reason, declining under the rigors of natural selection long before the arrival of the Anglo-Saxons. When the first whites arrived, Dilke asserts, "all the native quadrupeds save one, and nearly all the birds and river-fishes, were extinct," and "the Maories themselves were [already] dying out," perhaps because of lack of things to eat, apart from each other (1:393–94). Cannibalism, Dilke thinks, was not practiced for pleasure or for ceremonial purposes but out of necessity (1:394). He claims, however, that war and cannibalism, although contributing to "depopulation," were not the major causes, which were instead environmental. Dilke also claims that "the British Government has been less guilty than is commonly believed as regards the destruction of the Maories. Since the original misdeed of the annexation of the isles, we have done the Maories no serious wrong" (1:394–95).[21]

Dilke dodges or rationalizes several issues, including the wars of the 1840s and 1860s, which were sometimes viewed as, it was hoped, leading to the extermination of the Maori.[22] Whatever factors recent scholars may emphasize to explain Maori depopulation, for most nineteenth-century observers there was no doubt that "the race" would soon become extinct. For many, especially during and after the warfare of the 1860s, the wish was rather that it *should* become extinct to make room for the superior, colonizing race. In *The Last of the Tasmanians*, James Bonwick quotes the Wellington *Independent* for 10 September 1868:

> What are we to do with these bloodthirsty [Maori] rebels? These men must be shown no mercy. They should be treated as wild beasts, hunted down, and slain. Modern history teaches us that irreclaimable savages, who rendered colonization impossible, and the lives of peaceful settlers insecure, have been, in the interests of society, exterminated. It does not matter what means are em-

ployed, so long as the work is done effectually. Head-money, blood-money, killing by contract—any of these means may be adopted. (77)

Bonwick comments: "So once felt the Saxons toward the Britons, the English toward the wild Irish, the Lowlanders of Scotland toward the Highlanders, the Russians toward the Circassians" (77).

8. Darwin and After

Although the "Darwinian revolution" produced new ideas about human races, societies, and cultures, it did not much alter and in several ways strengthened extinction discourse. Starting with Thomas Henry Huxley's *Man's Place in Nature* (1863), evolutionists offered what quickly became the dominant view, accepted by most scientists and intellectuals, concerning racial variation.[1] *Homo sapiens* was one species, not several; the separate races had a single origin; they evolved through the same processes and stages; and the differences among them were insignificant compared to the similarities. Nevertheless, some races—the Australians, for example—had been isolated for millennia, and hence occupied the very lowest rungs of the evolutionary ladder. Whether this meant that they lacked the ability to become civilized was less than clear, but most evolutionists believed they were slated for extinction.

Darwin himself is usually pessimistic about the fate of the "dark races." In *The Descent of Man*, however, he rejects the biblically based notion that those races have degenerated from the original, Adamite, white race:

> To believe that man was aboriginally civilized and then suffered utter degradation in so many regions, is to take a pitiably low view of human nature. It is apparently a truer and more cheerful view that progress has been much more

general than retrogression; that man has risen, though by slow and interrupted steps, from a lowly condition to the highest standard as yet attained by him in knowledge, morals and religion. (151)

In contrast to the "more cheerful view," from *The Voyage of the Beagle* on, Darwin's notion of the savage condition is distinctly Hobbesian. He agrees with his friend and ally, John Lubbock, whom he quotes in *Descent*: "It is not too much to say that the horrible dread of unknown evil hangs like a thick cloud over savage life, and embitters every pleasure" (99).[2] In the famous conclusion to *Descent*, Darwin suggests that the gulf between savages and civilized humans is almost unbridgeable. "He who has seen a savage in his native land will not feel much shame," he writes, "if forced to acknowledge that the blood of some more humble creature flows in his veins":

For my own part I would as soon be descended from that heroic little monkey, who braved his dreaded enemy in order to save the life of his keeper . . . as from a savage who delights to torture his enemies, offers up bloody sacrifices, practises infanticide without remorse, treats his wives like slaves, knows no decency, and is haunted by the grossest superstitions. (643)

From the 1830s on, Darwin believed that, though humanity formed a single species, certain primitive races were so far behind civilization—so lost in the immense past of social evolution—that their extinction was likely if not inevitable. With a few exceptions—Lewis Henry Morgan and Alfred Russel Wallace are perhaps the main ones—most evolutionists treat primitive races and cultures negatively, not only as doomed by the inexorable laws of nature but also as meriting their pending extinctions.

Darwin's reaction to the Tierra del Fuegians was one of repulsion and disbelief that such primitive humans could be his "fellow creatures." He puzzled: "One's mind hurries back over past centuries, and then asks, could our progenitors have been men like these?" And his instinctive response was no: "men, whose very signs and expressions are less intelligible to us than those of domesticated animals; men who do not possess the instinct of those animals, nor yet appear to boast of human reason, or at least of arts consequent upon that reason. I do not believe it is possible to describe or paint the difference between savage and civilized man. It is the difference between a wild and tame animal" (*Voyage*, 501), only greater, "inasmuch as in man there is a greater power of improvement" (205).[3] Darwin was impressed by the intelligence and progress toward civilization of the Fuegians whom Captain Fitzroy was returning to their homeland—Jemmy Button, Fuegia Basket, and York Minster, as they had been renamed. Together with a white missionary, they were to provide the spark, at least, for civilizing and Christianizing their fellow Fuegians. But he was even more astonished at how subhuman the indigenous Fuegians seemed, and his opinion of all "savages" remained quite negative.

Influenced by both Malthus and Charles Lyell, Darwin, in *Voyage*, stresses the extinction of species and of primitive races more than he puzzles about their origin. "Certainly," he writes, "no fact in the long history of the world is so startling as the wide and repeated exterminations of its inhabitants" (175). Darwin notes the "war of extermination" against the natives in South America (104); comments on the situations of savage versus Christianized Tahitians and other Polynesians by way of Ellis's *Polynesian Researches* (412–43); compares the still-savage Maori unfavorably to the Tahitians (419); points out that the Australian aborigines are "rapidly decreasing" (433); and recounts in some detail the demise of the Tasmanians, despite the "intrepid exertions of Mr. Robinson" (445–46). In his *Journal of Researches*, Darwin writes: "All the [Tasmanian] aborigines have been removed to an island in Bass's Straits [*sic*], so that Van Diemen's Land enjoys the great advantage of being free from a native population"—a sentence he omitted from *Voyage*. But he adds, in language that reappears in *Voyage*:

This most cruel step [of removal] seems to have been quite unavoidable, as the only means of stopping a fearful succession of robberies, burnings, and murders, committed by the blacks; and which sooner or later would have ended in their utter destruction. I fear there is no doubt, that this train of evil and its consequences originated in the infamous conduct of some of our countrymen. Thirty years is a short period in which to have banished the last aboriginal from his native island—and that island nearly as large as Ireland. (*Journal*, 504)

Both in *Voyage* and in his later writings, Darwin at times looked forward to the complete triumph of civilized over primitive or "lower" races.[4] "How long will the wretched inhabitants of N.W. Australia go on blinking their eyes without extermination?" Darwin wondered in 1839; and in 1860 he wrote that "the white man is 'improving off the face of the earth' even races nearly his equals" (quoted in Gruber, 169; Darwin, *Life and Letters*, 2:136). Further, the progress of the world seemed to dictate not just the peaceful transformation of "savagery" into its opposite but, for better or worse, its violent liquidation: "Looking to the world at no very distant date, what an endless number of the lower races will have been eliminated by the higher civilized races throughout the world" (*Life and Letters*, 1:286).

Early in *Descent* Darwin asks: "Do the races or species of men, whichever term may be applied, encroach on and replace one another, so that some finally become extinct?" (6). His answer in the chapter on race, with the extinction of the Tasmanians as key instance, is yes. In his usual painstaking manner, Darwin surveys other peoples' theories about the causes of the extinction of primitive races before he arrives at his own. He opines that Malthus and other authorities have underestimated the impact of infanticide on savage populations (47), and he offers the by-then standard opinion that "if savages of any race are induced suddenly to change their habits of life, they become more or less sterile, and their young offspring suffer in health," just as wild animals in new environments do (198). In short, Darwin accepts his predecessors' basic views about the extinction of primitive races without much question. Thus, minus his evolutionary speculations about the fate of "the anthropomorphous apes," this statement from *Descent* could as easily have come from Robert Knox or James Hunt as from Darwin:

> At some future period, not very distant as measured by centuries, the civilized races of man will almost certainly exterminate, and replace, the savage races throughout the world. At the same time the anthropomorphous apes . . . will no doubt be exterminated. The break between man and his nearest allies will then be wider, for it will intervene between man in a more civilized state, as we may hope, even than the Caucasian, and some ape as low as a baboon, instead of as now between the negro or Australian and the gorilla. (167–68)

Throughout his writings Darwin emphasizes the great, chronological, and cultural distance between the savage and the civilized conditions of human existence. What has produced that distance is progress, although not all races seem capable of moving up the scale from savagery. Further, even when insisting on the progress of civilization or of the "advanced races" (usually with progress in scientific discovery as a key piece of the evidence), Darwin and his allies recognized that there is nothing inherently progressive about evolutionary processes and also that all creatures and species are mutable and finite. Thus, in his *Autobiography*, Darwin declares: "There seems to be no more design in the variability of organic beings and in the action of natural selection, than in the course which the wind blows" (87). If there is a tendency that can be called progress, it is the accidental outcome of natural selection, and it is progress only for the temporary victors in the struggle for life.[5]

Darwin, Huxley, and their immediate followers also believed that "the survival of the fittest" had nothing to do with ethics. Human survival, however, depended on social cooperation, and progress could be defined as the strengthening of such cooperation. Nevertheless, there was no denying that, as Tennyson had written in *In Memoriam*, nature was "red in tooth and claw." Both new species and the advanced human races supplanted—or extinguished—older, supposedly less fit or less adaptable ones. Revolution may eat its children, but the reverse is true of evolution, at least according to Darwin: the children consume the parents. "Hence the improved and modified descendants of a species," writes Darwin, "will generally *cause the extermination* of the parent-species" (*Origin*, 453; my emphasis). And yet primitive races were said to be children, not the parents of modern civilization. In one sense, this metaphorical confusion did not matter: whether seen as antiquated or infantile, all savages were lost, misplaced in time. Darwin and his followers, of course, accepted geological "deep time"; applied to humans, that meant a vast temporal difference between history and prehistory, and between civilization and savagery. In contrast to the ancestors of the progressive races, modern savages were like dead branches on the tree of life, born out of their due time. The first generation of evolutionists did not give them much credit for the fact that they had survived for millennia and that they must therefore have been quite remarkably "fit" somehow. On the contrary, for the evolutionists as for the pre-Darwinian race scientists, eons of savagery and the extant savages themselves were about to vanish, defeated in the struggle for life.

Although in 1859 Darwin did not address the evolution of *Homo sapiens*, *The Origin of Species* has more to say about "man," human races, and the extinction of both species and races than has always been recognized. Besides stressing the human selection or breeding of animal and plant varieties, one of the ways *Origin* does so is through terminology and concepts drawn from economics, especially from Malthus. The theory of evolution, Darwin acknowledges, "is the doctrine of Malthus applied with manifold force to the whole animal and vegetable kingdoms" — "with manifold force" because "in this case [i.e., in nature as opposed to human society] there can be no artificial increase of food, and no prudential restraint from marriage" (*Origin*, 91). And another way *Origin*, at least covertly, relates to the history of the human species has to do with Darwin's particular use of extinction discourse. Indeed, *The Origin of Species* could well have been entitled *The Origin and Extinction of Species*, because, as Darwin frequently insists, "extinction and natural selection go hand in hand" (213). "No one can have marvelled more than I have done at the extinction of species," he writes (450); and he devotes a section of chapter 11 to that topic ("On Extinction," 449–55).

Darwin contends that "the production of new forms" in nature entails "almost" inevitably the "extinction of old forms" (*Origin*, 479). Nature "selects" qualities that enable "fit" individuals and species to survive; what nature rejects is, to use a verb that recurs throughout both *Origin* and *Descent*, "exterminated." Darwin often uses this term even when another, more neutral term such as *supplanted* or *superseded* would be more accurate. Thus at one point he writes, "under nature we have every reason to believe that parent forms are generally supplanted *and* exterminated by their improved offspring," when just the word *supplanted* would do (*Origin*, 447–48; my emphasis). To take another example:

> Though Nature grants long periods of time for the work of natural selection, she does not grant an indefinite period; for as all organic beings are striving to seize on each place in the economy of nature, if any one species does not become modified and improved in a corresponding degree with its competitors, it will be exterminated. (*Origin*, 133–34)

Darwin here leaves unclear whether he means that the unimproved species will be directly, violently "exterminated" by "its competitors," or whether instead it will gradually disappear through diminishing access to the means of subsistence that the improved species gradually monopolize.

In any event, whether consciously or not, Darwin often applies the active, violent rhetoric of the discourse about racial extinction to processes that are long-term and nonviolent. Further, as Peter Bowler notes, "the mechanism of the survival of the fittest could be used to justify a more ruthless approach toward conquered peoples, in which extinction was both a symbol and a consequence of inferiority" (*Evolution*, 300). After all, the subtitle of *The Origin of Species by Means of Natural Selection* reads: *The Preservation of Favored Races in the Struggle for Life*. Although "races" here refers to varieties and species of nonhuman organisms, in *Darwinism and Politics* (1889) D. G. Ritchie not unfairly claims that Darwin "looks forward to the elimination of the lower races by the higher civilized races throughout the world" and also that social Darwinism is a "scheme of salvation for the elect by the damnation of the vast majority" whether abroad or at home (7).

From *Man's Place in Nature* forward, Huxley's "ethnological" writings present a vision of the human past as "the struggle for existence" among "races." Huxley is less prone than many nineteenth-century scientists to attribute specific moral, emotional, and intellectual qualities to races, and he also stresses the influence of geographical and climatic factors in the "struggle" through which the "fittest" races have survived while apparently "unfit" ones such as the Neanderthals and the Tasmanians have perished. Huxley stresses that, though there are apparently great differences between races, with the "lower" ones not far removed from the gorilla and chimpanzee, humanity forms a single species. No extant race or species is the "missing link" between humans and the anthropoid apes. Yet in *Man's Place in Nature* Huxley cites evidence suggesting the similarities between sub-Saharan Africans, on the one hand, and chimpanzees and gorillas, on the other, including a gratuitous reference to "African cannibalism in the sixteenth century," based on a Portuguese account he admits is irrelevant to his argument. He illustrates it with an even more gratuitous woodcut of a "human butcher shop" (7:73–74).

For Huxley, ethnology is not primarily about customs and culture but about the physical and mental characteristics of the human races. In "On the Methods and Results of Ethnology" (1865), he writes: "ethnology is the science which determines the distinctive characters of the persistent modifications of mankind" (7:209). The important modifications are morphological, involving bodily structure; these are what differentiate one "race" from another—or, rather, these are the differences that Huxley believes can be scientifically measured and compared. At the outset of his essay, Huxley insists that the terms "persistent modifications" and "stocks" should be used instead of "varieties," "races," or "species" "because each of these last well-known terms implies, on the part of its employer, a preconceived opinion touching one of those problems, the solution of which is the ultimate object of the science" of ethnology (7:209). But Huxley's solution elsewhere is to use "race" while insisting that humanity forms one "species." Anyway, Huxley considers "ethnology" to be a branch of zoology, "which again is the animal half of BI-OLOGY—the science of life and living things" (7:210). In contrast to Edward Burnett Tylor, Lewis Henry Morgan, and John F. McLennan, among early cultural anthropologists, for Huxley neither language nor artifacts offer reliable evidence about the real differences between the human races or about their past: "That two nations use calabashes or shells for drinking-vessels, or that they employ spears, or clubs, or swords and axes of stone and metal . . . cannot be regarded as evidence that these two nations had a common origin, or even that intercommunication ever took place between them" (7:213). Nor can the fact that two nations or races speak the same language prove much: Frenchmen speak French, says Huxley, but so do Haitians. Huxley here, as in later essays such as "The Aryan Question and Prehistoric Man" (1890), dismisses the language-based speculations of the philologist Max Müller and his followers, who claimed to be able to read the ethnological past and present from the distribution of languages and dialects.

The supposed physical differences between the races provides Huxley with evidence for a taxonomy that, in "On the Methods and Results of Ethnology," includes eleven distinct racial "stocks" (7:234–37): Australians, "Negritos" (such as Tasmanians and Papuans), "Amphinesians" (Polynesians, the Maori), American Indians, "Esquimaux," Mongolians, Negroes, Bushmen, "Mincopies" (the Andaman Islanders), and the two great groups that make up most of the population of Europe, North Africa, and much of western Asia: the blond "Xanthochroi" who may be either "short" or "long-headed" (though in other essays they are described as "long-headed" only), and the dark, "long-headed" "Melanochroi." Huxley remarks that "of the eleven different stocks enumerated, seven have been known to us for less than 400 years; and of these seven not one possessed a fragment of written history at the time it came into contact with European civilization" (7:237–38).

This lack of history and its opposite is, indeed, the main nonmorphological difference that Huxley cites among the eleven "stocks." Only three of the eleven "stocks" have been capable of producing written histories, or—to emphasize the point—have had histories as opposed to evolutionary prehistories. The Negro "stock" has been known to Europeans for centuries but is also history-less. Only the Xanthochroi, the Melanochroi, and, though within limits, the Mongolian "stocks" have entered history—that is, written, Western history. Huxley says that "archaeological and historical investigations are of great value for all those peoples whose ancient state has differed widely from their present condition, and who have the good or evil fortune to possess a history. But on taking a broad survey of the world, it is astonishing that few nations present either condition. Respecting five-sixths of the persistent modifications of mankind, history and archaeology are absolutely silent" (7:212). Like Hegel, John Stuart Mill, and many other nineteenth-century thinkers, Huxley identifies history with progress toward civilization (and therefore with the eventual capacity to compose written histories, even when these are largely mythological). The Xanthochroi and the Melanochroi alone, he claims, are currently civilized and still making progress.

While the Mongolians—or that branch of this "stock" identified as Chinese, at any rate—"have attained a remarkable and apparently indigenous civilization, only surpassed by that of Europe" (7:229), they have stalled (as in *The Wealth of Nations*: the Chinese were Adam Smith's main example of a "stationary" social condition). In contrast to the Chinese, says Huxley, "everything that is highest in science, in art, in law, in politics, and in mechanical inventions" has "originated" with the Xanthochroi and the Melanochroi. "In their hands, at the present moment, lies the order of the social world, and to them its progress is committed" (7:232). Huxley implies, of course, that if the other racial "stocks" are ever to become progressive or to achieve even a modicum of civilization, then one or both of the European "stocks" must lead them. This is the same message implicit in the colony-as-garden metaphor at the outset of *Evolution and Ethics,* where the actual colony named—Tasmania—suggests the fate of those "native savages" incapable of gardening or, in other words, of entering historical time and becoming civilized.

Huxley's stress on morphology and his skepticism about languages and cultural artifacts as historical evidence means that history, for him, as for earlier race scientists, is a spectacle of races in collision. Rather than cultural diffusion and economic exchange, the primary interactions of races are war and colonization; in his essay, "On Some Fixed Points in British Ethnology" (1871), the Roman, barbarian, and Norman invasions of Britain are key examples.[6] Further, the main motivator of the great racial migrations and collisions of the past has been economic scarcity, brought on by Malthusian population pressure on available resources.[7] Writing in "The Aryan Question" about "the Teutonic inroads upon the Empire of Rome," Huxley declares: "Whatever the causes which led to the breaking out of bounds of the blond long-heads, in mass, at particular epochs, the natural increase in numbers of a vigorous and fertile race must always have impelled them to press upon their neighbours" (7:287).

For Huxley, there is apparently not much more to be understood about human history or prehistory unless it sheds light on the evolutionary changes that the physical structures of the different races have undergone. But on this score, he thinks, there is little to be said, because the main racial "stocks," despite much intermingling as in the case of Britain, appear to have been almost fixed during most or all recorded history:

> On the whole . . . it is wonderful how little change has been effected by these mutual invasions and intermixtures. As at the present time, so at the dawn of history, the Melanochroi fringed the Atlantic and the Mediterranean; the Xanthochroi occupied most of Central and Eastern Europe, and much of Western and Central Asia; while Mongolians held the extreme east of the Old World. So far as history teaches us, the populations of Europe, Asia and Africa were, twenty centuries ago, just what they are now. (7:238)

Compared to evolutionary time, recorded historical time is insignificant. During the short span of history, civilization may have begun to allay "the struggle for existence" within the bounds of certain societies, but that is hardly the case, Huxley thinks, with savagery; anyway, modern intersocietal relations are just more of the same—the struggle for survival among races continues.

Like other Victorian ethnologists, including his antagonist, James Hunt, of the Anthropological Society (see Stocking, 247–55), Huxley believed that ethnology was a science capable of providing much useful information to British imperial administrators and colonists. As president of the Ethnological Society in 1868, he "launched what amounted to an ethnological census of the populations of the British possessions," starting with India (Di Gregorio, 175). Huxley's goal was the mapping and measurement of all the races of the world. Only such a total mapping would provide the evidence necessary to develop an accurate taxonomy of the races, to understand how they had evolved and interacted through prehistory and history, and to judge their greatly varying capacities for civilization or progress. No doubt Huxley believed that such a mapping of races would also provide the answer to the mystery that absorbed Darwin in the chapter on race in *Descent of Man*—namely, why some or perhaps all primitive races were dying out, apparently on mere contact with civilization. The ethnological map of human races would, of course, also be a hierarchy, and it would help in the general process of eradicating savagery, if not the savages themselves.

In common with other evolutionists including Darwin, Huxley identifies the progress of science unproblematically with social progress; he also identifies it more generally with evolutionary progress, upward from the apes. Thus, in *Man's Place in Nature*, Huxley offers multiple, overlapping narratives of "progressive development." There is, first and most obviously, the evolution of "man" literally upward from the apes (or, rather, from the apes' ancestors). Paralleling this evolution but in much foreshortened chronology is the development of scientific knowledge, banishing ignorance, as in the opening sentence: "Ancient traditions, when tested by the severe processes of modern investigation, commonly enough fade away into mere dreams" (7:1). This second narrative is the intellectual version of eliminating "savagery" from the world. It is also the recent, most important version of a more general, third narrative of progress, "from blind force to conscious intellect and will" (7:151), which is, in turn, a version of "Nature's great progression, from the formless to the formed—from the inorganic to the organic" (7:151). Every individual organism, moreover, and every species (also every society), undergoes a related "progressive development" from the simple to the complex, from the acorn to the oak tree or the embryo to the adult animal. However, that organisms also peak, degenerate, and die, and that all previously recorded or unrecorded empires have declined and fallen, make all the processes of nature and history ultimately "cyclical," revolving in "the procession of the great year" (9:85), as in Lyell's *Principles of Geology*. Huxley bases this view in part on the second law of thermodynamics:

> If our globe is proceeding from a condition in which it was too hot to support any but the lowest living thing to a condition in which it will be too cold to permit of the existence of any others, the course of life upon its surface must describe a trajectory like that of a ball fired from a mortar; and the sinking half of that course is as much a part of the general process of evolution as the rising. (9:199)

Ordinarily, however, Huxley emphasizes only the "rising" half, or "the doctrine of progressive development" (9:208). In the vanguard of "the cosmic struggle" of nature against itself, and therefore in the vanguard of "the ethical process" (9:35), the European nations and some of their imperial offshoots (the areas of white colonization) are the most complex, successful examples yet of humanity's ascent out of mere brutality. For Huxley, "civilization" is the usual name for this vanguard, though a near synonym is scientific enlightenment. However named, science for Huxley is that accurate knowledge or consciousness of nature and society that is progressively enabling civilized humanity to control its own destiny, to turn wilderness into garden.

"The theory of evolution encourages no millennial anticipations" (9:85), Huxley writes in *Evolution and Ethics*. But the gardening metaphor, pointing to an ultimate civilization, product of the empire of science and reason, suggests otherwise.[8] The "ethical process" in history does not contradict but instead leads to imperialism as the natural outcome of competition among human groups. That process gradually mitigates or even eliminates the "struggle for existence" within a given society. Huxley's "categorical imperative" (9:75), however, is not a secular version of the golden rule as in Kant but rather the pressure from the "struggle for existence" on individuals to band together for mutual protection against other individuals or groups. Those groups or societies that learn best how to mitigate internal competition among individuals, substituting for such competition cooperation and the "gradual strengthening of the social bond," are "fittest" for survival in the broader struggle—that is, the struggle (competition for scarce resources, warfare) of societies against one another—which Huxley explicitly identifies with and not against "the ethical process" (9:35).

Although Huxley deplores "the unfortunate ambiguity of the phrase 'survival of the fittest'" because it equates might with right or, in other words, because it confounds what is "fittest" in the "struggle" in and against nature with what is morally "best" (9:80), throughout *Evolution and Ethics* he implicitly and sometimes explicitly identifies those societies that succeed in dominating others with progress and civilization, and the dominated with unfitness, barbarism, savagery. Though Huxley does not spell out this conclusion, it follows that those societies capable of constructing empires are more "ethical" than those that are imperialized. (This conclusion is already implicit in the opposition between "savagery" and "civilization" that informs all evolutionary anthropology.) Huxley places his (secular) faith concerning the gradual "improvement" of the human condition in that "intelligence" and "science" that he everywhere identifies with both "civilization" and the "ethical process." Though all evolutionary processes are ultimately "cyclical" rather than "progressive" (9:49), so that beyond whatever heights of civilization humanity may attain there looms a future decline and fall, during the "progressive" upswing of social evolution Huxley sees "no limit to the extent to which intelligence and will, guided by sound principles of investigation, and organized in common effort, may modify the conditions of existence" for the better (9:85). Humanity has the capacity to alter both external and internal nature, Huxley declares: "much may be done to change the nature of man himself. The intelligence which has converted the brother of the wolf into the faithful guardian of the flock ought to be able to do something towards curbing the instincts of savagery in civilized men" (9:85).

Viewed through the lens of Huxley's "ethical process," "civilization" means nothing more nor less than "curbing the instincts of savagery"— or just curbing "savagery." The savage within—not distinguishable from the beast within—must be tamed, repressed. But so must the savage without. In the external struggle between societies, civilization is virtually identical to imperialism, because both entail the conquest and domestication of savages. In his 1888 essay "The Struggle for Existence in Human Society," Huxley writes: "the course shaped by the ethical man—the member of society or citizen—necessarily runs counter to that which the non-ethical man—the primitive savage, or man as a mere member of the animal kingdom—tends to adopt. The latter fights out the struggle for existence to the bitter end, like any other animal; the former devotes his best energies to the object of setting limits to the struggle" (9:203). Once again, as in most extinction discourse, savages turn out to be self-exterminating "to the bitter end."

Two years before the appearance of *Origin of Species*, Herbert Spencer, who coined the phrase "survival of the fittest," pronounced progress to be a universal "law" of nature and defined that law as "the transformation of the homogeneous into the heterogeneous" ("Progress," 40, 46). This supposed law of progress applied to the inorganic as well as organic, to "the development of the Earth" as well as to "the development of Life upon its surface" (40). Above all, it applied to "the social organism"—to human history, and to all societies and cultures. According to Spencer's Panglossian notion, the universe was a place where everything was constantly getting better. True, there were earlier stages that had to be surpassed, just as snakes had to shed their skins or trees their leaves. Occasionally, too, among species and also among human societies, "there will be retrogradation" (48), if only to make room for the new. But, on the whole, progress was the universal movement of everything in existence.

> It will be seen that . . . from the beginning, the decomposition of every expended force into several forces has been perpetually producing a higher complication; that the increase of heterogeneity so brought about is still going on, and must continue to go on; and that thus Progress is not an accident, not a thing within human control, but a beneficent necessity. ("Progress," 52)

The last phrase suggests a providential view of both natural and human history; although Spencer would later identify his deity as the "Unknowable," the concepts he really worshipped were, he believed, completely knowable. These were "Progress" and "Nature," and they were virtually the same for him.

Spencer is regarded today as a pioneer sociologist rather than anthropologist, and yet the first volume of his *Principles of Sociology* (1874) summarizes a vast amount of evidence and speculation about "primitive man" and also about race. So, too, his methodological treatise, *The Study of Sociology* (1873), surveys the various "biases" that impede scientific observation, especially of societies and cultures different from one's own, including the "mistaken estimates of other races [that] result from over-estimation of one's own race" (*Study*, 188). Despite that cautionary note, most evolutionists including Darwin and Huxley agreed with Spencer's general assumptions that, as he says in *Principles*, "primitive man" is "less evolved" than, say, the average Englishman (55); that "primitive man" lacks the "ability to think" (89); that there are "inferior" and "superior" races; and that "the lighter-skinned races are habitually the dominant races" (23). Further, history is a matter of "survival of the fittest" among the races, which means that, at least "occasionally," the "inferior varieties" of mankind meet with "extermination" (40).

Not all evolutionists, however, were so certain as Spencer about the universal "law of progress." Nevertheless, such evolutionary anthropologists as Edward Burnett Tylor and Lewis Henry Morgan provided the generally optimistic message that all the races of the single human species were progressing through identical stages of cultural development, from savagery through barbarism to civilization. In *Ancient Society* (1877), Morgan elaborated this old, tripartite division of cultures and societies into seven distinct "ethnical periods," through which all humanity was evolving (16–18). "Progress has been found to be substantially the same in kind in tribes and nations inhabiting different and even disconnected continents," Morgan declared; "the argument when extended tends to establish the unity of origin of mankind" (23).[9]

Prior to Morgan's *Ancient Society*, Tylor, in his 1865 *Early History of Mankind*, argued that "the wide differences in the civilization and mental state of the various races of mankind are rather differences of development than of origin, rather of degree than of kind" (232). In both *Early History* and his magnum opus, *Primitive Culture* (1871), Tylor defines the chief goal of his version of anthropology as the "working out [of] the problem of the Origin and Progress of Culture" among all "races" (*Early History*, 141), which are ultimately one "race" (or species). His subject, in other words, is cultural progress, but that progress is shadowed by a long history of losses and of forgetting. Humans are signifying animals, endowed with language, but, as Christopher Herbert remarks in his discussion of Tylor, "the distinctive characteristic of *Homo significans* is *not to know*, in effect to have forgotten, what he 'means'" (261). Anthropology is therefore a science of remembrance, using the "survivals" or traces of the past that linger on into the present to reconstruct that past.

Tylor is concerned, in part, to refute contentions that primitive "races" have, on the whole, regressed or "degenerated" from a higher condition:

> An inspection of the geographical distribution of art and knowledge among mankind, seems to give some grounds for the belief that the history of the lower races, as of the higher, is not the history of a course of degeneration, or even of equal oscillations to and fro, but of a movement which, in spite of frequent stops and relapses, has on the whole been forward; that there has been from age to age a growth in Man's power over Nature, which no degrading influences have been able permanently to check. (*Early History*, 166)

Tylor recognizes that the results of contact between "the low races" and "the high races" have been hugely destructive for the former. Even with all the destruction, however, the general tendency of the human species is upward from the apes:

> The disappearance of savage arts in presence of a higher civilization is . . . mostly caused by their being superseded by something higher, and this can hardly be called a decline of culture, which must not be confounded with the physical and moral decline of so many tribes under the oppression and temptation of civilized men. (*Early History*, 159)

Perhaps because all "tribes" and societies pass through the same stages of development, Tylor does not express much concern about "the oppression and temptation of civilized men" that were main causes of the extinction of many primitive races.

Throughout his career, Tylor did an unanalyzed balancing act between a nascent cultural relativism that adumbrated modern anthropology and an "easy ethnocentrism" that allowed him to claim the "educated" elites of Europe and North America as the "standard" whereby to judge all "lower" cultures (Stocking, 162). Civilization both contains and supersedes the earlier stages of social and cultural evolution, so in a sense nothing is lost. As Tylor announces in the famous first paragraph of *Primitive Culture*:

> On the one hand, the uniformity which so largely pervades civilization may be ascribed, in great measure, to the uniform action of uniform causes: while on the other hand its various grades may be regarded as stages of development or

evolution, each the outcome of previous history, and about to do its proper part in shaping the history of the future. (1:1)

While the rapid disappearance of many savage cultures, societies, and races is mournful, it is so largely because evidence about mankind's unitary history gets buried as the new emerges. Tylor's attitude toward primitive peoples is basically humane; but his theory of cultural evolution as progress, while more cautious than Spencer's, is both optimistic and generally approving of what has transpired among the "races" of the world.

Tylor offers a definition of culture as the stuff of everyday experience, shared by all humans, one basic to modern anthropology. Although there are "lower" and "higher" stages of culture, the tendency of the "lower" is invariably to evolve into the "higher." Neither race nor environment determines the outcome in any absolute sense. "The ancient Swiss lake-dweller may be set beside the medieval Aztec, and the Ojibwa of North America beside the Zulu of South Africa," he writes in *Primitive Culture*; "As Dr. Johnson contemptuously said when he had read about Patagonians and South Sea Islanders in Hawkesworth's Voyages, 'one set of savages is like another'" (1:6).

But it is not just that groups of savages resemble one another; civilized peoples also resemble savages, as "higher" stages of culture continue to reflect "lower" ones. "When it comes to comparing barbarous hordes with civilized nations, the consideration thrusts itself upon our minds, how far item after item of the life of the lower races passes into analogous proceedings of the higher, in forms not too far changed . . . and sometimes hardly changed at all" (1:6–7). Despite evolutionary stages, such a claim has a leveling effect that leads Tylor in the direction of satire. The survivals of many savage traits and beliefs in the midst of civilization—belief in ghosts, for example—suggest how childish modern, supposedly educated people can be.

Tylor thinks of anthropology as a reformer's science, especially regarding religion. His patient accumulation of examples of mythic and superstitious survivals implies that religion itself is a survival or anachronism in the modern world. In lines he contributed to Andrew Lang's "Double Ballade of a Primitive Man," Tylor writes:

First epoch, the human began,
Theologians all to expose,—

'Tis the *mission* of primitive man.
(Quoted in Stocking, 190–94)

Tylor also strikes a politically reforming note when he mentions the discovery of white savages within the confines of civilization: "In our great cities, the so-called 'dangerous classes' are sunk in hideous misery and depravity. If we have to strike a balance between the Papuans of New Caledonia and the communities of European beggars and thieves, we may sadly acknowledge that we have in our midst something worse than savagery" (1:42–43). This passage occurs, however, in the midst of Tylor's rejection of the degeneration theories of Archbishop Richard Whately and others. Tylor contends that the general trend of evolution has been upward, through savagery and barbarism to civilization, and that there is no "known savage tribe [which] would not be improved by judicious civilization" (1:31).

In his 1874 essay on "the principles of classifying" cultural artifacts from an evolutionary standpoint, as also in his 1875 "On the Evolution of Culture" and elsewhere, Augustus Lane-Fox Pitt-Rivers agreed with Tylor, Lubbock, and other Darwinian anthropologists and archaeologists: savagery and savages were rapidly, necessarily disappearing from the world. Presiding over the Anthropological Institute, Pitt-Rivers worried that contact with white civilization would soon render it impossible to study primitive cultures and races (Lorimer, 216). And Britain, which had "done more than any other [nation] to destroy all those races and to obliterate their culture," was morally obligated at the very least to construct a "scientific record of that which we destroy" (quoted in Lorimer, 216). Concerning the evidence that would fill the pages of such a record, Pitt-Rivers proclaimed:

As we find amongst existing animals and plants, species akin to what geology teaches us were primitive species, and as among existing species we find the representatives of successive stages of geological species, so amongst the arts of existing savages we find forms which, being adapted to a low condition of culture, have survived from the earliest times, and also the representatives of many successive stages through which development has taken place in times past. (18)

Pitt-Rivers had earlier (1867) declared that it must "strike even the most superficial observer of nature [that] there can be little doubt that in a few years all the most barbarous races will have disappeared from

the earth, or will have ceased to preserve their native arts" (54). He
went on to speak of "the law which consigns to destruction all savage
races when brought in contact with a civilization much higher than
their own" and asserted that this law "is now operating with unrelent-
ing fury in every part of the world":

> Of the aborigines of Tasmania, not a single individual remains; those of New
> Zealand are fast disappearing. The Australian savage dies out before the ad-
> vancing European. North and South America, and the Polynesian Islands, all
> tell the same tale. (54)

Pitt-Rivers added, with antireligious irony, that "wherever the generous
influences of Christianity have set foot, there they have been accompanied by the scourge" (54). And he opined that "the savage is morally
and mentally an unfit instrument for the spread of civilization, except
when, like the higher mammalia, he is reduced to slavery; his occupation is gone, and his place is required for an improved race" (54–55).

The slow work that has gone into the evolution of surviving savagery is now, suddenly, to be terminated by "progress." Nature, which
supposedly does not take leaps, is taking one, it seems. No more than
Darwin, Huxley, or Tylor does Pitt-Rivers confront this problem—
contradiction, rather—though he does suggest that it has something
to do with the accelerating rate at which civilization is "progressing"
or evolving:

> Allowing for the rapidly increasing ratio in which progress advances, it is not
> too much to assume, that in half a century from the present time, savage life
> will have ceased to have a single true representative on the face of the globe,
> and the evidence which it has been the means of handing down to our gener-
> ation will have perished with it. (55)

With its "rapidly increasing ratio," progress leaves "savage life" in its
wake, although present-day savages—many of them only recently discovered by Europeans because of progress in science and technology—have survived the struggle with nature for ages. It is just the
struggle with their more progressive counterparts that curtails their
existence.

For his part the co-discoverer of natural selection, Alfred Russel Wallace, was something of a romantic—a Rousseauistic Darwinian, per-

haps.[10] In contrast to Darwin's, Lubbock's, and Huxley's Hobbesian view of savagery, Wallace developed an appreciation of the virtues of "savage life." Thus, while in Borneo, he could write: "The more I see of uncivilised people, the better I think of human nature on the whole, and the essential differences between so-called civilised and savage man seem to disappear" (quoted in Moore, 298). So, too, Wallace's ethnographic accounts of the likely futures of many of the "natives" and "primitive races" he observed during his global travels are often explicitly elegiac. In *Narrative of Travels on the Amazon and Rio Negro* (1853), Wallace writes that "the Indians" are peaceful, affectionate, ingenious, and civilizable: "they seem capable of being formed, by education and good government, into a peaceable and civilised community." This positive result, however, seems unlikely, because "they are exposed to the influence of the refuse of Brazilian society, and will probably, before many years, be reduced to the condition of the other half-civilised Indians of the country, who seem to have lost the good qualities of savage life, and gained only the vices of civilisation" (361). Except for a brief appendix "On Amazonian Picture-Writings," these are the final words of Wallace's natural history travelogue; in retrospect, the entire journey becomes a nonrepeatable experience of a wilderness and a savage innocence that are about to disappear.

The same elegiac message is evident in Wallace's 1869 *Malay Archipelago*, at least in regard to "the true Polynesians" and the "Papuan race" of New Guinea:

> If the past history of these varied races is obscure and uncertain, the future is no less so. The true Polynesians, inhabiting the farthest isles of the Pacific, are no doubt doomed to an early extinction. But the more numerous Malay race seems well adapted to survive as the cultivator of the soil, even when his country and government have passed into the hands of Europeans. If the tide of colonization should be turned to New Guinea, there can be little doubt of the early extinction of the Papuan race. A warlike and energetic people, who will not submit to national slavery or to domestic servitude, must disappear before the white man as surely as do the wolf and the tiger. (455)

Naturalists like Wallace will miss nature and all that it contains—wildlife as well as wild men—when it finally disappears.

Despite his romantic inclinations, in 1864 Wallace declared, quoting the subtitle of *Origin of Species*, that the "great law of 'the preser-

vation of favoured races in the struggle for life' . . . leads to the inevitable extinction of all those low and mentally undeveloped populations with which Europeans come in contact" ("Origin of Human
Races," clxiv–clxv). Darwin had his "Malthusian moment," and so
did Wallace. Both were led to their insights about the mechanism of
evolution by Malthus's account of savage customs and the "struggle
for survival" among human populations. As James Moore puts it:
"Reading Malthus, [Wallace] grasped that living nature was in effect
the workhouse world writ large. Ruthless struggle was everywhere the
law, not just among London's starving poor. Adaptation comes
through competition. Progress costs lives" (293). Nevertheless, Wallace was more humane or at least more conflicted in his political out-
look than either Darwin or Huxley. Despite or perhaps because of his
application of the "great law" of survival of the fittest to savages and
barbarians, Wallace became both a socialist and "a spirited critic of
modern war and imperialism" (Crook, 57). Thus Wallace could
write:

> Naturalists need not be bound by the same rule as politicians, and may be per-
> mitted to recognize the just claims of the more ancient inhabitants, and to
> raise up fallen nationalities. The aborigines and not the invaders must be
> looked upon as the rightful owners of the soil. (Quoted in Moore, 290)

In contrast to most social Darwinists, who agreed with Huxley,
Spencer, and Francis Galton in opposing state interference in the
operations of the capitalist marketplace, Wallace added so-called free
trade to the causes of the extinction of primitive races. As George
Stocking notes, Wallace held that the "paternal despotism" of Dutch
imperialism in Indonesia was superior to British rule in India and
elsewhere, because the Dutch apparently understood that there were
"certain stages through which society must pass in its onward march
from barbarism to civilization" (Stocking, 100; Wallace, *Malay Archipelago*, 195–97). In contrast, the British insisted on immediate
change or conversion to civilization, so that "we demoralize and we
extirpate, but we never really civilize" (*Malay Archipelago*, 197).
British so-called free trade, as opposed to Dutch mercantilist monopoly, "invariably results in the extinction or degradation of 'the lower
race'" (*Malay Archipelago*, 223).

In considering "the action of natural selection on man," Wallace
contended that "from the time . . . when the social and sympathetic

feelings came into active operation, and the intellectual and moral faculties became fairly developed, man would cease to be influenced by 'natural selection' in his physical form and structure" ("Origin of Human Races," clxiii–clxiv). Indeed, already in "the rudest tribes" the force of "natural selection is . . . checked; the weaker, the dwarfish, those of less active limbs, or less piercing eyesight, do not suffer the extreme penalty which falls upon animals so defective" (11). Paradoxically, however, tribes able to protect their weaker members "would therefore have an advantage in the struggle for existence over other tribes in which they [the social virtues] were less developed, would live and maintain their numbers, while the others would decrease and finally succumb" (12). But this thought, in turn, leads to the conclusion, with which Galton certainly agreed, that the very ability of civilization to lessen or eliminate the operation of natural selection within its confines—a lessening that threatened, in turn, the eventual degeneration of the civilized—was the same process by which civilization was exterminating savagery throughout the world. "If my conclusions are just," writes Wallace, "it must inevitably follow that the higher—the more intellectual and moral—must displace the lower and more degraded races . . . till the world is again inhabited by a single nearly homogeneous race, no individual of which will be inferior to the noblest specimens of existing humanity" (26–27).

Wallace contends, then, that in its effects on humans, natural selection leads first to the survival of those humans who, at least within their own small groups, treat one another with moral consideration; morality enables such groups to eliminate less moral groups; the progress toward civilization is also moral progress, leading to the nearly total elimination of the operation of natural selection on humans; although this, in turn, threatens a weakening or degeneration of the highly civilized. Here morality, virtually identical with social organization, is the product of nature and natural selection; the elimination of less moral—that is, more savage—groups is simply an inevitable aspect of progress. In line with this theory of progress by way of natural selection, Wallace, like Huxley, offers a version of the gardening metaphor, only this time European colonists are the "weeds," exterminating "native productions":

> The red Indian in North America and in Brazil; the Tasmanian, Australian, and New Zealander in the southern hemisphere, die out, not from any one special cause, but from the inevitable effects of an unequal mental and physi-

cal struggle. The intellectual and moral, as well as the physical qualities of the European are superior; the same powers and capacities which have made him rise in a few centuries from the condition of the wandering savage with a scanty and stationary population, to his present state of culture and advancement, with a greater average longevity, a greater average strength, and a capacity for more rapid increase, — enable him when in contact with the savage man, to conquer in the struggle for existence, and to increase at the expense of the less adapted varieties in the animal and vegetable kingdoms, — just as the weeds of Europe overrun North America and Australia, extinguishing native productions by the inherent vigor of their organization, and by their greater capacity for existence and multiplication. (17)

Wallace reverses Huxley's identification of colonies with gardens and natives with weeds. This reversal expresses the division in Wallace's thinking between romantic primitivism and evolutionary theory, and between his anti-imperialist and anti-capitalist political inclinations and social Darwinism. Throughout his writings, Wallace attempted to combine these positions, just as he also sought to reconcile science and spiritualism.

In the conclusion to *The Malay Archipelago*, Wallace contends that, if the progress of civilization is at all a meaningful concept, then that progress must be leading humanity toward an "ideally perfect social state" (456). In such a state, every individual would be able to maximize his or her freedom, "intellectual organization," and morality, and to do so only by following "the free impulses of [human] nature" (456). Sounding like the Lévi-Strauss of *Tristes Tropiques* or, for that matter, like Rousseau, Wallace continues:

Now it is very remarkable that among people in a very low stage of civilization we find some approach to such a perfect social state. I have lived with communities of savages in South America and in the East, who have no laws or law courts but the public opinion of the village freely expressed. Each man scrupulously respects the rights of his fellow, and any infraction of those rights rarely or never takes place. In such a community, all are nearly equal. There are none of those wide distinctions, of education and ignorance, wealth and poverty, master and servant, which are the product of our civilization.

There is not even, Wallace continues, "that severe competition and struggle for existence, or for wealth, which the dense population of civilized countries inevitably creates" (456). This is still Wallace in

Malthusian mode, only reversing both Malthus's and most social Darwinian judgments about savagery, and also about the weakening and eventual elimination of the "struggle for existence" within civilized societies.

Wallace's *Wonderful Century* (1898) is mainly a paean to progress on many fronts of nineteenth-century European civilization, though he also considers its "failures." Among these are "the plunder of the earth," by which Wallace means both imperialism and capitalism. Here the operation of civilization on the noncivilized parts of the world is not merely the neutral action of natural selection or survival of the fittest but the immoral action of power and greed. In the chapter on "plunder of the earth," Wallace condemns the scramble for Africa that began in earnest after the Berlin Conference of 1884:

> The result, so far, has been the sale of vast quantities of rum and gunpowder; much bloodshed, owing to the objection of the natives to the seizure of their lands and their cattle; great demoralization both of black and white; and the condemnation of the conquered tribes to a modified form of slavery. (372)

So, too, in India and Ireland the results of British domination have been, says Wallace, "rebellion, recurrent famines, and plague in India; discontent, chronic want and misery; famines more or less severe, and continuous depopulation in our sister-island at home — these must surely be reckoned among the most terrible and most disastrous failures of the Nineteenth Century" (375). What is more, "if the Spaniards exterminated the natives of the West Indies, we have done the same thing in Tasmania, and almost the same in temperate Australia." Wallace adds that "in the estimation of the historian of the future," the Spaniards will be recognized as having "surpassed us," in part because:

> Their belief that they were really serving God in converting the heathen, even at the point of the sword, was a genuine belief shared by priests and conquerors alike — not a mere sham, as is ours when we defend our conduct by the plea of introducing the "blessings of civilization." (372–73)

Wallace may have been something of a "crank" or an intellectual faddist (see, e.g., Ruse, 156), but he was also less willing than Darwin, Huxley, Spencer, or even Tylor to biologize — that is, naturalize —

capitalism, war, imperialism, and the extinction of the noncivilized races through the supposed progress of white civilization. Both his socialist sympathies for the working class at home and his lengthy sojourns among "savage" peoples in South America and Indonesia helped Wallace approximate "the perceptive modes of modern anthropology," including its cultural relativism (Stocking, 99).

9. Conclusion
White Twilights

In *Gone Primitive* Marianna Torgovnick points out that modernist artists and intellectuals often placed a positive, even fetishistic premium on "savage" art and customs, but also that "ideas about primitive societies" have continued to support much less benign projects and politics: "Many events in this [twentieth] century would have been less possible without operative notions of how groups or societies deemed primitive become available to 'higher' cultures for conquest, exploitation, or extermination: the partition of Africa, the invasion of Ethiopia, the Nazi 'final solution' for Gypsies and Jews" (13). Torgovnick goes on to mention Vietnam, the Gulf War, and Western support for dictatorships in Zaire and elsewhere. The extent to which extinction discourse has contributed to such modern and now postmodern events is unclear, but Torgovnick is surely right to see even in positive conceptions of "primitive societies" imperialist and racist forms of othering that entail ideological temptations, at least, toward eliminating "the primitive" altogether. After all, once it is "gone," it can continue to be mourned and celebrated in both art and "salvage ethnography."

The national mourning involved in proleptic elegy, whether in the United States, Australia, or South Africa, is always also, whether explicitly or not, nationalist celebration. The creation first of the new white colony in the wilderness and then of the new nation-state demands the vanishing of the primeval others who cannot become or supposedly refuse to be part of its future. The most lethal aspect of extinction discourse has probably been its stress on the inevitability of that vanishing. The sense of doom has often been rendered all the more powerful by the combination of three elements: belief in the progress of at least some (chosen) peoples from savagery to civilization; the faith that progress is either providential or natural—God's or Nature's wise plan; and the idea that the white and dark races of the world are separated from each other by biological essences that, translated into Darwinian terms, equal "fitness" versus "unfitness" to survive. In all these ways, extinction discourse forms a powerful nexus of ideas that has been hegemonic for countless European explorers, colonists, writers, artists, officials, missionaries, humanitarians, and anthropologists. Albeit in less overtly racist terms, that general nexus of ideas is still at work in the insistence by the West that the rest of the planet must travel the road of capitalist economic development.

Today indigenous peoples, whether primitive or not, perhaps number 357 million (Hitchcock and Twedt, 487), most of them in China and India (only about 7 million inhabit the main regions covered by this study).[1] Many belong to societies and cultures that have been subjected to genocide in one form or another over the last three centuries. Many continue to be victims of genocidal practices. In their survey of the "physical and cultural genocide of indigenous peoples," Robert Hitchcock and Tara Twedt point out that during the twentieth century, "indigenous groups . . . disappeared at an unprecedented rate" (495); nor has anything changed in that regard in the twenty-first century.[2]

Deplorable though many of the effects of extinction discourse have been, at least that discourse has brought the vanishings of "the primitive" and of "savages" under some public and governmental scrutiny in many parts of the world. Despite contemporary sociobiology, the racial and social Darwinian components of extinction discourse have mostly given way to ideas and attitudes influenced by contemporary anthropology and cultural relativism. But these new, nonracist ideas have little purchase on the continuing destruction of so-called primitive or underdeveloped societies and cultures. What now seems inexorably destructive is not the auto-genocide of savagery nor the biological (racially determined) demise of the unfit, but the juggernaut of economic development, which to peoples trying to maintain traditional ways of life can be just as destructive as armed massacres.

Decolonization has brought few benefits to many indigenous peoples, largely because postcolonial governments have pursued the "one line of development" prescribed by the world's superpowers (Burger, *Report*, 8).[3] The vanishings of indigenous ways of life and populations continue to be mourned, of course, in postmodern, postcolonial literature, art, and anthropology. And yet with increasing frequency and sometimes effectiveness, indigenous peoples have been organizing and speaking up for themselves. The American Indian Movement and the Aboriginal Rights movement in Australia are just two examples; there exist today "many hundreds of indigenous peoples' organizations," such as the World Council of Indigenous Peoples (Burger, *Report*, 284).[4] "After 1950," writes James Clifford, "peoples long spoken for by Western ethnographers, administrators, and missionaries began to speak and act more powerfully for themselves on a global stage. It was increasingly difficult to keep them in their (traditional) places. Distinct ways of life once destined to merge into 'the modern world' reasserted their difference, in novel ways" (*Predicament*, 6). That is one hopeful aspect, at least, of our postmodern, supposedly postcolonial era.

From the 1880s to World War II, however, social Darwinism and the eugenics movement gave rise to much less hopeful ideas about the prospects of what many commentators called "the ruling race," or peoples of European origin. Toward the beginning of F. Scott Fitzgerald's *The Great Gatsby* (1925), Tom Buchanan announces, "Civilization's going to pieces. . . . I've gotten to be a terrible pessimist about things. Have you read 'The Rise of the Colored Empires' by this man Goddard?" (13). There is no book of that title, but Fitzgerald may be alluding to American eugenicist Henry Goddard, although another candidate is Lothrop Stoddard, author of *The Rising Tide of Color* (1920). Leading up to World War II, many books and articles expressing the same racial pessimism were published, among them *The Passing of the Great Race* (1916), by Madison Grant; *The Decline of the West*, by Oswald Spengler (1918); *The Menace of Colour* (1925), by John Walter Gregory; and *The Twilight of the White Races* (1926), by Maurice Muret.

With the troubling idea that the white race is "passing" while one or more of the "colored" races may supersede it, extinction discourse comes full circle. A variation of the "decline of the west" theme stressed that, through the civilizing process itself, the white race was committing suicide. The masses, so it was frequently claimed, were swamping the classes and subverting traditional values. Western civilization or indeed the entire human species was said to be devolving into its opposite, as in H. G. Wells's *Time Machine* (1895). Often, too, some non-white race was depicted as hugely prolific—hardly about to self-exterminate—and as threatening to invade and destroy white civilization. This is the premise, for example, of M. P. Shiel's 1898 invasion-scare novel, *The Yellow Danger*.[5]

Despite the hegemonic belief in the inevitable progress of (white) civilization, neither pre-Darwinian race science nor social Darwinism provided unequivocal support for that belief. If all species and races evolved, the white race was evolving, too, perhaps in a progressive, superhuman direction, though that was uncertain. Moreover, even if it was turning into something greater than itself, the white race would sooner or later vanish, experiencing the doom of the inferior races it had bested in the struggle for existence.

In *Vestiges of the Natural History of Creation* (1844), Robert Chambers had wondered: "Is our race but the initial of the grand crowning type?" (276). If *development*, Chambers's term for evolution, is the general rule throughout nature and for all time, why should it stop with "man" or with any other species? Moreover, if the development of a higher out of a lower species causes the extinction of the lower one, would not all existing humans one day be supplanted or exterminated by a superior species? Chambers imagines higher species, plural, ruling over a still extant humanity: "Are there yet to be species superior to us in organization, purer in feeling, more powerful in device and act, and who shall take a rule over us!" (276). He also briefly imagines the bleaker prospect of the extinction of humanity, one that Mary Shelley had explored in her apocalyptic fantasy, *The Last Man* (1826).[6] From the romantic era forward, the nightmare of the extinction of European civilization was a recurrent one, in part because progress could not go on forever and might even be its own undoing. These possibilities inform the greatest elegy of the Victorian era, Tennyson's *In Memoriam*, and also serve as increasingly standard themes in the emergent genre of science fiction, from *The Last Man* through Edward Bulwer-Lytton's *The Coming Race* (1872) to Wells's *Time Machine* (1895) and beyond.[7]

The thought that progress has limits haunted classical economics as well as natural history. Malthus's argument that population, unless checked, always outruns subsistence expresses this thought, as does David Ricardo's thesis of the declining rate of profits from the increased use of land or any other finite resource. So, too, in his *Principles of Political Economy* (1848), John Stuart Mill speculates anxiously about the culmination of social and economic progress in what he calls, echoing Adam Smith, "the stationary state" (2:753–56). Regarding race and evolution, however, the fear that white civilization might cause its own downfall was most dramatically expressed by Darwin's cousin Francis Galton and by the eugenics movement he pioneered.[8]

Galton drew from Darwin's work the conclusion that the blind mechanism of natural selection could and should be brought under control by human selection or eugenics, a term he coined in 1883. For his part, Darwin in *The Descent of Man* wrote of "the admirable labors of Mr. Galton" (28). With Galton, Darwin worried about how civilization protected its less fit specimens from the weeding-out effects of natural selection: "Thus the weak members of civilized societies propagate their kind," which "leads to the degeneration of a domestic race" (*Descent*, 138–39). At the same time, as George Searle notes, Darwin "doubted whether people could ever be persuaded to co-operate intelligently in the matter" (*Eugenics*, 4)—that is, in breeding a superior race that would not degenerate.

First in an 1865 article and then in *Hereditary Genius* (1869) Galton asserted that "Darwin's law of natural selection acts with unimpassioned, merciless severity. The weakly die in the battle for life; the stronger and more capable individuals are alone permitted to survive" ("Hereditary Talent," 323). But "modern industrial civilization," by permitting the propagation and survival of weaklings, "deteriorates the breed" ("Hereditary Talent," 326). According to Galton:

> One of the effects of civilization is to diminish the rigour of the application of the law of natural selection. It preserves weakly lives, that would have perished in barbarous lands. The sickly children of a wealthy family have a better chance of living and rearing offspring than the stalwart children of a poor one. ("Hereditary Talent," 326)

In contrast to what was happening within civilized societies (the "deterioration" of "the breed"), what was happening to uncivilized societies and races was the direct outcome of the "law" of natural selection, which was also—though only up to the point where civilization began—the main "law" of progress. Although Galton's travels in Africa and the Middle East gave him some appreciation of the great diversity of societies and cultures in the world, he nevertheless held stereotypic notions about "negroes" and "savages" and about the inevitable extinction of all "races" which were unable to meet the severe demands of the civilizing process (Kevles, 8; Stocking, 95). "The number of the races of mankind that have been entirely destroyed under the pressure of the requirements of an incoming civilization, reads us a terrible lesson," Galton asserts in a chapter entitled "The Comparative Worth of Different Races." He continues:

> Probably in no former period of the world has the destruction of the races of any animal whatever been effected over such wide areas and with such startling rapidity as in the case of savage man. In the North American Continent, in the West Indian Islands, in the Cape of Good Hope, in Australia, New Zealand, and Van Diemen's Land, the human denizens of vast regions have been entirely swept away in the short space of three centuries, less by the pressure of a stronger race than through the influence of a civilization they were incapable of supporting. (*Hereditary Genius*, 332–33)

As so often in other versions of extinction discourse, Galton blames "savage man" for self-extinguishing: rather than "the pressure of a stronger race," the main lethal mechanism is the inability of savages to "support" the "incoming civilization."

That primitive races perish on contact with civilization is, Galton believes, just as it should be—natural and inevitable. "The feeble nations of the world are necessarily giving way before the nobler varieties of mankind," he writes ("Hereditary Talent," 166). Those "feeble nations" or races are "unfit" to "support" civilization, which on his account is a hard taskmaster even for the civilized. Indeed, the "terrible lesson" Galton reads in the extinction of primitive races does not concern the possibility or impossibility of preserving even the remnants of those races. Rather, Galton thinks that the ordinary "denizens" of civilization are themselves not as capable as they should be to "support" it and to continue the work of progress.

> And we too, the foremost labourers in creating this civilization, are beginning to show ourselves incapable of keeping pace with our own work. The needs of centralization, communication, and culture call for more brains and stamina than the average of our race possess. (*Hereditary Genius*, 333)

In short, "our race" is threatened with "degeneracy," if not yet with extinction. Improving the white (or just the Anglo-Saxon) race both physically and mentally was the central aim of the eugenics movement that Galton pioneered. And while Galton imagined giving prizes to very "fit" young men and women who agreed to marry ("Hereditary Talent," 165), other eugenicists such as Karl Pearson, R. R. Rentoul, and Arnold White emphasized the sterilization of the "unfit"—indeed, their "extirpation" (White, *Efficiency and Empire*, 117). Both the rhetoric and the main emphasis of the eugenics movement were thus negative in tendency: it was more concerned with preventing degeneration and "race suicide" than with rescuing or improving races abroad or even with a possible utopia of racial fitness at home (Childs, 2; Stocking, 145).

The key problem for Galton and his followers was to reverse the process through which civilization blunted the natural selection of the fittest while encouraging the unfit to spawn. Galton opined that "England has certainly got rid of a great deal of refuse through . . . emigration," but that only transplanted the problem to the colonies, while merely treating the symptom instead of the disease at home (*Hereditary Genius*, 346). In eugenics discourse from Galton forward, the unfit were typically identified with the "refuse" or "residuum"— that is, with the "lower classes"—of London and other cities, as in White's 1886 diatribe, *The Problems of a Great City*.[9] "Compared with the nomadic tribes of tropic countries, where the curse of civilization is unknown," White asserted, "the nomads of London are but miserable savages" who should not be allowed to propagate their kind (14). Indeed, though without quite advocating killing them (his favored methods are sterilization and lifelong incarceration), White looks for ways that "would lead to the extermination of the unfit as a class" (*Problems*, 31). The slums are breeding grounds, eugenicists maintain, for "degenerates" of all sorts—criminals, lunatics, sexual deviants, the mentally and physically "feeble." In *Hereditary Genius*, Galton claims that the overcrowded life of the great cities is physically and mentally corrupting, so that "the race gradually deteriorates, becoming in each successive generation less fitted for a high civilization . . . until . . . the whole political and social fabric caves in, and a greater or less relapse to barbarism takes place" (346–47).

White believed that the claims he had made about racial degeneration in *The Problems of a Great City* were borne out by the Boer War (*Efficiency*, 18–32; see also Searle, *Quest*, 34–53). So bad was the situation by 1901 that "unfitness" and "ineffeciency" ruled. Although maintaining that the "unfit" triumphed over the "fit" by out-populating the latter, White could nevertheless declare: "The present generation of the unfit is doomed" (*Efficiency*, 116). This is a familiar contradiction in turn-of-the-century European and American thinking, based as much on Malthus as on Darwin or Francis Galton. How could the "unfit" be doomed if they were swamping the "fit"? On the contrary, from the eugenics standpoint, it was the "fit" that were doomed, unless the eugenics program of better breeding was quickly adopted.

Between the 1890s and World War II, the eugenicist movement became a major influence in the development of cultural modernisms in many countries, ranging from Britain to Brazil and the United States to Russia (Bradshaw, 35). According to William Greenslade, the appeal of eugenics stemmed from the "growing sense" of contradiction "between the rhetoric of progress . . . and the facts on the ground, the evidence in front of people's eyes, of poverty and degradation at the heart of ever richer empires" (15). Not only had Alfred Russel Wallace's "wonderful century" not led to the abolition of poverty, but it had ended in a new set of anxieties about the threat of the unruly masses. Though the "residuum" disappointed Marxists and socialists by appearing to have little or no interest in revolution, its members continued to reproduce their numbers and, hence, "poverty and degradation," just as Malthus had predicted in 1798. So the fear of racial decline and the desire to do something about it were expressed across the gamut of political positions, from socialist to reactionary.

Starting with his 1893 essay "On Extinction," in which he meditates on the demise both of numerous plant and animal species and of human races, H. G. Wells expresses similar anxieties about racial degeneration in many of his stories and essays. Like other Fabian Socialists, Wells advocated eugenics including, as he put it in *Anticipations* (1901), the elimination of "countless, needless, and unhappy lives" (328) through "the euthanasia of the weak" (332). In *The Time Machine*, some eight hundred thousand years into the future, Wells's inventive hero comes upon the entropic ruins of humanity, which has degenerated into two hostile but symbiotic species, the Elois and Morlocks. The cause of this dismal outcome is progress itself—indeed, nothing less than the "triumph" of "the true civilising process" (26). Though in their symbiosis the two species may be the ossified result of class conflict, they seem just as clearly to reflect the violence and insanity of racial conflict, themes also in Wells's *War of the*

Worlds and *The Island of Dr. Moreau*. The narrator of *War* says that, before judging the Martian invaders "too harshly,"

> we must remember what ruthless and utter destruction our own species has wrought, not only upon animals, such as vanished bison and the dodo, but upon its own inferior races. The Tasmanians . . . were entirely swept out of existence in a war of extermination waged by European immigrants, in the space of fifty years. Are we such apostles of mercy as to complain if the Martians warred in the same spirit? (311)

Between 1871 and World War I, many works of fiction depicted invasions of Britain, North America, or Western Europe by races or species from other continents and sometimes planets.[10] Besides anxiety about the inevitable degeneration and demise even of successful races and species, after Darwin there were at least two other reasons for the pessimistic application of extinction discourse to the white race. One was the huge and evidently growing populations of several non-white races, notably the Chinese and Japanese, but also central Africans and African Americans, the former slaves. The second was that many of the supposedly feeble races—the Australians, for instance—were not dying out as rapidly and completely as had often been predicted. In the American context, by the turn of the century, though versions of extinction discourse still maintained otherwise, Native Americans did not show signs of completely vanishing, and wishful thinking about the disappearance of "the Negro race" found little or no supporting evidence. Although predictions of the demise of the former slaves were made through the 1890s and beyond, the census figures of 1870, 1880, and 1890 offered contrary data, and even supported one forecast that, by 1980, the black population of the United States would reach 192 million (Frederickson, 240). Here was a "black-population peril" to match fantasies about the "yellow peril" inspired by Chinese immigration to North America and Australia, by the Boxer Rebellion of 1900, and by the Russo-Japanese War of 1904–5.

In *Passing of the Great Race*, Madison Grant comments on the "bitter opposition of the [white] Australians and Californians to the admission of Chinese coolies and Japanese farmers," and adds that this opposition "is due primarily to a blind but absolutely justified determination to keep those lands as white man's countries" (79).[11] Perhaps the most sensationally paranoid expression of the "yellow peril" theme came just two years before the Boxer uprising of 1900, in Shiel's *Yellow Danger*.[12] Its villain, Dr. Yen How, who is of both Chinese and Japanese descent, devises a nearly successful plan to overwhelm and exterminate the entire white race. As in Knox's *Races of Men*, hatred of other races, apparently innate or instinctual, is the main motivating factor in history. Shiel's representation of the white race, moreover, is not much more positive than that of the yellow race, because Yen How almost succeeds: "the cupidity and blind greed of the white races [*sic*] could be used by the yellow man as a means to the yellow man's triumph; the white races could be made to exterminate each other preparatory to the sweep, in hundreds of millions, of the yellow man over an exhausted and decimated Europe" (49). This diabolical scheme is thwarted, however, by one Thomas Hardy, a young naval genius with the very best Anglo-Saxon, seafaring blood in his veins, who destroys hundreds of enemy ships (French, German, Russian, Italian, Chinese, Japanese—it doesn't matter, Hardy's brilliant tactics sink them all), and partly through capturing and infecting several hundred "Chinamen" with cholera and then releasing them back on the continent, now almost wholly overrun by the "yellow race." This bit of biological warfare exterminates 150 million of the "yellow" invaders, with Shiel's apparent approval.[13]

In *Colonial Desire*, Robert Young notes: "There is always something comforting about the doom and gloom that the threat of deterioration holds, providing a solace of inevitability as it re-affirms the fall" (100). The mode of proleptic elegy, typical of extinction discourse, is indeed "obliquely comforting," even when its object is not some dark, supposedly inferior race, but the supposedly superior white race, founder and ruler of civilizations and empires. The mourning and moralizing doomster loses his or her sense of personal inadequacy in the grand apocalypse of nations, empires, or races. Nothing can be one's personal fault if everything is falling to pieces. That is one reason why "terminal visions," to use Warren Wagar's phrase for end-of-the-world fantasies, have flourished for the last century and more. Writing about the decades prior to 1914, Wagar declares that "almost every sort of world's end story . . . was written, published, and accepted by a wide reading public":

> Great world wars that devastated civilization were fought in the skies and on imaginary battlefields dwarfing those of Verdun and Stalingrad. Fascist dicta-

torships led to a new Dark Age, class and race struggles plunged civilization into Neolithic savagery, terrorists armed with super-weapons menaced global peace. Floods, volcanic eruptions, plagues, epochs of ice, colliding comets, exploding or cooling suns, and alien invaders laid waste to the world. (20)

Whether this flourishing of apocalyptic fantasy was a result of end-of-century, millennialist dreaming or more specifically foreshadowed "the real-life cataclysm of 1914," writers of such "terminal visions," Wagar notes, "did not miss their chances" (20). Through the last century into this one, moreover, those who prophesy the demise of the white race or Western civilization have been just as vociferous as those who continue to maintain that so-called primitive races will soon vanish from the face of the earth. Unless it comes true in the most total, apocalyptic sense, it seems that extinction discourse is here to stay.

Notes

Chapter 1. Introduction

1. Linear-temporal hierarchizing of the races both preceded and was reinforced by Darwinian evolutionary theory. But Darwin's *Origin* offered a different way of thinking about the emergence and spread of species (and all populations of organisms) on the analogy of trees or "bushes" rather than "ladders." See Gould, *Ever since Darwin*, 56–62.

2. On racial otherness in relation to Gothic literary conventions, see Malchow, *Gothic Images of Race in Nineteenth-Century Britain*.

3. For the three stages of historical development, see, for example, Tylor, *Anthropology*:

> The lowest or *savage* state is that in which man subsists on wild plants and animals, neither tilling the soil nor domesticating creatures for his food. . . . Men may be considered to have risen into the next or *barbaric* state when they take to agriculture. . . . Lastly, *civilized* life may be taken as beginning with the art of writing, which by recording history, law, knowledge and religion for the service of ages to come, binds together the past and the future in an unbroken chain of intellectual and moral progress. (24)

4. Thus, in New South Wales in 1838, Eliza Hamilton Dunlop responded to the Myall's Creek massacre, in which twenty-eight aboriginals were slaughtered and their corpses burned by a gang of white stock herders, with her poem, "The Aboriginal Mother (From Myall's Creek)." In a lullaby of horror, the mother croons to her infant her grief for her murdered husband and firstborn son:

> Oh hush thee, dear—for weary
>   And faint I bear thee on—
> His name is on thy gentle lips,
>   My child, my child, *he's gone!*
> Gone o'er the golden fields that lie
>   Beyond the rolling cloud,

To *bring thy people's murder cry*
Before the Christian's God.

Yes! o'er the stars that guide us,
    He brings my slaughter'd boy:
To shew their God how treacherously
    The stranger men destroy;
To tell how hands in friendship pledged
    Piled high the fatal pire;
To tell—to tell of the gloomy ridge!
    And the *stockmen's human fire.*
                    (Leonard, 391)

Later in the century the Melbourne poet Henry Kendall also penned a number of last-savage "songs," including "The Last of His Tribe" (1864) and "Aboriginal Death Song" (1869). Both these poems mention war, loss, and death, but the aboriginals' enemies are not white invaders; instead, they are other aboriginals—instances of savagery extirpating savagery. See also my comments in chapter 3 on Longfellow's *Hiawatha* and in chapter 4 on Thomas Pringle's poetry.

5. See, for instance, Žižek, *The Sublime Object of Ideology*: "The Lacanian subject is . . . identical to a lack" (122). From such a perspective, nationalism, or just national identity, is a form of fetishism covering over or disguising that lack.

6. Claude Lévi-Strauss's *Tristes Tropiques* is perhaps the best-known example of anthropological mourning. "In the America of the Indians," Lévi-Strauss writes, "I cherish the reflection, however fleeting it may have now become, of an era when the human species was in proportion to the world it occupied" (150). On this account, anthropology is not only a mournful science but an impossible one because, as Rousseau put it in his "Discourse on Inequality," "philosophers who have examined the foundations of society have all felt the necessity of going back to the state of nature, but none of them has ever reached it" (*The Essential Rousseau*, 144).

7. These figures are, needless to say, suspect. For the Maori population, see Ian Pool and also Belich, *Making Peoples*, 178.

8. This American publication was based on Wood's multipart *Natural History of Man*. For Wood and his role as a "popular science" writer who "refused to accept the application of Darwin's ideas to human beings," see Lorimer (218–19), who argues that post-Darwinian popularizers such as Wood, Brown, Edward Clodd, and Augustus Henry Keane, not all of whom supported the theory of evolution, were much more influential in terms of public opinion than Robert Knox and other pre-Darwinian race scientists. Given the usual lag between supposedly expert ideas and public opinion, this is a reasonable assessment.

9. Reviewing several 1992 books, including David Stannard's *American Holocaust*, the historian J. H. Elliott declares that "holocaust," "genocide," and "even 'racism'" and "imperialism" are an "emotive vocabulary" of "moral outrage" inappropriate for explaining what really happened to Native Americans. Needless to say, Native American authors do not shy away from "emotive" terms such as "genocide": see, for instance, Churchill, *Little Matter of Genocide*; Churchill's contributions to Charny's *Encyclopedia of Genocide*; and also the essays in Jaimes. For the text of the UN Convention on Genocide, as well as a variety of social-scientific attempts to define and analyze genocide, see Hinton, 1–23.

10. Diamond's study of "the fates of human societies" offers a sweeping account of the thirteen thousand years since the last Ice Age, a story of human populations and cultures in collision, often with fatal results for the technologically less-advanced populations. In this way it is similar to nineteenth-century versions of world history as the collision of races, with the key difference that race has no part in Diamond's narrative. On the contrary, the main factor is technological innovation: at its most basic, Diamond's thesis is that "empires with steel weapons were able to conquer or exterminate tribes with weapons of stone and wood" (16). See also Michael Adas, *Machines as the Measure of Man*. Nevertheless, "germs" were just as destructive as guns. For disease as a factor in the age of

modern imperialism, see, besides Diamond, Arnold, *Imperial Medicine and Indigenous Societies;* Crosby, *Ecological Imperialism;* Kunitz, *Disease and Social Diversity;* and MacLeod and Lewis, *Disease, Medicine, and Empire.*

11. In his *Victims of Progress,* John Bodley offers figures on "tribal depopulation" around the world; the estimated total depopulation is 27,860,000, and, of that total, 9,310,000 is the figure for North America since 1800 (40). Of course, depopulation was going on long before 1800. Moreover, given the persistent temptation to underestimate indigenous populations at the time of European invasions, the figure since 1800 may well be greater. See also Hitchcock and Twedt, "Physical and Cultural Genocide of Various Indigenous Peoples."

12. For another recent estimate that an indigenous population was much larger than earlier estimates, see Stannard, *Before the Horror.*

13. As we shall see in chapter 5, however, the claim of total extinction of the Tasmanians is questionable.

14. As proleptic elegy or premature celebration or both, extinction discourse has also downplayed or ignored the resistance, survival, and achievements of "first peoples" throughout the world. "If the victims of progress and empire are weak," writes Clifford, "they are seldom passive": "Throughout the world indigenous populations have had to reckon with the forces of progress and national unification. The results have been both destructive and inventive. Many traditions, languages, cosmologies, and values are lost, some literally murdered; but much has simultaneously been invented and revived in complex, oppositional contexts" (*Predicament,* 16).

15. Compare Marx and Engels, who, in *The Communist Manifesto,* declare: "The bourgeoisie, by the rapid improvement of all instruments of production . . . draws all, even the most barbarian, nations into civilisation. The cheap prices of its commodities are the heavy artillery with which it batters down all Chinese walls. . . . It compels all nations, *on pain of extinction,* to adopt the bourgeois mode of production" (477; my emphasis). The elimination of the primitive is not just a tragic side effect of modernization; as this passage suggests, it is its definition and destination.

Bauman also contends, with Hannah Arendt, that too much emphasis on the uniqueness of the Nazi holocaust can lead to underestimating or overlooking the routine ways it came about—through perfectly normal bureaucratic decision making, for example. And no matter how unique the Nazi holocaust may have been in some respects, there have been numerous genocides—or attempted genocides—throughout history. See Rosenbaum, Charny, Hinton, and Rummel, among others. For the case that modernization, in the sense of economic and industrial "development," has been the main cause of the extinction of primitive societies and cultures, see Bodley.

16. For "twentieth-century cases of genocide of indigenous peoples," see Hitchcock and Twedt, table 2 at 496–97.

Chapter 2. Pre-Darwinian Theories on the Extinction of Primitive Races

1. In this regard, although Elazar Barkan is certainly right that "scientific racism" has been in "retreat" since World War II, it has hardly disappeared. See his *Retreat of Scientific Racism* but compare Chase, Dubow, Graves, and Jacoby and Glauberman.

2. On the history and influence of Chambers's bestseller, see Secord.

3. As Martin Rudwick points out in *The Meaning of Fossils,* Georges Cuvier's comparative anatomical studies of the fossilized remains, especially of mammoths and mastodons, made the topic of the extinction of species unavoidable. Cuvier's 1796 paper, "On the Species of Living and Fossil Elephants," first presented "the world of science . . . with detailed and almost irrefutable evidence for the reality of extinction" (Rudwick, 101).

4. Both Ricardo's and Smith's proto-capitalist hunters and herdsmen are versions of Lévi-Strauss's savage *bricoleurs:* they are quasi-scientists—economists, anyway—*avant la lettre.* But unlike Lévi-Strauss's claims against the civilized and for the savage mind, Smith's and Ricardo's attributions of modern economic behavior to the precivilized express the failure of ethnographic imagination in economics. In doing so, they foreshadow

the World Bank and IMF ideology of capitalist development. As Marx also insisted, every society, no matter how different from the European model, must either become capitalist or perish (477). This is one Marxist prediction that has proven all too accurate.

5. For Prichard and the origins of British ethnology (or anthropology) in general, see Stocking. As Stocking observes, "In Britain in the 1850s, 'ethnology' was . . . the most general scientific framework for the study of the linguistic, physical, and cultural characteristics of dark-skinned, non-European, 'uncivilized' peoples" (47).

6. Because American ethnologists and race scientists are of special significance in relation to Native America, I examine Morton, Nott, and Glidden in more detail in the next chapter. But their work is of a piece with that of Count Gobineau in France and of Charles Hamilton Smith, Robert Knox, and James Hunt in Britain.

7. So, too, in his 1841 *Natural History of Society*, W. Cooke Taylor points to much evidence of "lost civilizations," with Rome an obvious illustration. Turning to the Americas, Taylor presents the descendants of the mound builders as the "savage" remnants of earlier "civilizations" which, however, were well on the way to self-liquidation before the advent of Europeans.

8. However, Smith then stresses "the duty of all to assert . . . the rights of humanity, in their indisputable plenitude; although to us . . . as mere naturalists, it is a bounden duty to confine ourselves to known historical and scientific facts" (168).

9. The *Dictionary of National Biography* accords Knox a good deal of respect as a scientist, and lists several major appointments and honors he received for his scientific work after 1850. According to his 1870 biographer, Henry Lonsdale: "Previous to his time, little or nothing was heard about Race in the medical schools: he changed all this. . . . Race became as familiar as household words . . . [and his ideas were] disseminated far and wide, both at home and abroad" (quoted in Banton, 59).

Douglas Lorimer argues, however, that both Knox and James Hunt were less influential than twentieth-century scholars have made them out to be. Perhaps so, but compare Stocking (64–65, 247). In terms of general readership, at least, such "popularizers" of "scientific images of race in the 1860s" and after as the Reverend John G. Wood, Robert Brown, Edward Clodd, and Augustus Henry Keane may well have been more influential. But in the 1850s and 1860s, Knox's and Hunt's version of racial determinism seems to have been just as prevalent as the views of the later figures, which were not all that different.

10. Matthew Arnold accepted the main terms of his father's race-based philosophy of history, while seeking to chasten and qualify Thomas Arnold's excessive Teutonism (Faverty, 76–77).

11. As Theodor Adorno puts it, "The world spirit's Hegelian migration . . . is the Migration of Nations blown up into metaphysics; the human steamroller of world history," whose "unity . . . animat[ing] the philosopher . . . is the unity of terror rolling over mankind" (341).

12. The idea that the separate races consist somehow of antagonistic, unchanging essences places Knox, like James Hunt, Gobineau, Nott, and Gliddon, closer to the modern, virulently paranoid, fascist, and Nazi varieties of racism than to Darwinism. The separate races, as pure essences, can only conquer and obliterate one another, or—just as tragically, Knox thinks—merge with one another through colonial hybridization (that is, through miscegenation). All racial amalgamations lead, sooner or later, to the infertility of the crossbreeds and to the absorption or dying out of the weaker races. History is thus always a downward spiral, a degeneration from a sort of edenic racial purity, with the biblical wages of sin—that is, death—at the end of the spiral. This is not to say that Knox invokes biblical authority to support what he considers to be his scientific, strictly materialist argument. But the pattern of history that any theory of racial essentialism entails is necessarily antiprogressive, a decline-and-fall narrative that at least parallels the Bible. Things fall apart, including races: once disintegration—that is, history—sets in, there is no reversing the process.

13. This elegiac language can also be heard in Ernest Renan's 1854 essay, "On the Poetry of the Celtic Races," which directly influenced Arnold's *On the Study of Celtic Literature* (Young, 68). According to Renan, all the Celtic races—Welsh, Scottish, Breton, and

Irish—are dying out, and with them their poetic "Gaelic genius." "Alas! it, too, is doomed to disappear, this emerald set in the western seas," Renan declares; "it is high time to note, before they shall have passed away, the divine tones thus expiring on the horizon before the growing tumult of uniform civilization" (412).

Chapter 3. Vanishing Americans

1. As in other contexts of colonization and empire, in the Americas estimates of aboriginal populations carry great ideological and political significance. For most of the twentieth century, the original indigenous population in North America was held to be no more than one million, the figure accepted by the Smithsonian Institute. Starting in the 1970s, anthropologists and demographers have revised that figure dramatically upward. Recent estimates place it at between nine and eighteen million. See Churchill, *Little Matter of Genocide*; Dippie; Jennings, 15–31; and Stannard.

2. A case in point is Roy Harvey Pearce's 1953 *Savagism and Civilization*, which reinforces even as it critiques the stereotypic antithesis of its title. In a variation on Frederick Jackson Turner's influential frontier thesis, Pearce argues that, from Puritan times to the present, "savagism" and "civilization" have been the poles around which white American culture has circulated. Further, though obviously sympathetic to "the Indian," Pearce is eager to pronounce the near-extinction of Native America as an episode of *early* United States history, one essentially completed before the 1850s. By that decade, Pearce claims, "psychological as well as physical Removal had been effected, and the Indian had become a creature of philanthropic agencies, scientific ethnology, and dime novels" (76). But "psychological" "removal" had hardly been effected, as the vast amount of discourse about "the Indian problem" spawned by "philanthropic agencies, scientific ethnology, and dime novels" indicates. Nor had "physical Removal . . . been effected": thousands of Indians remained east of the Mississippi; the western so-called Indian wars continued to the end of the nineteenth century; and Native American resistance has continued to the present, as Pearce well knew. But his assertion expresses a quite common, white American wish to get "the Indian problem" over and done with.

3. Besides Bergland, see Berkhofer, Dippie, Jennings, Lubbers, Maddox, Pearce, and many others.

4. In his *Two Treatises of Government*, Locke relates property to the ownership and cultivation of land, and its noncultivation to waste. He identifies "waste land" both with "Nature" and with the potential for great wealth, readily available throughout the world (he has North America especially in mind) for those who will settle on it, cultivate it, and convert it into productive property. And he also identifies property with the use of money. Throughout the world, he writes, "there are still great tracts of ground to be found, which the inhabitants thereof, not having joined with the rest of mankind in the consent of the use of their common money, lie waste, and are more than the people who dwell on it, do, or can make use of, and so still lie in common; though this can scarce happen amongst that part of mankind that have consented to the use of money" (139).

5. In *The Invasion of America*, Francis Jennings points out that the first English colonists were dependent on the Indians for food and for learning "how to grow strange crops under new conditions of soil and climate" as well as other survival techniques (40). "How, then," he asks, "did the observed data of the Indian peasant turn into the myth of the roaming savage?" In his 1822 *Report* on Indian affairs to the Secretary of War, Jedidiah Morse declared that "Indian title to their respective territories, is imperfect," in part because "in the *hunter state*" the amount of land "necessary to give support to any number of people . . . is vastly greater than is required . . . in the agricultural state" (68). Whereas Morse held out the hope that the Indians could be taught to settle down and farm, that notion seems to have evaporated with Indian "removal" in the 1830s. Contemplating the disappearance of the Sauks and Foxes from what is now Illinois, Thomas Farnham, in 1843, called the vanishing of "all the tribes" a "melancholy fact." Because they were wild and unwilling to buckle down to the routines of farming and improving the land, "The Indians' bones must enrich the soil, before the plough of the civilized man can open it" (Farnham, 142).

6. The causes Morgan lists for the decimations of the Iroquois and other Indian populations are, except for disease, cultural, not biological (*League*, 57, for example). Morgan also repeatedly uses the phrase "Indian races"; the plural noun does not refer to biological categories but to social groupings and is synonymous with "nations" and "tribes" (he uses all three terms interchangably).

7. The key texts are Lawrence Krader, ed., *The Ethnological Notebooks of Karl Marx*, and Friedrich Engels, *The Origin of the Family, Private Property and the State* (1884).

8. For the Removal Act, see Dippie, 56–78; Wallace.

9. According to another, more liberal but distinctly minority view, the quickest, surest way to civilize or assimilate the Indians was through intermarriage and miscegenation. Of course, even this pacific route to racial harmony involved the absorption and dilution of the Indian race by the white race, and of Indian culture by white culture. Nevertheless, this was the view espoused by the secretary of war William Crawford in 1816: "The utter extinction of the Indian race must be abhorrent to the feelings of an enlightened and benevolent nation. . . . When every effort to introduce among them ideas of separate property . . . shall fail, let intermarriages between them and the whites be encouraged by the Government. This cannot fail to preserve the race" (Prucha, 28).

10. "What can be more melancholy than their history?" wrote Justice Joseph Story in 1828: "By a law of their nature, they seem destined to a slow, but sure extinction" (quoted in Dippie, 1).

11. Within just the two years of 1823–24, notes Louise Barnett, "eight works of fiction" dealing with Indian–white conflicts appeared; from then "until the disappearance of the genre [the frontier romance] in the 1850s, the conventions of fiction which portrayed Indians and whites in a frontier setting were fixed" (61). But that genre did not disappear: it has reappeared in seemingly endless variations down to the present, if not in the form of canonical literature, accepted and taught in classes on American fiction, then as popular literature, dime novels, and "westerns" of the Hollywood variety, including Michael Mann's 1992 film adaptation of *The Last of the Mohicans* and beyond.

12. At the end of chapter 3, Natty announces that he is "a man, who, his very enemies will own, has no cross in his blood" (35); later references to his being a "man without a cross" refer back to this assertion about his racial purity. Earlier in the same chapter, Natty says to Chingachgook and Uncas: "I am not a prejudiced man, nor one who vaunts himself on his natural privileges, though the worst enemy I have on earth, and he is an Iroquois, daren't deny that I am genuine white" (31).

13. For the concept of the "Great Zero," see Lyotard, 1–13.

14. See also Irving's "Traits of Indian Character" in *The Sketchbook of Geoffrey Crayon*, 225–33.

15. For the question of the extinction of African-Americans, both before and after the Civil War, see Frederickson, 154–59, 245–52.

16. On racial "gifts" in the Leatherstocking novels, see Pearce, 196–212.

17. Here is a sampling of the adjectives that both the narrator and Natty apply to the Hurons and to other non–Delaware Indians: merciless, treacherous, thievish, greedy, lying, malignant, fierce, cunning, gluttonous, vindictive, and malicious. At times these ignoble qualities are attributed to *all* Indians, as when Natty says that "revenge is an Indian feeling" (183) or when he speaks of "Indian treachery" (52). Throughout, he refers to his "redskin" enemies as demons or devils: they are "imps," "hell-hounds" (70), "children of the devil" (76, 231), and "malicious demons" (237). He often also calls them "sarpents" or "skulking reptyle[s]" bent on "deviltry" (202). This is true even though the name of his bosom buddy Chingachgook means "big sarpent" (57), and even though, when the Bible-toting David Gamut says of Indians in general that "they are among the profanest of the idolatrous" (226), Natty jumps to their defense: "Therein you belie the nature of an Indian. Even the Mingo adores but the true and living God! 'Tis a wicked fabrication of the whites . . . that would make a warrior bow down before images of his own creation. It is true, they endeavour to make truces with the wicked one—as who would not with an enemy he cannot conquer!—but they look up for favor and assistance to the Great and Good Spirit only" (226).

18. In *Regeneration through Violence*, Richard Slotkin demonstrates the mythic centrality of captivity narratives to white American culture from the 1660s on (94–115). Slotkin notes that of the four prose narratives that were "bestsellers" between 1680 and 1720, three were captivity narratives and the fourth was John Bunyan's *Pilgrim's Progress*. So, too, Annette Kolodny points out that captivity narratives have been a staple of American culture down to our own time in fiction and film, and also that they were more complicated and contradictory than is usually acknowledged. While they were often provocations to intervention and even to the extermination of "the savages" who sometimes did capture whites, including white women and children, they sometimes also, by performing a sort of amateur ethnography, offer sympathetic accounts of Indian ways of life. Cooper's novel does both. On the one hand, it presents a sympathetic portrait of Natty Bumppo's favorite Indians, the "honest" Delawares and their "noble" but vanishing offshoot, the Mohicans. On the other hand, it presents Magua and the thieving, diabolical Hurons in a lurid light every bit as stereotypic as anything to be found in the crudest captivity narratives.

19. Quite apart from the evil machinations of Magua, who lusts after Cora, the grisliest episode in Cooper's novel reveals a "savagery" so ferocious as to demand its total extinction. When the British decamp from Fort William Henry, the French leave them at the mercy of the Hurons. One Huron, attracted by a shawl in which a mother has wrapped her baby, snatches both away and, with "a gleam of ferocity . . . dashed the head of the infant against a rock, and cast its quivering remains to her very feet" (175). When the mother falls on her knees to pray for deliverance, the Huron, "maddened" because another has grabbed the shawl, "and excited at the sight of blood . . . mercifully drove his tomahawk into her . . . brain" (175). There ensues a general massacre of the innocents by "more than two thousand raving savages" (176), during which "the flow of blood [became] a torrent; and as the natives became heated and maddened by the sight, many among them even kneeled to the earth, and drank freely, exultingly, hellishly, of the crimson tide" (176). This is the one instance in the story of cannibalism, which everywhere in imperialist discourse represents the absolute nadir of inhumanity—a sure sign that its practitioners are incapable of becoming civilized.

20. For the metaphor of Indians as children, see Rogin.

21. A famous example of the maturation metaphor occurs in Kant's 1784 essay, "Was ist Aufklärung?" Kant's answer is that Enlightenment as both a historical process and a period—the period that inaugurates *modern* history—is the progress of society from immaturity to adulthood. And maturity, Kant says, means the achievement of full Enlightenment or of the full exercise of public, democratic, and scientific reason for human betterment. A version of Kant's argument is inscribed today in development discourse, according to which societies that possess advanced economic and political capacities are said to be "mature"; the so-called underdeveloped societies of the so-called Third World are said to be "immature," like Cooper's "childish" Indians. But as André Gunther Frank and other critics of the ideology of "development" have contended, it is not the case that the supposed immaturity of, say, Iraq, Bosnia, or Vietnam is just a natural stage through which those nation-states are inevitably passing, on the progressive road to modern "maturity." Frank contends that the "underdevelopment" of the so-called Third World is the result of the "development" of the First World. In other words, the supposed "maturation" or modernization of some nation-states occurs at the expense of the *imposed* "immaturity" or infantilization of others.

22. Given Mann's "obsession with even the smallest detail" regarding everything from "the colors and patterns of each tribe's war paints" to finding "the few remaining old-growth forests that most resembled the terrain Cooper wrote about," the film's erasure of Cooper's sentimental racism is, to say the least, ironic. Mann "insisted on building everything from the muskets to the fort from scratch, using original materials" (Ansen, 49). But although Mann pursued historical details obsessively, he failed to see the big picture— that is, *the* central message of Cooper's proleptic elegy. Mann even reverses the roles of Cora and Alice, thereby obliterating the tragic mulatta motif of the novel: in the film, not Cora but the blonde, blue-eyed Alice dies at the end, committing suicide to escape from Magua.

Perhaps the movie semi-compensates for its erasure of Cooper's sentimental racism by converting the aging Natty Bumppo into the young, gorgeous Daniel Day-Lewis, who falls in love with the equally gorgeous, albeit raven-haired, Cora, played by Madeleine Stowe. The movie is certainly sexier than the novel, but the film love affair between Natty and Cora also obliterates the erotic element in Cooper's story, which is specifically *both* interracial and racist: the attraction both Magua and Uncas feel toward Cora. When it comes to sex, Cooper's Natty Bumppo is even more childlike than the Indians.

For other renditions of *Last of the Mohicans*, see Barker and Sabin; in their not always very critical compilation, they declare Mann's movie to be simply "splendid" (vii).

23. See, for example, H. Daniel Peck, who compares Cooper to more "realistic" (that is, partly, less philanthropically sentimental) "writers of the frontier" like Robert Montgomery Bird, whose *Nick of the Woods* (1837) depicts all Indians as diabolical savages deserving only to be slaughtered. In contrast to Bird, Peck's Cooper is an almost saintly early American mythologizer who faithfully records "the tragedy" of the Indians' "dispossession" (Peck does not use any stronger term like "genocide").

Chapter 4. Humanitarian Causes

1. So, too, as Mary Wollstonecraft argued in A *Vindication of the Rights of Women*, the rights of men applied to women, and at least by implication—especially through her application of the word *slavery* to women's situation everywhere—to the human race, singular.

2. In 1838 Buxton claimed that the slave trade, even after Britain had outlawed it, "requires at the rate of a thousand human beings per diem, in order to satisfy its enormous maw" (448).

3. According to Blackburn: "Just as abolitionist legislation helped the [British] oligarchy to assert its right to rule and deflect middle-class agitation for reform, so in the industrial districts middle-class abolitionism helped manufacturers to outface menacing combinations, cement ties with other respectable persons and assert their social conscience" (315).

4. Exeter Hall was the London meeting place of evangelical groups, including missionary societies. The London *Times* for May 10, 1854, declared: "It is of no use to say that there is misery enough in Bethnal-green, and ignorance enough within a mile of St. Paul's, to occupy all the energies of philanthropy or charity. . . . This is not the kind of wretchedness to be purveyed every May for the Exeter-hall sympathisers" (quoted in Galbraith, 75).

5. English terminology for African populations is variable, to say the least. I use "Caffre War" to refer to the 1834–35 conflict, because that is the spelling in the *Report* of the Aborigines Committee. I use "Xhosa" rather than either "Caffre" or "Kaffir"—sometimes spelled "Kafir"—because that is the current term for the "ama-Xhosa" or "Xhosas," plural.

6. Besides Buxton, the other members of the Aborigines Committee were also abolitionists. These included, among others, Joseph Pease, the first Quaker member of Parliament; the abolitionist leader Charles Lushington; the colonial administrator Sir George Grey; and William Gladstone, the future prime minister, then at the start of his career. Gladstone was the only Tory member of the committee (he later became a Liberal).

7. The evangelical bent of the committee is also evident from its summary: "He who has made Great Britain what she is, will inquire at our hands how we have employed the influence He has lent to us in our dealings with the untutored and defenceless savage" (*Report*, 2:76).

8. Cf. MacCrone: "It was not until some time after the beginning of the eighteenth century that the commando system, as a characteristic feature of frontier life, began to take shape. In 1715 the raids by Bushmen on the herds of the farmers were more than usually serious" (102). The commando system reached one climax in "the elaborately organized campaign of 1774 in which the whole of the northern frontier from the Camdeboo to the Oliphants River was involved. . . . From this time on, the northern frontier remained in a state of chronic border warfare and the Bushman became a sort of 'public

enemy (No. 1)' to be shot at sight and out of existence" (104). Further, there was "no question of exercising any kind of official control over the activities of individual comman-dos. . . . The decline of the [Dutch East India] Company's authority over the frontier dis-tricts that were most exposed to the attacks of the Bushmen was very nearly complete by this time. The official policy itself had become one of 'extirpation of the said rapacious tribes'; and there could be no more effective instrument in the service of that policy than a commando of aggrieved frontier farmers" (105). See also L. Thompson (49).

9. Promoting both the antislavery and the aborigines protection movements were missionaries of many denominations in colonial outposts. The evangelical revival of the late eighteenth century had led to a proliferation of missionary societies from the 1790s on, including the Baptist Missionary Society (1792), the London Missionary Society (1795), the Glasgow Missionary Society (1796), the Church Missionary Society (1799), the British and Foreign Bible Society (1804), the American Board of Commissioners for For-eign Missions (1810), and the Wesleyan Methodist Missionary Society (1813).

10. As Buxton's *Memoirs* puts it, Glenelg "had come to the conclusion that the Ade-laide territory had been unjustly taken away from the Caffre people. Accordingly, with a regard for justice as rare as it was noble, his lordship determined not to acquiesce in our usurpation of the territory, but to restore it to its rightful possessors" (379).

11. See also Robert Ross: "The power of evangelical humanitarians in Britain, whose allies a number of the South African missionaries were, resulted in a major restructuring of the legal relationships in the [Cape] Colony. First, in 1828, all legal disabilities on the free people of colour, particularly the Khoisan [Hottentots], were removed by Ordinance 50. The impulse for this measure . . . derived from . . . Dr. John Philip" (37). Ross goes on to name the abolition of slavery as the second "major restructuring," one that for many Boers was a last straw, the final motivating factor behind the Great Trek, which in turn led to the creation of a series of transient "republics," at first beyond British influence and then claimed as British: Natal, the Orange Free State, the Transvaal.

12. According to Monica Wilson, "Between 1715 and 1862 the hunters were hunted, al-most as they themselves hunted animals, for many white farmers thought and spoke of them as if they were animals, and thousands were killed. . . . After 1715 *trekboers* en-croached further into 'Bushman country.' By the 1770s conflict was so intense that *trek-boer* commandos systematically exterminated the San, while San raids forced *trekboers* to abandon farms" ("The Hunters and Herders," 71). In short, throughout the eighteenth century, according to M. F. Katzen, "the San were systematically exterminated" (184). Other recent histories and ethnographies bear Philip out about the deliberate, obviously genocidal attempts to exterminate the Bushmen. Thus, according to Robert Ross: "The burgher (citizen) militias known as commandos received permission from the Cape gov-ernment to 'extirpate' the San [Bushmen], thus formalising their genocidal practice which had been in operation for most of the century. Hundreds of San were killed in these operations, and the children were taken as *de facto* slaves" (23).

13. Macmillan notes that "generations of South African children have learnt from teachers and textbooks of a Philip they must deem to have been *wicked*; even in the 1960's hardly a month or a week passed without some example of a Nationalist politician or scribe resorting to the use of the name 'Dr. Philip' as the most comprehensive term of abuse possible" (10).

14. Not to be mistaken for the *Edinburgh Review*, the *Edinburgh Magazine* was later renamed *Blackwood's Magazine*.

15. There are several reasons not to treat Pringle's *African Sketches* as some kind of originary work or fountainhead of South African literature in English, though it has been so treated by Stephen Gray and earlier critics. First, like H. Rider Haggard and a number of other later writers, Pringle was in South Africa for only a few years. Second, the creation of a more or less unified nation-state in South Africa was nearly a century away. Third, Pringle's poetry is highly derivative, imitative of other romantic writers, including Pringle's patron and friend, Sir Walter Scott.

16. For *Makanna* and also Kendall's *The English Boy*, see, besides Stephen Gray, Ian Glenn's "The Bushman in Early South African Literature." Glenn, in turn, cites Mar-

tineau's *Life in the Wild* (1832) as the "first English South African novel" (46), even though Martineau had never been to South Africa.

17. Pringle writes: "That the ignorant Dutch-African boors should exhibit great jealousy of the political importance and equal privileges conferred on a race of people whom they had from infancy been accustomed to regard as an inferior caste, doomed to be hewers of wood and drawers of water to the 'Christians,' was not at all surprising" (250).

18. Hodgkin's disease is named for his research on it.

19. From the start, Hodgkin "did most of the work" of the organization (Kass, 271), sometimes serving as its sole source of money and its only publicist.

20. In Namibia and Botswana, the few San or Bushmen who remained in the Kalahari Desert have been relocated in settlements outside the boundaries of the new national parks.

21. Governor D'Urban wanted to banish the Xhosas totally from the Albany and Queen Adelaide areas but, as already noted, Lord Glenelg reversed D'Urban's policy. This minor triumph for the humanitarian cause fueled Boer resentment and did nothing to prevent future conflicts (Wilson, "Co-Operation and Conflict," 243).

22. Wilson points out that this response, though extreme especially in the extent of the sacrifice of property to bring about the millennium, was similar to the reactions of other aboriginal groups to invasion and defeat elsewhere in the world ("Co-Operation and Conflict," 260).

23. At the time of the 1834–35 war, Robert Godlonton and other supporters of colonial expansion portrayed the Xhosas as "marauding hordes" of savages streaming into the peaceful settlements of Albany without cause or warning, even though Albany was their territory. The Xhosas were not often depicted as so totally warlike and ferocious as the Zulus, but they were nevertheless, according to Godlonton, treacherous, thieving, and bloodthirsty. And they were behaving like the Zulus: waging war for the sake of war, and threatening, at least, to exterminate white colonists and peaceful blacks alike. For Godlonton, the complete destruction of the Xhosas or any other savage tribe that refused to accept the great boon of white civilization was not too high a price to pay for turning all of South Africa into white-owned territory.

24. The historian of the APS, H. R. Fox Bourne, has nothing but praise for Sir George Grey, whose "policy was in substantial agreement with that persistently urged by the Society . . . and the splendid work done by him was most gratifying proof of the soundness of the views it had so repeatedly put forward" (19). This, even though Grey had been governor of the Cape during the cattle-killing and famine of 1857–58 and was suspected by the Xhosas to have been "hiding in the reeds by the Gxarha [River], whispering to Nongqawuse" (Ross, 53; see also Trollope, *South Africa*, 1:44).

25. G. M. Theal speaks of "the awful destruction of human life by the wars of Tshaka," but says "European dominion" brought this to a halt, so that "the surviving Bantu could emerge from the mountains and deserts and cultivate the ground and breed cattle once more" (341). With peace, the Bantu flourished, because European law removed the Malthusian checks in the form of murderous savage customs against population growth, and the Bantu are "a people possessing greater power of increasing their number rapidly than any other on the face of the earth" (Theal, *The Yellow and Dark-Skinned People*, 341). Instead of the automatically depopulating savage, the Bantu represent the specter of the overpopulating savage—the threat implicit in the word *horde*, which, of course, also suggests anarchy rather than organization.

26. In *The Destruction of Aboriginal Society*, C. D. Rowley notes that the legislative implications of the *Report* are obvious: "the 'native' must be protected; and to be protected he must be the subject of special legislation." This leads, in turn, to legalized patterns of discrimination, because "protective legislation is inevitably discriminatory in effect. Moreover, the categories of protected persons are often most easily defined in racial terms. The very attempt to protect the 'native' British subject in such rights as are to be left to him involves a separate status in law, which places him at the discretion and the mercy of the protecting agencies" (20).

Chapter 5. The Irish Famine

1. For parallels between the Irish and Native Americans in the discourse of the conquering and colonizing English, see also Canny, O'Toole, and Rawson. Other historians of white representations of Native Americans also note these parallels (Drinnon, 32–33; Jennings, 45–46).

2. On the Western, ideological stereotyping of non-Western peoples as cannibals, see Barker, Hulme, and Iverson.

3. In *Paddy and Mr. Punch* (1993), R. F. Foster points out that the historical revisionism of twenty (now thirty) years ago has been re-revised, partly by restoring earlier verdicts—although this "does not make [the revisionists'] new-wave critics anti-revisionist" (79). For reviews of revisionist historiography on the Famine, see Mary Daly and Graham Davis.

4. According to Senior, "The English resolved that the Irish should not starve. We resolved that, for one year at least, we would feed them. But we came to a third resolution, inconsistent with the first, that we would not feed them for *more* than a year" (1:209). It is this third resolution that, from Senior's perspective, returns the English safely to scientific principles. But Senior's opinions and proposals about Ireland evolved from the 1830s through the period of the Famine and its aftermath. During the Famine itself, he became more, not less orthodox in terms of the Malthusian and laissez-faire doctrines of capitalist economics. For the development of Senior's views about Ireland, and for a nuanced account of views and proposals among especially liberal, English leaders during the Famine itself, see Gray, "Nassau Senior."

5. In *The Condition of the Working Class in England in 1844*, Engels declared: "It is . . . Malthus's theory of population—and the new poor law to which it gave rise—which represent the most flagrant warlike aggression of the middle classes against the workers" (320). But the aggression was committed in the name of science, and policies shaped by Malthusian doctrine were held to be for the ultimate benefit of the poor—even the starving poor.

6. Instead of the proverbial snowstorm into which the fallen woman of melodrama is evicted, the forlorn, starving, anti-Madonnas of Ireland ("anti-" precisely because they were unable to feed their children) were cast out into the Famine, as if into a storm of their own making.

7. For Bauman, see Richard Rubenstein's *Age of Triage*, chap. 1. Rubenstein identifies genocide as one solution—the most drastic and destructive—that modern nation-states have devised to deal with "surplus" populations. Rubenstein sees the enclosure movements in British agriculture, starting as early as the Tudor period, as a less violent process of uprooting an economically unprofitable peasantry, causing them to swell the ranks of the rural and urban poor, the unemployed, but also the industrial proletariat. In the case of the Irish peasantry, the uprooting came later and with greater violence, in part because the system of land distribution was even more retrograde than it had been in England, Wales, and Scotland. In Rubenstein's opinion, "The Irish catastrophe can be seen as the outcome of an early attempt by a modern government systematically to eliminate a population it deemed undesirable. Having been indifferent to the fate of their own peasants in the enclosures, many of the same British leaders had even less concern for the fate of the peasants of a people they regarded as a conquered enemy" (11). Compare Donnelly, "The Administration of Relief," on the Encumbered Estates Bill (316–17), including his commentary on A. J. P. Taylor's judgment of "genocide" (330).

8. As William Trench put it, the Famine "was an awful remedy" (quoted in Senior, 2:2).

9. As James Donnelly says, "This . . . was to make a religion of the market, and to herald its cruel dictates as blessings in disguise" ("Administration," 299).

10. According to Terry Eagleton, the various "measures, half-measures and non-measures" taken by the British government, including its "failure to stop the grain harvest of 1846 from being exported" from Ireland, "despatched hundreds of thousands to their needless deaths" (24).

11. Even so sympathetic and astute an observer as Friedrich Engels thought of the Irish as an inferior race. Engels quotes Carlyle's moralizing discourse on the dissolute

moral traits of the Irish. He then says: "Carlyle's description is a perfectly true one, if we overlook his exaggerated and prejudiced defamation of the Irish national character" (105). But in describing the slums of Dublin, Engels himself says: "The national character of the Irish is partly responsible for this" (40). Moreover, through the admixture of the Irish, "the working classes have become a race apart from the English bourgeoisie. . . . They are two quite different nations, as unlike as if they were differentiated by race" (139). Certainly the Irish are "differentiated by race" from the English in such a passage as this: "The Englishman, who is not yet wholly uncivilised, needs more than the Irishman, who goes about in rags, eats potatoes and lives in pigsties. This does not prevent the Irishman competing with the Englishman and gradually dragging down his wages and standard of living to his own level" (89). Early in Condition of the Working Class, Engels also strikes an elegiac note for a vanishing race—one that can be heard as well in Matthew Arnold's On the Study of Celtic Literature: "The language and customs of the Celt are rapidly vanishing before the triumphant march of English civilisation" (22).

12. Like the Chronicle, the Illustrated London News also stressed bad land distribution and English imperialism as the main causes both of chronic Irish poverty and of the Famine.

13. R. F. Foster calls The Landleaguers "a crude treatise against Irish rural savagery" (293). He also notes, however, that The Kellys offers "an unwinking, accurate and thoughtful observation of Irish conditions just before the Famine" (293). For some reason, though offering a thorough, sympathetic account of Trollope's Palliser or parliamentary novels, Foster deals with the Irish novels only in passing and does not deal at all with Castle Richmond.

14. For Trollope, Philip Jones represents the new, responsible, and solvent English landlords that the Encumbered Estates Act of 1849 was supposed to attract. Most of the investors in encumbered estates after the Famine were, however, Irish.

15. That Herbert, his sisters, and Clara try to relieve some of the suffering of the peasants is a good thing at least for themselves, Trollope thinks, but, despite mass starvation, the government's relief measures were sufficient unto the day. Through the workings of the Poor Law in particular, Trollope says,

> life and soul were kept together, the government . . . having wisely seen what, at so short a notice, was possible for them to do, and what was absolutely impossible. It is in such emergencies as these that the watching and the wisdom of a government are necessary; and I shall always think . . . that the wisdom of its action and the wisdom of its abstinence from action were very good. (346)

16. After Herbert and Clara are engaged, the bad news arrives that he is not the legal heir to Castle Richmond; on the contrary, the legal heir is cousin Owen. Lady Fitzgerald's first husband of long ago, one Matthew Mollett, is not dead; instead, this old scapegrace surfaces to blackmail Sir John Fitzgerald. Lady Fitzgerald has unwittingly committed bigamy, Herbert is legally a bastard, and the estate therefore goes to the nearest legitimate male relative, Owen. Thus Castle Richmond replays the theme of the fall of an estate or "house" that Trollope had taken up in The Macdermots of Ballycloran. But the tragic reversal of the fortunes of Herbert and his family reverses again when the lawyer Mr. Prendergast proves that Mollett had been legally married to another woman before he illegally married Lady Fitzgerald. This means that her marriage to Sir John is legal, and Herbert has all along been the legitimate heir of Castle Richmond, and of course an appropriate husband for Clara Desmond.

17. "In Language and Silence, George Steiner writes: 'The world of Auschwitz lies outside speech as it lies outside reason.' The same could be said of the world of the Famine" (Morash, Introduction, 37). Cf. Eagleton: There is "something recalcitrant" at the "core" of the Famine "which defeats articulation, some 'real' which stubbornly refuses to be symbolized. . . . this 'real' is a voracious desire which was beaten back and defeated, which could find no place in the symbolic order of social time and was expunged from it . . . some primordial trauma has taken place, which fixates your development at one level

even as you continue to unfold at another, so that time in Irish history . . . would seem to move backwards and forwards simultaneously" (15).

18. In his Australian travelogue, Trollope wrote that the "doom" of the Australian aboriginals "is to be exterminated; and the sooner that their doom is accomplished—so that there be no cruelty—the better it will be for civilization" (564). And in *South Africa*, he wrote that "Nature's first planting [will] wither and die wherever come the hardier plants, which science added to nature has produced" (2:332). Apparently he felt the same way about the Irish peasantry with whom he claimed an intimate knowledge and sympathy.

19. In his *Autobiography* Trollope declares that he is an "advanced conservative liberal."

Chapter 6. The Dusk of the Dreamtime

1. Carter adds that "the Aborigines' crime was to be primitive, to have no history. In this sense it was quite natural that nineteenth-century ethnologists meticulously compared the skull measurements of slaughtered Aborigines with those of executed white criminals, as if the volume of unreason might be plotted on a graph. The dead were more informative than the living" (321).

2. At best, as Carter notes, "the Aborigines were made to speak a language which was not theirs," although in naming the country the white colonists utilized numerous aboriginal terms (327).

3. In North America, New Zealand, and South Africa, there was at least the supposition that colonial officials and settlers were obligated to purchase or otherwise compensate indigenous peoples for the lands they seized and occupied. This was not the case in Australia.

4. Besides the poems by Eliza Hamilton Dunlop and Henry Kendall mentioned earlier, see Charles Tompson's "Black Town" (1826) in Elliott and Mitchell, *Bards in the Wilderness*, and the pseudonymous Hugo's "The Gin" (1831) in John Leonard, *Australian Verse*. In W. Howitt's *A Boy's Adventures in the Wilds of Australia. Or Herbert's Note-Book* (1845), "the white man" comes to the outback just in time to save the aboriginals from their savage customs, including cannibalism and infanticide, which would otherwise have "exterminated the race" (quoted in Pickering, 64). J. J. Healy notes also the echoes of James Fenimore Cooper in the novels of Rolf Boldrewood (51).

5. For the Mabo decision, see Attwood; for Wik, see Brennan. As Justices Deane and Gaudron declared in the Mabo case: "The acts and events by which that dispossession in legal theory was carried into practical effect constitute the darkest aspect of the history of this nation. The nation as a whole must remain diminished unless and until there is an acknowledgment of, and retreat from, those past injustices. . . . The lands of this continent were not terra nullius or 'practically unoccupied in 1788'" (quoted in Bourke and Cox, 66).

6. See also Butlin's more recent *Economics and the Dreamtime*, 102–39. In *Guns, Germs, and Steel*, Jared Diamond uses the estimate of 300,000 by anthropologist A. R. Radcliffe-Brown without citation and as if it were still uncontested (313).

7. Breton appears to accept this improbable piece of misinformation, though, in a more skeptical vein, he adds: "This [custom] has been absurdly attributed to the circumstance of Providence having decreed the final destruction or extinction of all the people in [New South Wales]; as if we have any right to suppose Providence capable of an act of such absolute supererogation as that of creating a race of human beings merely to destroy them" (167).

8. As late as 1824 the *Hobart Gazette* could declare: "Perhaps, taken collectively, the sable natives of this colony are the most peaceful people in the world" (quoted in Bonwick, *Lost*, 29). Certainly they were no more warlike among themselves than were the mainland aboriginals. Conflicts between tribes or groups were usually ritual skirmishes and probably never resulted in many deaths.

9. On such narratives, see my *Rule of Darkness*, 19–32.

10. Meanwhile, "the aboriginal police," according to Robinson, "take a general sur-

veillance over the entire of the aborigines" (401), but it seems that Robinson's own sur-
veillance was even more thorough. Their dances, the main feature of their corroborees,
Robinson held, were not only heathen but damaging to "the health of the natives" (402)—
one more cause of their demise—though this may only have been his official stance. According to his son, Robinson occasionally "threw off his boat cloak along with his inhibi-
tions" and joined in the revelries of his charges, just as he is also suspected by his recent
biographer, Vivienne Rae-Ellis, of being motivated through much of his humanitarian activity by his sexual fixation on Truganini (Rae-Ellis, *Trucanini*, 38–40, 83). That Robinson
and Truganini may have been lovers seems likely even to Henry Reynolds, who disagrees
with many of Rae-Ellis's other opinions, including her absurd claim that Truganini,
through her cooperation with Robinson, was a "traitor" to her people (Reynolds, *Fate*,
140–42). In any event, Robinson may have been something of a Tasmanian Kurtz—he certainly enjoyed and profited from his expeditions away from civilization—though the jury
is still out and is likely, for lack of evidence, to remain that way.

11. Robinson insisted on giving his charges European names, though he claimed that
they wanted him to do so. Many of the new names express a patronizing racism—Nep-
tune, Romeo, Queen Cleopatra, and so forth. He called Truganini "Lalla Rookh." He
even gave new names to aboriginals whom he apparently only knew by imposed, European names: thus "Charley" became "Algernon," "Big Billy" became "Alfred," and "Kangaroo Billy" became "Nimrod" (Bonwick, *Last*, 257–58).

12. According to Bonwick: "The more *civilized* they became, the more dependent
were the Blacks upon their masters for supplies, and the less disposed were they to exert
themselves. Listless and good, they wanted energy to pursue the bounding kangaroo, or
clamber after an opossum" (*Last*, 256).

13. On other "King Billys," see Rowley, 25.

14. After the Risdon massacre of aboriginals by British troops in 1804, the surgeon attached to the fledgling convict colony, Jacob Mountgarrett, had "salted down a couple of
casks of their bones and sent them to Sydney," but what became of them is not known
(Hughes, 414).

15. Bonwick provides a detailed account in *The Last of the Tasmanians*, 395–400; see
also Ryan, 214–17.

16. The whole sorry tale grew even sorrier a few years later, through claims that Lanney had not been of pure Tasmanian blood but partly of Australian aboriginal descent. If
so, the value of his invaluable bones, at least from the standpoint of Victorian race science, would have been nil.

17. In *What the Bones Say*, John Cove writes: "A review of the literature prior to 1950
shows no evidence that Truganini's skeleton had been used in any published research"
(147).

18. The Beothuks of Newfoundland were not a distinct race and nor were the Arawaks
of the West Indies or the Guanches of the Canary Islands, extinct by the 1550s (Crosby,
71–103).

19. Hughes writes that the extinction of the Tasmanian aborigines "was the only true
genocide in English colonial history" and adds that, by "the standards of Pol Pot, let alone
Josef Stalin or Adolf Hitler, this was a small slaughter. But not to the Tasmanian Aborigines" (120). In this passage Hughes perpetuates the myth of the total extinction of the Tasmanians (although on 641–42 n. 98 he quotes Lyndall Ryan at length on the ideological
functions of that "myth" and calls it a "myth" himself). He also equates genocide with the
total extinction of one race or people by another, although, by this standard, neither the
Holocaust nor the other examples he gives qualify as genocides. *Only* the extinction of the
Tasmanians—assuming it was total—qualifies, Hughes suggests, not just as the *only* genocide in "English colonial history" but in all history, or at least in all modern history. Yet it
was comparatively a "small slaughter," except to the Tasmanians!

20. So, too, as the Reverend James Günther claimed, "the aborigines themselves have
the impression that their ancestors knew much more than themselves" (quoted in Reece,
75).

21. That Robinson's and Threlkeld's failures were part of a general trend, at least in

Australia, seems clear. In 1842 Lord Stanley, head of the Colonial Office in London, opined that Australian missions were not effective, and two years later Governor Gipps reported that he had ended support for the Wellington mission as well as the Moravian mission at Moreton Bay, both of which were failing because they were too near to the corrupting influence of white settlers (Rowley, 100). So, too, shortly after the Church Missionary Society established its Yarra mission in 1837, thirty-six children were attending its school. But less than two years later no children were in attendance, and the head missionary concluded that it would be futile to continue (Rowley, 55). Also by the 1840s the aboriginals were mounting stiffer resistance to the expansion of white settlement than in the past. And there was the more general reaction against "Exeter Hall," evangelical humanitarianism that marked a new mood of caution and pessimism in the Colonial Office in London. This is not to say that missions and missionary activity came to an end. David Livingstone's enormous influence began in the 1850s. But no one looked too carefully at Livingstone's missionary efforts; he was viewed as a hero for his feats of exploration, and his being a missionary only added the halo to his portrait. There was a growing skepticism and a sense that, in the future, missionaries would have to work much longer and harder, with different, more gradualist expectations, while also moving farther away from the areas of white settlement, if they were to have any chance of success. See also Ferry, and Woolmington. For the failure of missionary and humanitarian activism in South Africa, see Bank.

22. The evidence of aboriginal cannibalism is always second- or thirdhand; in accepting such evidence, Backhouse is more typical than Breton. As another nineteenth-century writer put it:

> Certainly in conversation, [the aborigines] admitted the fact [of cannibalism]; but this does not prove it, because . . . they will at any time admit or say anything which they think will please their interlocutors . . . if leading questions are put to them, as is usually done by enthusiastic enquirers . . . they may be made to say anything. (Quoted in Mulvaney, 21)

Michael Pickering, having analyzed several hundred accounts, concludes that "there is no reliable evidence to support the claim that Australian Aboriginal societies engaged in institutional cannibalism" (51). In his recent survey of anthropological disagreements about aboriginal culture, L. R. Hiatt makes no mention of cannibalism. On the weakness or nonexistence of evidence about cannibalism in Polynesia, New Guinea, New Zealand, and some other parts of the world, see Arens; Barker, Hulme, and Iversen; and Jahoda, 97–127.

23. Besides his stress on cannibalism, Lumholtz expresses the standard, "doomed race" view:

> They have proved themselves almost incapable of receiving either culture or Christianity, and they have not the power to resist the onward march of civilisation. They are therefore without a future, without a home, without a hope, a doomed race. . . . The philanthropist is filled with sadness when he sees the original inhabitants of this strange land succumbing according to the inexorable law of degeneration. Invading civilisation has not brought development and progress to the Australian native; after a few generations his race will have disappeared from the face of the earth. (Quoted in Webb and Enstice, 110)

For cannibalism in the African context, see my *Rule of Darkness*, 185, 260–61.

24. "Social anthropologists at the University of Sydney in the 1920s pronounced unequivocally on the doom of Aboriginal culture," writes McGregor. "On the fate of the bearers of that culture, they were more ambivalent. Other anthropologists of the day also allowed a remote possibility of Aboriginal survival, although the dominant scientific viewpoint could scarcely be characterised as optimistic" (113).

Chapter 7. Islands of Death and the Devil

1. "The paradox in which [missionary] literature is involved," writes Christopher Herbert, "is that it calls for the minute, sympathetic study, at the cost of arduous training, of social phenomena defined from the outset as worthless and marked out for the speediest possible forcible elimination" (166).

2. George Vason is an interesting case of a missionary turned native. See Lamb, Smith, and Thomas, 156–69.

3. Since the publication of William Arens's *Man-Eating Myth* in 1979, the evidence about any form of customary cannibalism anywhere in the world has been hotly debated among anthropologists.

4. When the native missionary or "teacher" in *Coral Island* tells Ralph, Jack, and Peterkin about his failure to prevent the strangulation of a dying chief's wives, and also to prevent the murder of the dying chief, he seems to have borrowed the episode, almost verbatim, from Thomas Williams's *Fiji and the Fijians*, even though that missionary text was published in the same year (1858) as *Coral Island* (Williams, 194–95; Ballantyne, 294–95). The point is not to accuse Ballantyne of plagiarism, much less to attempt to prove that he borrowed from this or that missionary text, but rather to suggest that missionary authors include very similar episodes and responses to "horrid customs" in all their writings. The upshot is a cumulative record of sin and savagery that both dramatizes the urgency (and bravery) of missionary work and offers an unambiguous explanation for the evident, ongoing depopulation of the South Pacific.

5. Of the Tahitians, Cook also writes that "we have reason to beleive [sic] there was a time when they were Canibals," though he presents no eyewitness evidence (3:204). Cook and his men twice performed experiments by having pieces of recently slain corpses roasted and presented to two Maori, who were encouraged to eat them; they did so, thus providing the only eyewitness evidence to cannibalism in Cook's journals (Hulme, 21–23).

6. "In Britain it was women who fell," writes Edmond; "in Tahiti it was missionaries" (99).

7. Ellis testified before the Aborigines Committee in 1836 about the depopulation of the South Pacific:

I am not aware that it is traceable to the operation of the cruelty of Europeans. It is traceable, in a great measure, to the demoralizing effects of intercourse with Europeans; the introduction of diseases, of ardent spirits, and of fire-arms. These results of intercourse with Europeans have produced a destruction of human life that is truly awful. When Captain Cook was at the Sandwich Islands he estimated the population at 400,000. In 1823, when, with other missionaries, I made a tour of some of the islands, we counted every house in one of the largest islands, which is 300 miles in circumference, and endeavoured to obtain as accurate a census as several months' labour would afford, and there was not in the entire group of islands at that time above 150,000 people. That diminution is [to] be ascribed to the above causes—wars promoted by fire-arms, ardent spirits, and foreign diseases, and also to the superstitions of the people, the offering of human sacrifices. The practice of infanticide, which destroyed so many in the southern islands, did not prevail to any extent in the Sandwich Islands. . . . Captain Cook estimated the population of . . . Tahiti at 200,000. I have reason to believe, from actual observation, that his estimate was much too high; but the ruins of former dwellings, which still spread over every part of the island, show that it must have been much more densely peopled formerly than it is now. When the missionaries first arrived, there were not more than 16,000, and after they had been there 10 years or 14 years, such had been the extent of depopulation . . . that the entire population was not above 8,000, some supposed not even 6,000. Since Christianity has prevailed among the people there has been a reaction; the population is increasing, and perhaps it has increased one-fourth since Christianity has been introduced. I do not ascribe the depopulation . . . to overt acts of cruelty, but chiefly to the indirect operation of intercourse with Europeans. (*Report* 1:502)

8. Rod Edmond rightly points out that "any discussion of depopulation must be aware of the insistent and ubiquitous nineteenth-century narrative of the inevitable extinction of Pacific populations, which by the end of the century had become a colonialist mantra. There was an overdetermined European cultural investment in this myth of the dying Polynesian. It legitimated many different kinds of incursion into the Pacific, from imperialist dispossession to romantic or primitivist appropriation" (14–15).

9. In one of his recent surveys of Polynesian "depopulation," Donald Denoon corroborates much of what Melville has to say. During the nineteenth century most "Polynesian populations fell by at least half, and Micronesian societies risked complete extinction when new diseases compounded the effects of natural disasters. . . . On islets, decline could be irreversible" (244). Denoon cites venereal disease as a major cause of "demographic collapse" in Polynesia, including "the scything down of the Hawaiian population." That deadly "scything down" Denoon sees as the most significant aspect of modern Hawaiian history (244). Moreover, Denoon points out that the missionary practice of resettling converts in "village-congregations" facilitated the spread of contagious diseases and also that missionary medicine, "in the days before germ theory or quinine," was no more effective than indigenous medicine—"consolation," perhaps, but not cure (246). See also Blackman, 208–28; Kunitz, 44–81; and Stannard, *Before the Horror.*

10. According to Craik:

The character of this people, both moral and intellectual, exhibits . . . a much richer and more interesting variety of peculiarities than that of most other savages. Its very anomalies constitute much of its attraction. They belong . . . to the class of the energetic, bold, and haughty nations; and both their virtues and their vices wear the same general air . . . of independence, decision, and fearlessness. (365)

11. In Butler's novel and its sequel, *Erewhon Revisited,* the exact connections between the Maori and the Erewhonians are not entirely clear, although Chowbok—who is not an Erewhonian—is clearly a Maori. See J. Jones, 132–54; and Lamb, 294–96.

12. Wakefield's propagandizing for "systematic colonization" in New Zealand and elsewhere offered, according to Jonathan Lamb, "a neo-Malthusian thesis with a utopian solution" (*Preserving the Self,* 290). In his *View of the Art of Colonization* (1849), Wakefield writes about "the paradise which a colony is for the poor" (137).

13. Like the Tahitians and Hawaiians, the Maori also appeared ripe for conversion to Christianity. The Maori were eager learners, quickly gaining literacy, and many also became Christians. While the missionaries at first opposed further white settlement in New Zealand, they were nevertheless advocates of official British intervention to protect both the Maori and law-abiding British citizens (Yarwood, 191–93; Mellor, 326–31). Buxton's Aborigines Committee and the APS added to the humanitarian pressure to turn New Zealand into yet another piece of the British Empire. Peter Adams contends that the *Report* of the Aborigines Committee "merely reiterated the sentiments and ideas of the missionary societies without offering any new proposals" (93), which is true but does not contradict the view that the committee was a factor in the humanitarian pressure for annexation. So, too, the APS may have taken an illogical position in supporting Wakefield's "New Zealand Company and its native reserve scheme," but that does not mean it was "uninfluential as a pressure group" (Adams, 93).

14. In *Manners and Customs of the New Zealanders,* published in 1840, the same year the Treaty of Waitangi was signed, Joel Samuel Polack writes: "Colonization by a European power having happily interfered, could alone retard, and it is to be hoped will eventually stop, the extermination of this interesting people" (2:91).

15. Owens claims that humanitarian arguments for official annexation were "grossly exaggerated" (53). He also contends that the evidence for rapid demographic collapse "is not clear" (49), though he does not dispute that there was a sizable decline in the indige-

nous population between 1800 and 1900. Although measles, tuberculosis, and some other diseases killed many Maori, Belich argues, the major European diseases that wreaked havoc in Australia and elsewhere including smallpox, typhus, and cholera "did not manage the jump to New Zealand." The relatively late colonization of New Zealand meant also that new medical techniques, especially vaccination, could limit the spread of some diseases. The notion that venereal disease was widespread among the Maori also appears to have been exaggerated (Belich, *Making Peoples*, 174–75; Owens, 49). Further, I am not aware of any revisionary studies like those by Ned Butlin for Australia and David Stannard for Hawaii and North America that argue that the Maori population on first contact was far higher than the early estimates of between 90,000 and 200,000.

16. The main evidence is that adult males far outnumber females, which Thomson believes stems from either the deliberate killing or the neglect of female infants.

17. "In 1890 the fate of the Maori remained in [the] balance," writes M. P. K. Sorrenson; the population of the Maori "was still declining. The Darwinian prognosis that 'native' races confronted with European colonization were doomed to extinction seemed to be confirmed. . . . The best that could be hoped for was that a remnant of the Maori would, through miscegenation, survive in the 'blood' of many Pakeha New Zealanders" (189).

18. The allusion is to chapter 25 of Gibbon's *Decline and Fall of the Roman Empire*.

19. Dilke thinks that the Maori themselves were originally Malay invaders of New Zealand, who "found a numerous horde of blacks of the Australian race living in the forests of the South Island" and promptly exterminated them (1:347). But as a tropical race, the Malays who migrated to the colder climate of New Zealand "unknowingly broke one of Nature's laws, and their descendants are paying the penalty in extinction" (1:354). Here is the theme of changed circumstances, coupled with climate, as explanation for the demise of a race quite apart from contact and conflict with Europeans.

20. "Nature's work in New Zealand," says Dilke, "is not the same as that which she is quickly doing in North America, in Tasmania, in Queensland." And, according to Dilke,

> It is not merely that a hunting and fighting people is being replaced by an agricultural and pastoral people, and must farm or die: the Maori does farm; Maori chiefs own villages, build houses, which they let to European settlers; we have here Maori sheep-farmers, Maori ship-owners, Maori mechanics, Maori soldiers, Maori rough-riders, Maori sailors, and even Maori traders. There is nothing which the average Englishman can do which the average Maori cannot be taught to do as cheaply and as well. Nevertheless, the race dies out. The Red Indian dies because he cannot farm; the Maori farms, and dies. (1:393)

21. Compare A. K. Newman, who, in his 1882 "Study of the Causes Leading to the Extinction of the Maori" writes: "Taking all things into consideration, the disappearance of the race is scarcely subject for much regret. They are dying out in a quick, easy way, and are being supplanted by a superior race" (quoted in Belich, *Victorian Interpretation*, 299). So, too, the globetrotting novelist Anthony Trollope opined that the Maori "are certainly more highly gifted than other savage nations I have seen. . . . One can understand the hope . . . of the first . . . missionaries. . . . But contact with Europeans does not improve them. At the touch of the higher race they are poisoned and melt away. There is scope for poetry in their past history. There is room for philanthropy as to their present condition. But in regard to their future,—there is hardly a place for hope" (*Australia and New Zealand*, 2:488).

22. Thus the London *Times* for 16 December 1864 declared: "All questions between the British colonists of New Zealand and the Maoris are now merged in a war of sovereignty—probably of extermination" (quoted in Orange, 159).

Chapter 8. Darwin and After

1. To lessen the controversy that he knew *The Origin of Species* would provoke when it appeared in 1859, Darwin chose not to discuss how his theory of evolution applied to humans. *Man's Place in Nature* was the first work addressed to "the general public applying the Darwinian hypothesis systematically to man" (Stocking, 147), and others quickly followed. Darwin himself would fill in *Origin's* blank about humans with its 1871 sequel, *The Descent of Man*.

2. In *Pre-Historic Times* (1865), Lubbock combines archaeology, ethnology, and Darwinism in a major synthesis that, among other things, portrays life both among the earliest and among present-day "savages," to quote Hobbes, as "nasty, brutish, and short." Lubbock claims that the Hottentots are "the filthiest people in the world" (432); "the natives of New South Wales" are "miserable savages" (450); and, if not the lowest, the Fuegians certainly appear to be among "the most miserable specimens of the human race" (542). Lubbock rarely emphasizes such factors as geographical isolation that might help to explain why certain "savage tribes" have remained, as he sees it, stationary or nonprogressive—or just plain "miserable"—perhaps since the very origin of the human species. Like Cooper's final Mohicans, moreover, Lubbock's prehistoric *and* "modern savages" are "children" unable to grow up, and hence doomed to a sort of self-inflicted infanticide (569).

3. In *Voyage*, Darwin offers this comparison of the different human races:

> I believe, in this extreme part of South America, man exists in a lower state of improvement than in any other part of the world. The South Sea Islanders of the two races inhabiting the Pacific, are comparatively civilized. The Esquimaux, in his subterranean hut, enjoys some of the comforts of life, and in his canoe, when fully equipped, manifests much skill. Some of the tribes of Southern Africa, prowling about in search of roots, and living concealed on the wild and arid plains, are sufficiently wretched. The Australian, in the simplicity of the arts of life, comes nearest the Fuegian: he can, however, boast of his boomerang, his spear and throwing-stick, his method of climbing trees, of tracking animals, and of hunting. Although the Australian may be superior in acquirements, it by no means follows that he is likewise superior in mental capacity: indeed, from what I saw of the Fuegians when [they were] on board [the *Beagle*], and from what I have read of the Australians, I should think the case was exactly the reverse. (231)

4. George Stocking notes that in *Voyage* "Darwin's rhetoric upon occasion suggests that he still thought of savage man as fallen man, who must redeem himself (or be redeemed) through progress" or else become extinct (106–7). But that is also true of Darwin's rhetoric in *Descent of Man* and elsewhere.

5. So, too, in "Social Diseases and Worse Remedies" (1891), Huxley insists: "it is an error to imagine that evolution signifies a constant tendency to increased perfection. . . . Retrogressive is as practicable as progressive metamorphosis" (9:199). Usually optimistic, Darwin believed that "man in the distant future will be a far more perfect creature than he now is," but he also had to accept the "intolerable thought," based on the second law of thermodynamics and the idea of the heat-death of the universe, that man "and all other sentient beings are doomed to complete annihilation after such long-continued slow progress" toward perfection (*Autobiography*, 92).

6. In contrast to other "social Darwinists" (and Darwinism was always "social") such as Benjamin Kidd, Karl Pearson, and the founder of the eugenics movement, Francis Galton, Darwin, Huxley, and Wallace perhaps took a "mild attitude to the question of race" (Di Gregorio, 170). This relative mildness seems evident in Huxley's lack of emphasis on war as an instrument of natural selection, although Paul Crook's alignment of Huxley with Wallace as an opponent of "imperial biology" and therefore as tending toward Wallace's pacifism is misleading (Crook, 54–62). In Walter Bagehot's *Physics and Politics* (1872) and in other instances of social Darwinism down to Kidd's *Social Evolution* (1894) and beyond, war is a primary mechanism of history as well as of human evolution. This is

also true for Huxley, though more implicitly than explicitly. The social Darwinist vision of history is one of race war, with the "survival of the fittest" as the outcome. As in Bagehot's construction, war is also a primary mechanism of progress and therefore of civilization. And, of course, to the "fittest" go the spoils of war, including empires which, in modern times at least, carry with them "the white man's burden" to try to civilize those perhaps semi-fit "savages" and "barbarians" who, though vanquished, do not always vanish.

7. However, in *Evolution and Ethics*, Huxley recasts economic scarcity in quasi-Nietzschean terms as the desire for increased "enjoyment."

8. Di Gregorio calls Huxley "an open-minded conservative" (174), and Irvine, canvassing Huxley's anti-socialist essays, points out that Huxley's essay, "The Natural Inequality of Men" (1890), reverses Rousseau's *Discourse on the Origins of Inequality* (334–35). Huxley regarded "all forms of socialism . . . as utopian illusion rendered dangerous by grave and widespread poverty" (Irvine, 334). However, like Darwin, Huxley took the liberal side in the Governor Eyre controversy and the American Civil War; he was a liberal individualist and utilitarian who nevertheless espoused a Burkean conservatism about the slow, organic, or natural processes of the evolution of social institutions and about the great, natural inequalities among individuals, races, and species in the "struggle for existence." Huxley argues in "Emancipation—Black and White" (1865) that slavery should be abolished not because Africans are the equals of Europeans but because slavery interferes with natural selection; "the struggle for existence" works to render the great inequalities among the races historically manifest, and "the highest places in the hierarchy of civilisation will assuredly not be within the reach of our dusky cousins" (3:67).

9. The final paragraph of *Ancient Society* declares that the attainment of "civilization" some "five thousand years ago" is a "marvelous fact," and adds: "In strictness but two families, the Semitic and the Aryan, accomplished the work through unassisted self-development. The Aryan family represents the central stream of human progress, because it produced the highest type of mankind, and because it has proved its intrinsic superiority by gradually assuming the control of the earth." This is as close as Morgan comes to insisting that racial (or biological) "superiority," rather than environmental advantages, have led to European imperial dominance of most of the planet. But he immediately qualifies this notion: "And yet civilization must be regarded as an accident of circumstances" (468).

10. Darwin's scientific modesty and caution extends to the fact that he only finally published *Origin* after Wallace sent him a paper outlining what Darwin would later call "exactly the same theory as mine" (*Autobiography*, 121). Wallace and Darwin had been exchanging views for several years. Darwin acknowledged Wallace as co-discoverer of the theory, and Wallace gave Darwin his due as his more original and authoritative colleague in natural history (White and Gribbin, 188–95).

Chapter 9. Conclusion

1. In *Report from the Frontier*, Julian Burger estimates the worldwide number for indigenous peoples to be more than 200 million; the discrepancy between that figure and the 357 million offered by Hitchcock and Twedt has to do both with the definition of "indigenous peoples" and with the difficulties of counting.

2. Hitchcock and Twedt list more than thirty genocides of indigenous peoples that have occurred since the 1960s (some ongoing), even though they do not include the genocides in the former Yugoslavia or, for some reason, the decimation of the East Timorese by the government of Indonesia (496–97).

3. The militant orthodoxy of both the International Monetary Fund and the World Bank has insisted that "there is only one line of development and that indigenous peoples benefit from following it" (Burger, *Report* 8; see also Adas, 402–18).

4. Burger also lists many more organizations, both official and nongovernmental, that now concern themselves with the rights, health, and cultural survival of indigenous people around the world. Burger's *Report* was published under the auspices of both the Anti-Slavery Society (direct descendant of the Aborigines Protection Society and Buxton's

nineteenth-century Anti-Slavery Society) and of the U.S.-based organization Cultural Survival.

5. Translated into English in 1895, Max Nordau's *Degeneration* diagnosed virtually everything modern and Western as diseased and dying. For many more examples of the decline-and-fall theme, see Daniel Pick, *Faces of Degeneration*, and also my *Bread and Circuses*.

6. Chambers immediately softens this terrific prospect. Rather than something entirely different and inimical to mankind, the new dominant species may be "a nobler type of humanity, which shall complete the zoological circle on this planet, and realize some of the dreams of the purest spirits of the present race" (276). Thus Chambers broaches and then quickly turns away from the threatening fantasy of the extermination of "the present race" by a higher one. Despite the Lyellian notion of "the zoological circle," Chambers's version of evolution is a progressively Whiggish, even Benthamite one.

7. The narrator of Bulwer-Lytton's novella discovers the subterranean realm of the Vril-ya, a race far superior to *Homo sapiens* (and yet all-too-human in several respects: they still use money and they treat other "nations" with "more disdain than citizens of New York regard the negroes" [725]). The narrator speculates that the Vril-ya will one day emerge "into sunlight [as] our inevitable destroyers"; nonetheless, they are supposedly a superior race compared to mere Victorian mortals, in part because they use their mysterious form of energy, vril, to exterminate any creatures (human or otherwise) whom they consider inferior or inimical to themselves.

8. The eugenics movement was purely Malthusian in its anxiety about the overpopulating tendencies of the poor and "unfit." But whereas Malthus argued that all government could do to prevent poverty via overpopulation was to educate the poor in sexual restraint and to promote emigration (only a temporary "palliative"), the eugenicists held that more could be done, not through socialism or even social welfare programs, but by encouraging the fit—which usually meant the successful bourgeoisie (or, in Galton's case, people very much like himself)—to have larger families, and by sterilizing or locking up the unfit. As Daniel Pick remarks, after Darwin, and increasingly through the writings and influence of Galton and the eugenics movement, the "condition of England question" became "centrally concerned with the condition of the English body" (195).

9. See, in general, G. S. Jones, 127–51, 281–314. One theorist of "urban degeneration" opined that "a pure Londoner of the fourth generation is not capable of existing" (quoted in G. S. Jones, 127).

10. The year 1871 is the date of Sir George Chesney's *Battle of Dorking*. In *Voices Prophesying War*, I. F. Clarke surveys dozens of "imaginary war" novels published from then to World War I, and in many cases these entail invasions of Britain.

11. In *A Secret Country*, John Pilger quotes the Sydney *Bulletin* for November, 1898: "the European's dislike of the Chinaman is not a matter of taste, but a healthy racial instinct . . . in the case of the chinkies, this out-of-date instinctive dislike has lasted long enough to be useful again as a protection against a race that is more dangerous to civilisation than a savage with a club is to a fellow savage" (121). Pilger notes that white Australian opposition to Asian immigration has continued through the Vietnam era down to the present (119–34). And in the American context, although there has probably been even more concern about immigration from Mexico, the "yellow peril" theme has waxed and waned from the 1880s through the Korean and Vietnam war eras into the twenty-first century (see, for example, Greenfeld).

12. Shiel's novel was renamed *The Yellow Peril* in a 1900 edition. According to its recent editor, George Locke, *The Yellow Danger* was a popular success and went through "several editions" (Shiel, v).

13. It is hard to tell how seriously to take Shiel's potboiler, but there are not many signs of irony in it. Shiel evidently shares the anxiety he seeks to induce in his readers: "The yellow conquest meant, naturally, that wherever it passed, the very memory of the white races it encountered would disappear for ever." Shiel adds: "At this dark thought the heart quailed, and there was Panic" (256).

Shiel was the author of several other popular potboilers, starting with *Prince Zaleski* in 1895 and including *The Purple Cloud* (1901), another apocalyptic fantasy. Just what made his writing so popular is unclear, but it seems likely that Dr. Yen How served as a model for Sax Rohmer's Dr. Fu Manchu, starting in 1913 with *The Mystery of Dr. Fu Manchu*. And there were numerous other signs in the early 1900s, in Britain, Canada, the United States, and Australia, of "yellow peril" anxiety (Bradshaw, 39).

Works Cited

Adams, Peter. *Fatal Necessity: British Intervention in New Zealand, 1830–1847*. Auckland: Auckland University Press, 1977.

Adas, Michael. *Machines as the Measure of Men: Science, Technology, and Ideologies of Western Dominance*. Ithaca, N.Y.: Cornell University Press, 1989.

Adorno, Theodor. *Negative Dialectics*. Translated by E. B. Ashton. New York: Continuum, 1973.

Anderson, Charles Roberts. *Melville in the South Seas*. 1939. New York: Dover, 1966.

Angas, George French. *Savage Life and Scenes in Australia and New Zealand: Being an Artist's Impressions of Countries and People at the Antipodes*. 2 vols. 1847. New York: Johnson Reprint, 1967.

Ansen, David. "Mann in the Wilderness." *Newsweek*, September 28, 1992, 48–49.

Arendt, Hannah. *Imperialism*. Part 2 of *The Origins of Totalitarianism*. New York: Harcourt, Brace and World, 1968.

Arens, William. *The Man-Eating Myth: Anthropology and Anthropophagy*. New York: Oxford University Press, 1979.

Arnold, David, ed. *Imperial Medicine and Indigenous Societies*. Manchester: Manchester University Press, 1988.

Attwood, Bain, ed. *In the Age of Mabo: History, Aborigines, and Australia*. St. Leonards, NSW: Allen and Unwin, 1996.

Axtell, James. "The White Indians of Colonial America." In *The European and the Indian: Essays in the Ethnohistory of Colonial North America*, 168–206. New York: Oxford University Press, 1981.

Backhouse, James. *A Narrative of a Visit to the Australian Colonies*. 1843. New York: Johnson Reprint, 1967.

Ballantyne, Robert. *The Coral Island*. 1858. Oxford: Oxford World's Classics, 1990.

Bank, Andrew. "Losing Faith in the Civilizing Mission: The Premature Decline of

Humanitarian Liberalism at the Cape, 1840–60." In *Empire and Others: British Encounters with Indigenous Peoples, 1600–1850*, ed. Martin Daunton and Rick Halpern, 364–83. Philadelphia: University of Pennsylvania Press, 1999.

Banton, Michael. *Racial Theories*. Cambridge: Cambridge University Press, 1987.

Barkan, Elazar. *The Retreat of Scientific Racism: Changing Concepts of Race in Britain and the United States between the World Wars*. Cambridge: Cambridge University Press, 1992.

Barker, Francis, Peter Hulme, and Margaret Iversen, eds. *Cannibalism and the Colonial World*. Cambridge: Cambridge University Press, 1998.

Barker, Martin, and Roger Sabin. *The Lasting of the Mohicans: History of an American Myth*. Jackson: University Press of Mississippi, 1995.

Barnett, Louise K. *The Ignoble Savage: American Literary Racism, 1790–1890*. Westport, Conn.: Greenwood, 1975.

Barrow, John. *An Account of Travels into the Interior of Southern Africa in the Years 1797 and 1798 . . . 1801*. New York: Johnson Reprint, 1968.

Bates, Daisy. *The Passing of the Aborigines: A Lifetime Spent among the Natives of Australia*. 1938. New York: Praeger, 1967.

Bauman, Zygmunt. *Modernity and the Holocaust*. Ithaca, N.Y.: Cornell University Press, 1989.

Becker, Allienne R. *The Lost Worlds Romance: From Dawn till Dusk*. Westport, Conn.: Greenwood, 1992.

Belich, James. *The Victorian Interpretation of Racial Conflict: The Maori, the British, and the New Zealand Wars*. Montreal: McGill-Queens University Press, 1989.

——. *Making Peoples: A History of the New Zealanders from Polynesian Settlement to the End of the Nineteenth Century*. Honolulu: University of Hawaii Press, 1996.

Bergland, Renée L. *The National Uncanny: Indian Ghosts and American Subjects*. Hanover, N.H.: University Press of New England, 2000.

Bergonzi, Bernard. *The Early H. G. Wells: A Study of the Scientific Romances*. Manchester: Manchester University Press, 1961.

Berkhofer, Robert. *The White Man's Indian: Images of the American Indian from Columbus to the Present*. New York: Knopf, 1978.

Bernstein, George. "Liberals, the Irish Famine, and the Role of the State." *Irish Historical Studies* 29, no. 116 (November 1995): 513–36.

Bieder, Robert E. *Science Encounters the Indian, 1820–1880: The Early Years of American Ethnology*. Norman: University of Oklahoma Press, 1986.

Blackburn, Robin. *The Overthrow of Colonial Slavery, 1776–1848*. London: Verso, 1988.

Blackman, William Fremont. *The Making of Hawaii: A Study in Social Evolution*. New York: Macmillan, 1906.

Blumenbach, Johann Friedrich. *On the Natural Varieties of Mankind*. 1775. New York: Bergman, 1969.

Bodley, John H. *Victims of Progress*. Menlo Park, Calif.: Benjamin/Cummings, 1982.

Bonwick, James. *The Last of the Tasmanians; or, the Black War of Van Diemen's Land*. 1870. New York: Johnson Reprint, 1970.

——. *The Lost Tasmanian Race*. 1884. New York: Johnson Reprint, 1970.

Bourke, Colin, Eleanor Bourke, and Bill Edwards, eds. *Aboriginal Australia: An In-*

troductory Reader in Aboriginal Studies. 2d ed. St. Lucia: University of Queensland Press, 1998.

Bourke, Colin, and Helen Cox. "Two Laws: One Land." In Bourke, Bourke, and Edwards, *Aboriginal Australia,* 56–76.

Bourke, Eleanor. "Australia's First Peoples: Identity and Population." In Bourke, Bourke, and Edwards, *Aboriginal Australia,* 38–55.

Bourne, H. R. Fox. *The Aborigines Protection Society: Chapters in Its History.* London: P. S. King, 1899.

Bowler, Peter. *Fossils and Progress: Palaeontology and the Idea of Progressive Evolution in the Nineteenth Century.* New York: Science History Publications, 1976.

——. *Evolution: The History of an Idea.* Rev. ed. Berkeley: University of California Press, 1989.

Boylan, Thomas A., and Timothy P. Folan. "'A Nation Perishing of Political Economy'?" In Morash and Hayes, *"Fearful Realities,"* 138–150.

Bradshaw, David. "Eugenics: 'They Should Certainly Be Killed.'" In *A Concise Companion to Modernism,* ed. David Bradshaw, 34–55. Oxford: Blackwell, 2003.

Brantlinger, Patrick. *Bread and Circuses: Theories of Mass Culture as Social Decay.* Ithaca, N.Y.: Cornell University Press, 1983.

——. *Rule of Darkness: British Literature and Imperialism, 1830–1914.* Ithaca, N.Y.: Cornell University Press, 1986.

——. "'Dying Races': Rationalizing Genocide in the Nineteenth-Century." In *The Decolonization of Imagination,* ed. Bhikhu Parekh and Jan Nederveen Pieterse, 43–56. London: Zed, 1995.

Bratton, J. S. Introduction to *The Coral Island,* by Robert Ballantyne. 1858. Oxford: Oxford World's Classics, 1990.

Brennan, Frank. *The Wik Debate: Its Impact on Aborigines, Pastoralists, and Miners.* Sydney: University of New South Wales Press, 1998.

Breton, W. H. *Excursions in New South Wales, Western Australia, and Van Diemen's Land, during the Years 1830, 1831, 1832, and 1833.* 1834. New York: Johnson Reprint, 1970.

Brown, Charles Brockden. *Edgar Huntly, Or, Memoirs of a Sleep-Walker.* 1799. New York: Penguin, 1988.

Brown, Dee. *Bury My Heart at Wounded Knee: An Indian History of the American West.* New York: Holt, 1970.

Brown, Robert. *The Races of Mankind: Being a Popular Description of the Characteristics, Manners, and Customs of the Principal Varieties of the Human Family.* 4 vols. London: Cassell Petter and Galpin, 1873.

Bryant, William Cullen. *Poetical Works of William Cullen Bryant.* Edited by Henry C. Sturgis. New York: AMS Press, [1969].

Bulwer-Lytton, Edward. *The Coming Race.* In vol. 2 of *The Works of Edward Bulwer-Lytton,* 9 vols. New York: P. F. Collier, n.d.

Burger, Julian. *Report from the Frontier: The State of the World's Indigenous Peoples.* London: Zed, 1987.

——. *The Gaia Atlas of First Peoples: A Future for the Indigenous World.* London: Gaia, 1990.

Butlin, Noel George [Ned]. *Our Original Aggression: Aboriginal Populations of Southeastern Australia, 1788–1850.* Sydney: George Allen and Unwin, 1983.

——. *Economics and the Dreamtime: A Hypothetical History*. Cambridge: Cambridge University Press, 1993.

Buxton, Charles. *Memoirs of Sir Thomas Fowell Buxton, Bart*. London: John Murray, 1849.

Canny, Nicholas P. "The Ideology of English Colonization: From Ireland to America." *William and Mary Quarterly*, 3rd series, 30 (1973): 575–98.

Carlyle, Thomas. "Chartism." In *English and Other Critical Essays*, 165–238. London: Dent, 1964.

Carter, Paul. *The Road to Botany Bay: An Exploration of Landscape and History*. Chicago: University of Chicago Press, 1987.

Casey, Daniel, and Robert Rhodes, eds. *Views of the Irish Peasantry, 1800–1916*. Hamden, Conn.: Archon, 1977.

Castoriadis, Cornelius. "Reflections on 'Rationality' and 'Development.' " In *Philosophy, Politics, Autonomy: Essays in Political Philosophy*, 175–98. Oxford: Oxford University Press, 1991.

Chambers, Robert. *Vestiges of the Natural History of Creation*. 1844. New York: Humanities, 1969.

Charny, Israel W. *Encyclopedia of Genocide*. 2 vols. Santa Barbara, Calif.: ABC-CLIO, 1999.

Chase, Allan. *The Legacy of Malthus: The Social Costs of the New Scientific Racism*. New York: Knopf, 1977.

Chesterton, Gilbert Keith. *The Crimes of England*. London: Cecil Palmer and Hayward, 1915.

Childs, Donald J. *Modernism and Eugenics: Woolf, Eliot, Yeats, and the Culture of Degeneration*. Cambridge: Cambridge University Press, 2001.

Churchill, Ward. *Indians Are Us? Culture and Genocide in Native North America*. Monroe, Maine: Common Courage, 1994.

——. *A Little Matter of Genocide: Holocaust and Denial in the Americas, 1492 to the Present*. San Francisco: City Lights, 1997.

Clarke, I. F. *Voices Prophesying War, 1763–1984*. London: Oxford University Press, 1966.

Clifford, James. "On Ethnographic Allegory." In Clifford and Marcus, *Writing Culture*, 98–121.

——. *The Predicament of Culture: Twentieth-Century Ethnography, Literature, and Art*. Cambridge, Mass.: Harvard University Press, 1988.

Clifford, James, and George Marcus, eds. *Writing Culture: The Poetics and Politics of Ethnography*. Berkeley: University of California Press, 1986.

Cobbett, William. *Cobbett in Ireland: A Warning to England*. Edited by Denis Knight. London: Lawrence and Wishart, 1984.

Coetzee, J. M. *White Writing: On the Culture of Letters in South Africa*. New Haven: Yale University Press, 1988.

Colbert, Edwin H. *Men and Dinosaurs: The Search in Field and Laboratory*. New York: Dutton, 1968.

Congress of the United States. *Speeches on the Passage of the Bill for the Removal of the Indians . . . April and May, 1830*. Millwood, N.Y.: Kraus Reprint, 1973.

Connolly, S. J. "Revisions Revised? New Work on the Irish Famine." *Victorian Studies* 39, no. 2 (winter 1996): 205–16.

Conrad, Joseph. *Victory*. New York: Penguin, 1996.

Cook, James. *The Journals of Captain James Cook on His Voyages of Discovery*. 4 vols. Edited by J. C. Beaglehole. Cambridge: Cambridge University Press, 1969.

Cooper, James Fenimore. *The Deerslayer*. New York: Penguin, 1987.

——. *The Prairie*. New York: Penguin, 1987.

——. *The Last of the Mohicans*. Oxford: Oxford World's Classics, 1990.

——. *Notions of the Americans: Picked up by a Travelling Bachelor*. Albany: State University of New York Press, 1991.

Corbett, Mary Jean. *Allegories of Union in Irish and English Writing, 1790–1870: Politics, History, and the Family from Edgeworth to Arnold*. Cambridge: Cambridge University Press, 2000.

Cornell, Stephen. *The Return of the Native: American Indian Political Resurgence*. New York: Oxford University Press, 1988.

Cove, John J. *What the Bones Say: Tasmanian Aborigines, Science, and Domination*. Ottawa: Carleton University Press, 1995.

[Craik, George Lillie]. *The New Zealanders*. London: Charles Knight for the Society for the Diffusion of Useful Knowledge, 1830.

Crèvecoeur, Hector St. John. *Letters from an American Farmer and Sketches of Eighteenth-Century America*. New York: Penguin, 1986.

Crook, Paul. *Darwinism, War, and History: The Debate over the Biology of War from the "Origin of Species" to the First World War*. Cambridge: Cambridge University Press, 1994.

Crosby, A. W. *The Columbian Exchange: The Biological and Cultural Consequences of 1492*. Westport, Conn.: Greenwood, 1972.

Curtis, L. Perry. *Anglo-Saxons and Celts: A Study of Anti-Irish Prejudice in Victorian England*. Bridgeport, Conn.: University of Bridgeport Press, 1968.

——. *Apes and Angels: The Irishman in Victorian Caricature*. Washington, D.C.: Smithsonian Institution Press, 1971.

Cuvier, Georges. *The Animal Kingdom Arranged in Conformity with Its Organization*. Edited by Edward Griffith et al. Vol. 1. London: George Whittaker, 1827.

Daly, Mary. "Revisionism and Irish History: The Great Famine." In *The Making of Modern Irish History: Revisionism and the Revisionist Controversy*, ed. D. George Boyce and Alan O'Day, 71–89. London: Routledge, 1996.

Daniel, Glyn. *The Idea of Prehistory*. Harmondsworth: Penguin, 1971.

Darwin, Charles. *Journal of Researches*. New York: P. F. Collier, 1905.

——. *The Voyage of the Beagle*. Ed. Leonard Engel. Garden City, N.Y.: Doubleday, Natural History Library, 1962.

——. *The Autobiography of Charles Darwin, 1809–1882*. Edited by Nora Barlow. New York: Norton, 1969.

——. *The Origin of Species*. 1859. New York: Modern Library, 1998.

——. *The Descent of Man*. 1874. New York: Prometheus Books, 1998.

Darwin, Francis, ed. *The Life and Letters of Charles Darwin*. 2 vols. 1888. New York: Basic Books, 1959.

Davenport, T. R. H. "The Consolidation of a New Society: The Cape Colony." In Wilson and Thompson, *The Oxford History of South Africa*, 1:272–333.

Davies, David. *The Last of the Tasmanians*. London: Frederick Muller, 1973.

Davies, John. *The History of the Tahitian Mission, 1799–1830.* Edited by C. W. Newbury. Cambridge: Cambridge University Press, 1961.

Davis, Graham. "The Historiography of the Irish Famine." In O'Sullivan, *The Meaning of the Famine,* 15–39.

Denoon, Donald. "Depopulation." In *The Cambridge History of the Pacific Islanders,* 243–49. Cambridge: Cambridge University Press, 1997.

Derrida, Jacques. *Of Grammatology.* Translated by Gayatri Chakravorty Spivak. Baltimore: Johns Hopkins University Press, 1976.

Diamond, Jared. *Guns, Germs, and Steel: The Fates of Human Societies.* New York: Norton, 1997.

Dickens, Charles. "The Noble Savage." *Household Words,* June 11, 1853.

——. "The Niger Expedition." In *Miscellaneous Papers.* National Library edition. Vol. 18. New York: Bigelow, Brown, 1903. First published in *The Examiner,* August 19, 1848.

Di Gregorio, Mario A. *T. H. Huxley's Place in Natural Science.* New Haven: Yale University Press, 1984.

Dilke, Charles Wentworth. *Greater Britain: A Record of Travel in English-Speaking Countries during 1866 and 1867.* 2 vols. London: Macmillan, 1869.

Dippie, Brian. *The Vanishing American: White Attitudes and U.S. Indian Policy.* Lawrence: University Press of Kansas, 1982.

Donnelly, James S., Jr. "The Administration of Relief, 1846–7." In *New History of Ireland,* ed. W. E. Vaughan, 5:294–331. Oxford: Clarendon, 1989.

——. "The Construction of the Memory of the Famine in Ireland and the Irish Diaspora, 1850–1900." *Éire-Ireland* 31, nos. 1/2 (spring/summer 1996): 26–61.

Drewe, Robert. *The Savage Crows.* Sydney: Williams Collins, 1976.

Drinnon, Richard. *Facing West: The Metaphysics of Indian-Hating and Empire Building.* Minneapolis: University of Minnesota Press, 1980.

Dubow, Saul. *Scientific Racism in Modern South Africa.* Cambridge: Cambridge University Press, 1995.

Dupâquier, Jacques, ed. *Malthus Past and Present.* London: Academic Press, 1983.

Du Plessis, J. *A History of Christian Missions in South Africa.* 1911. Cape Town: Struik, 1965.

Eagleton, Terry. *Heathcliff and the Great Hunger: Studies in Irish Culture.* London: Verso, 1995.

Earle, Augustus. *Narrative of a Residence in New Zealand/Journal of a Residence in Tristan da Cunha.* Edited by E. H. McCormick. Oxford: Clarendon, 1966.

Edmond, Rod. *Representing the South Pacific: Colonial Discourse from Cook to Gauguin.* Cambridge: Cambridge University Press, 1997.

Edwards, Isobel Eirlys. *The 1820 Settlers in South Africa: A Study in British Colonial Policy.* London: Longmans, Green, 1934.

Elkin, A. P. *The Australian Aborigines.* 1938. 3rd ed. Garden City, N.Y.: Anchor, 1964.

Elliott, Brian, and Adrian Mitchell, eds. *Bards in the Wilderness: Australian Colonial Poetry to 1920.* Melbourne: Nelson, 1970.

Elliott, Emory, ed. *The Columbia Literary History of the United States.* New York: Columbia University Press, 1988.

Elliott, J. H. "The Rediscovery of America." *New York Review of Books,* June 24, 1993, 36–41.

Ellis, William. *Polynesian Researches, during a Residence of Nearly Eight Years in the Society and Sandwich Islands.* 4 vols. New York: Harper, 1833.

Elphick, Richard, and Hermann Giliomee, eds. *The Shaping of South African Society, 1652–1840.* Middletown, Conn.: Wesleyan University Press, 1989.

Engels, Friedrich. *The Condition of the Working Class in England.* Translated by W. O. Henderson and W. H. Chaloner. Stanford, Calif.: Stanford University Press, 1958.

Fabian, Johannes. *Time and the Other: How Anthropology Makes Its Object.* New York: Columbia University Press, 1983.

Fanon, Frantz. *The Wretched of the Earth.* Translated by Constance Farrington. New York: Grove, 1963.

Farnham, Thomas J. *Travels in the Great Western Prairies, the Anahuac and Rocky Mountains, and in the Oregon Territory.* Edited by Reuben Gold Thwaites. Vol. 28 of *Early Western Travels, 1748–1846.* Cleveland, Ohio: Arthur H. Clark, 1906.

Faverty, Frederic E. *Matthew Arnold the Ethnologist.* Evanston: Northwestern University Press, 1951.

Ferry, John. "The Failure of the New South Wales Missions to the Aborigines before 1845." *Aboriginal History* 3, nos. 1–2 (1979): 25–36.

Fitzgerald, F. Scott. *The Great Gatsby.* New York: Scribner's, 1953.

Flanagan, Roderick J. *The Aborigines of Australia.* Sydney: George Robertson, 1888.

Foley, Tadhg, and Seán Ryder, eds. *Ideology and Ireland in the Nineteenth Century.* Dublin: Four Courts, 1998.

Foster, Robert F. *Paddy and Mr Punch: Connections in Irish and English History.* London: Allen Lane, Penguin, 1993.

Frank, André Gunder. *Capitalism and Underdevelopment in Latin America.* New York: Monthly Review Press, 1967.

Franklin, Benjamin. *Autobiography and Selections from His Other Writings.* New York: Modern Library, 1950.

Frazier, Patrick. *The Mohicans of Stockbridge.* Lincoln: University of Nebraska Press, 1992.

Frederickson, George M. *The Black Image in the White Mind: The Debate on Afro-American Character and Destiny, 1817–1914.* Middletown, Conn.: Wesleyan University Press, 1987.

Freneau, Philip. *Poems of Freneau.* Edited by Harry Hayden Clark. New York: Hafner, 1929.

Frost, Alan. "New South Wales as *terra nullius*: The British Denial of Aboriginal Rights." In Janson and Macintyre, *Through White Eyes*, 65–76.

Froude, James Anthony. *Oceana; or, England and Her Colonies.* London: Longmans, Green, 1886.

Gailey, Andrew. *Ireland and the Death of Kindness: The Experience of Constructive Unionism, 1890–1905.* Cork: Cork University Press, 1987.

Galbraith, John S. *Reluctant Empire: British Policy on the South African Frontier, 1834–1854.* Berkeley: University of California Press, 1963.

Galton, Francis. "Hereditary Talent and Character." *Macmillan's Magazine* 12 (1865): 157–66, 318–27.

——— . *Hereditary Genius: An Inquiry into Its Laws and Consequences.* 1869. London: Macmillan, 1925.

Glenn, Ian. "The Bushman in Early South African Literature." In Skotnes, *Miscast*, 41–49.

Godelier, Maurice. "Malthus and Ethnography." In Dupâquier, *Malthus Past and Present*, 125–50.

Godlonton, Robert. *Narrative of the Irruption of the Kafir Hordes into the Eastern Province of the Cape of Good Hope, A.D. 1834–35*. Graham's Town: Meurant and Godlonton, 1835.

Gould, Stephen Jay. *Ever since Darwin: Reflections in Natural History*. New York: Norton, 1977.

——. *The Mismeasure of Man*. New York: Norton, 1981.

——. *Time's Arrow, Time's Cycle: Myth and Metaphor in the Discovery of Geological Time*. Cambridge, Mass.: Harvard University Press, 1987.

Grant, Madison. *The Passing of the Great Race*. 2nd ed. 1918. New York: Arno, 1970.

Graves, Joseph L. *The Emperor's New Clothes: Biological Theories of Race at the Millennium*. New Brunswick, N.J.: Rutgers University Press, 2001.

Gray, Peter. "Ideology and the Famine." In Póirtéir, *The Great Irish Famine*, 86–103.

——. "Nassau Senior, the *Edinburgh Review*, and Ireland 1843–49." In Foley and Ryder, *Ideology and Ireland in the Nineteenth Century*, 130–42.

Gray, Stephen. *South African Literature: An Introduction*. New York: Harper and Row, 1979.

Greenfeld, Karl Taro. "Return of the *Yellow Peril*." *The Nation* 254, no. 18 (May 11, 1992): 636–39.

Greenslade, William. *Degeneration, Culture, and the Novel, 1880–1940*. Cambridge: Cambridge University Press, 1994.

Grey, George. *Journals of Two Expeditions of Discovery in North-West and Western Australia, during the Years 1837, 38, and 39*. 2 vols. London: Boone, 1841.

Gruber, Howard E. *Darwin on Man: A Psychological Study of Scientific Creativity*. New York: Dutton, 1974.

Gunson, Niel. Introduction to *Australian Reminiscences and Papers of L. E. Threlkeld, Missionary to the Aborigines, 1824–1859*, by L[ancelot] E. Threlkeld, ed. Niel Gunson, 1:1–37. 2 vols. Canberra: Australian Institute of Aboriginal Studies, 1974.

——. *Messengers of Grace: Evangelical Missionaries in the South Seas, 1797–1860*. Melbourne: Oxford University Press, 1978.

Haggard, H. Rider. *Cetawayo and His White Neighbours*. London: Trubner, 1882.

Hall, Henry L. *The Colonial Office: A History*. London: Longmans, Green, 1937.

Haller, John S. *Outcasts from Evolution: Scientific Attitudes of Racial Inferiority, 1859–1900*. Urbana: University of Illinois Press, 1971.

Healy, J. J. *Literature and the Aborigine in Australia*. 2nd ed. St. Lucia: University of Queensland Press, 1989.

Hegel, Georg Wilhelm Friedrich. *The Philosophy of History*. Translated by J. Sibree. New York: Dover, 1956.

Hemming, Steve. "Changing History: New Images of Aboriginal History." In Bourke, Bourke, and Edwards, *Aboriginal Australia*, 16–37.

Herbert, Christopher. *Culture and Anomie: Ethnographic Imagination in the Nineteenth Century*. Chicago: University of Chicago Press, 1991.

Herbert, T. Walter, Jr. *Marquesan Encounters: Melville and the Meaning of Civilization*. Cambridge, Mass.: Harvard University Press, 1980.

Herskovits, Melville J. *Economic Anthropology: A Study in Comparative Economics.* New York: Knopf, 1952.

Hiatt, L. R. *Arguments about Aborigines: Australia and the Evolution of Social Anthropology.* Cambridge: Cambridge University Press, 1996.

Higman, B. W. "Slavery and the Development of Demographic Theory in the Age of the Industrial Revolution." In *Slavery and British Society, 1776–1846,* ed. James Walvin, 164–94. Baton Rouge: Lousiana State University Press, 1982.

Hinsley, Curtis M. *The Smithsonian and the American Indian: Making a Moral Anthropology in Victorian America.* Washington, D.C.: Smithsonian Institution Press, 1994.

Hinton, Alexander Laban, ed. *Genocide: An Anthropological Reader.* Oxford: Blackwell, 2002.

Hitchcock, Robert K., and Tara M. Twedt. "Physical and Cultural Genocide of Various Indigenous Peoples." In Totten, Parsons, and Charny, *Genocide in the Twentieth Century,* 483–534.

Hodge, Bob, and Vijay Mishra. *Dark Side of the Dream: Australian Literature and the Postcolonial Mind.* Sydney: Allen and Unwin, 1991.

Hopkins, Manley. *Hawaii: The Past, Present, and Future of Its Island-Kingdom.* London: Longmans, Green, 1866.

Hughes, Robert. *The Fatal Shore: The Epic of Australia's Founding.* New York: Vintage, 1986.

Hulme, Peter. Introduction to Barker, Hulme, and Iversen, *Cannibalism and the Colonial World.*

Huxley, Thomas Henry. *Collected Essays.* 9 vols. New York: Greenwood, 1968.

Ignatiev, Noel. *How the Irish Became White.* New York: Routledge, 1995.

Irvine, William. *Apes, Angels, and Victorians: Darwin, Huxley, and Evolution.* New York: McGraw-Hill, 1972.

Irving, Washington. *Astoria; or, Anecdotes of an Enterprise beyond the Rocky Mountains.* Boston: Twayne, 1976.

———. *The Sketchbook of Geoffrey Crayon, Gent.* New York: Penguin, 1988.

Jacoby, Russell, and Naomi Glauberman, eds. *The Bell Curve Debate: History, Documents, Opinions.* New York: Times Books, 1995.

Jahoda, Gustav. *Images of Savages: Ancient Roots of Modern Prejudice in Western Culture.* New York: Routledge, 1999.

Jaimes, M. Annette, ed. *The State of Native America: Genocide, Colonization, and Resistance.* Boston: South End, 1992.

JanMohamed, Abdul R. *Manichean Aesthetics: The Politics of Literature in Colonial Africa.* Amherst: University of Massachusetts Press, 1983.

Janson, Susan, and Stuart Macintyre, eds. *Through White Eyes.* Sydney: Allen and Unwin, 1990.

Jeal, Tim. *Livingstone.* New York: G. P. Putnam, 1973.

Jennings, Francis. *The Invasion of America: Indians, Colonialism, and the Cant of Conquest.* Chapel Hill: University of North Carolina Press, 1975.

Johnson, Paul. *Ireland: A Concise History from the Twelfth Century to the Present Day.* Chicago: Academy, 1984.

Jones, Gareth Stedman. *Outcast London: A Study of the Relationship between Classes in Victorian Society.* 1971. New York: Pantheon, 1984.

Jones, Howard Mumford. *O Strange New World: American Culture: The Formative Years*. New York: Viking, 1964.

Jones, Joseph. *The Cradle of Erewhon: Samuel Butler in New Zealand*. Austin: University of Texas Press, 1959.

Kass, Amalie M., and Edward H. Kass. *Perfecting the World: The Life and Times of Dr. Thomas Hodgkin, 1798–1866*. Boston: Harcourt Brace Jovanovich, 1988.

Katzen, M. F. "White Settlers and the Origin of a New Society, 1652–1778." In Wilson and Thompson, *The Oxford History of South Africa*, 1:183–232.

Keegan, Timothy. *Colonial South Africa and the Origins of the Racial Order*. Charlottesville: University of Virginia Press, 1996.

Keiser, Albert. *The Indian in American Literature*. New York: Oxford University Press, 1933.

Kelleher, Margaret. *The Feminization of Famine*. Durham: Duke University Press, 1997.

Kendall, Henry. *The Poetical Works of Henry Kendall*. Adelaide: Libraries Board of South Australia, 1966.

Kennedy, Roger G. *Hidden Cities: The Discovery and Loss of Ancient North American Civilization*. New York: Free Press, 1994.

Kevles, Daniel J. *In the Name of Eugenics: Genetics and the Uses of Human Heredity*. Cambridge, Mass.: Harvard University Press, 1995.

Kinealy, Christine. *The Great Calamity: The Irish Famine, 1845–52*. Boulder, Colo.: Roberts Rinehart, 1995.

Kingsley, Charles. *Charles Kingsley, His Letters and Memories of His Life*. London: Macmillan, 1921.

Knaplund, Paul. *James Stephen and the British Colonial System, 1813–1847*. Madison: University of Wisconsin Press, 1953.

Knelman, Judith. "Anthony Trollope, English Journalist and Novelist, Writing about the Famine in Ireland." *Éire-Ireland* 23, no. 3 (1988): 57–67.

Knox, Robert. *The Races of Men: A Fragment*. 1850. Miami: Mnemosyne, 1969.

Kolodny, Annette. "Among the Indians: The Uses of Captivity." *New York Times Book Review*, January 31, 1993, 1, 26–29.

Krader, Lawrence, ed. *The Ethnological Notebooks of Karl Marx*. Assen: Van Gorcum, 1972.

Kunitz, Stephen J. *Disease and Social Diversity: The European Impact on the Health of Non-Europeans*. New York: Oxford University Press, 1994.

Kupperman, Karen Ordahl. *Settling with the Indians: The Meeting of English and Indian Cultures in America, 1580–1640*. Totowa, N.J.: Rowman and Littlefield, 1980.

Lamb, Jonathan. *Preserving the Self in the South Seas, 1680–1840*. Chicago: University of Chicago Press, 2001.

Lamb, Jonathan, Vanessa Smith, and Nicholas Thomas, eds. *Exploration and Exchange: A South Seas Anthology, 1680–1900*. Chicago: University of Chicago Press, 2000.

Lang, Raeburn. *May the People Live: A History of Maori Health Development, 1900–1920*. Auckland: Auckland University Press, 1999.

Lankester, E. Ray. *Degeneration: A Chapter in Darwinism*. London: Macmillan, 1880.

Las Casas, Bartolomé de. *The Devastation of the Indies.* Translated by Herma Briffault. Baltimore, Md.: Johns Hopkins University Press, 1992.

Lebow, Ned. "British Images of Poverty in Pre-Famine Ireland." In Casey and Rhodes, *Views of the Irish Peasantry, 1800–1916,* 57–85.

Leonard, John, ed. *Australian Verse: An Oxford Anthology.* Melbourne: Oxford University Press, 1998.

Levine, Robert S., ed. *The Cambridge Companion to Herman Melville.* Cambridge: Cambridge University Press, 1998.

Lévi-Strauss, Claude. *Structural Anthropology.* Translated by Claire Jacobson and Brooke Grundfest Schoepf. Garden City, N.Y.: Anchor, 1967.

——. *Tristes Tropiques.* Translated by John and Doreen Weightman. New York: Atheneum, 1974.

Lewis, Milton." 'The Health of the Race' and Infant Health in New South Wales: Perspectives on Medicine and Empire." In MacLeod and Lewis, *Disease, Medicine, and Empire,* 301–15.

Lightman, Bernard, ed. *Victorian Science in Context.* Chicago: University of Chicago Press, 1997.

Locke, John. *Two Treatises of Government.* London: Dent, 1991.

Longfellow, Henry Wadsworth. *Poems.* New York: Modern Library, n.d.

Lorimer, Douglas. "Science and the Secularization of Victorian Images of Race." In Lightman, *Victorian Science in Context,* 212–35.

Lovett, Richard. *History of the London Missionary Society.* 2 vols. London: H. Frowde, 1899.

Lubbers, Klaus. *Born for the Shade: Stereotypes of the Native American in United States Literature and the Visual Arts, 1776–1894.* Amsterdam: Rodopi, 1994.

Lubbock, Sir John. *Pre-Historic Times as Illustrated by Ancient Remains and the Manners and Customs of Modern Savages.* 1865. 5th ed. New York: Appleton, 1890.

Lyell, Charles. *Principles of Geology.* Edited by James A. Secord. London: Penguin, 1997.

Lyotard, Jean-François. *Libidinal Economy.* Translated by Iain Hamilton Grant. Bloomington: Indiana University Press, 1993.

MacCrone, Ian Douglas. *Race Attitudes in South Africa: Historical, Experimental, and Psychological Studies.* London: Oxford University Press, 1937.

MacLeod, Roy, and Milton Lewis, eds. *Disease, Medicine, and Empire: Perspectives on Western Medicine and the Experience of European Expansion.* London: Routledge, 1988.

Macmillan, W. M. *Bantu, Boer, and Briton: The Making of the South African Native Problem.* Rev. ed. Oxford: Oxford University Press, 1963.

Maddox, Lucy. *Removals: Nineteenth-Century American Literature and the Politics of Indian Affairs.* New York: Oxford University Press, 1991.

Malchow, H. L. *Gothic Images of Race in Nineteenth-Century Britain.* Stanford, Calif.: Stanford University Press, 1996.

Malthus, Thomas Robert. *On Population.* New York: Random House, Modern Library, 1960.

Marsden, Rev. Samuel. *Letters and Journals.* Edited by John R. Elder. Dunedin: Coulls, Somerville, Wilkie: 1932.

Martin, Calvin, ed. *The American Indian and the Problem of History.* New York: Oxford University Press, 1987.

Martineau, Harriet. *Demarara.* In *Illustrations of Political Economy,* 2:1–143. London: Charles Fox, 1834.

———. *Life in the Wilds.* In *Illustrations of Political Economy,* 1:1–124. London: Charles Fox, 1834.

———. *Dawn Island, A Tale.* Manchester: Gadsby, 1845.

Marx, Karl, and Frederick [sic] Engels. *Ireland and the Irish Question.* New York: International, 1972.

Marx, Karl, and Friedrich Engels. *The Marx-Engels Reader.* Edited by Robert Tucker. New York: Norton, 1978.

Mather, Cotton. *Magnalia Christi Americana; or, The Ecclesiastical History of New-England.* 2 vols. New York: Russell and Russell, 1966.

McCaffrey, Lawrence J. *The Irish Question: Two Centuries of Conflict.* 2d ed. Lexington: University Press of Kentucky, 1995.

McCormick, E. H. *New Zealand Literature: A Survey.* London: Oxford University Press, 1959.

McGregor, Russell. *Imagined Destinies: Aboriginal Australians and the Doomed Race Theory, 1880–1939.* Melbourne: Melbourne University Press, 1997.

McNab, Robert, ed. *Historical Records of New Zealand.* Vol. 1. Wellington: John MacKay, 1908.

Mellor, George R. *British Imperial Trusteeship, 1783–1850.* London: Faber and Faber, 1951.

Melville, Herman. *Typee.* Harmondsworth: Penguin, 1972.

———. *The Confidence-Man: His Masquerade.* New York: Penguin, 1990.

Merivale, Herman. *Lectures on Colonization and Colonies, 1839–41.* London: Longman, Green, Longman, and Roberts, 1861.

Mill, John Stuart. "Civilization." In Schneewind, *Mill's Essays on Literature and Society,* 148–82.

———. *Principles of Political Economy.* 2 vols. Toronto: University of Toronto Press, 1965.

Moore, James. "Wallace's Malthusian Moment: The Common Context Revisited." In Lightman, *Victorian Science in Context,* 290–311.

Moorehead, Alan. *The Fatal Impact: An Account of the Invasion of the South Pacific, 1767–1840.* New York: Harper and Row, 1966.

Morash, Christopher. Introduction to *The Hungry Voice: The Poetry of the Irish Famine,* ed. Christopher Morash. Dublin: Irish Academic Press, 1989.

———. *Writing the Irish Famine.* Oxford: Clarendon, 1995.

Morash, Christopher, and Richard Hayes, eds. *'Fearful Realities': New Perspectives on the Irish Famine.* Dublin: Irish Academic Press, 1996.

Morgan, Lewis Henry. *Ancient Society.* 1877. Edited by Leslie White. Cambridge, Mass.: Harvard University Press, 1964.

———. *League of the Iroquois.* Secaucus, N.J.: Citadel, 1990.

Morse, Jedidiah. *A Report to the Secretary of War, on Indian Affairs.* 1822.

Mostert, Noël. *Frontiers: The Epic of South Africa's Creation and the Tragedy of the Xhosa People.* New York: Knopf, 1992.

Mulvaney, D. J. "The Australian Aborigines, 1606–1929: Opinion and Fieldwork." In Janson and Macintyre, *Through White Eyes*, 1–44.

Mulvaney, Derek J., and J. H. Calaby. *"So Much That Is New": Baldwin Spencer, 1860–1929*. Melbourne: University of Melbourne Press, 1985.

Newbury, C. W. Introduction to John Davies, *The History of the Tahitian Mission, 1799–1830*, edited by C. W. Newbury. Cambridge: Cambridge University Press, 1961.

Nicolson, Malcolm. "Medicine and Racial Politics: Changing Images of the New Zealand Maori in the Nineteenth Century." In Arnold, *Imperial Medicine and Indigenous Societies*, 66–104.

Nightingale, Florence. "Note on the Aboriginal Races in Australia." *National Association for the Promotion of Social Science Transactions* (1864): 552–58.

Nott, Josiah, and George Glidden. *Types of Mankind; or, Ethnological Researches.* 1854. 10th ed. Philadelphia: Lippincott, 1871.

O'Gráda, Cormac. *The Great Irish Famine*. New York: Macmillan, 1989.

Oliver, W. H., and B. R. Williams, eds. *The Oxford History of New Zealand*. Oxford: Oxford University Press, 1981.

Orange, Claudia. *The Treaty of Waitangi*. Wellington: Allen and Unwin, 1987.

Osborne, Sidney Godolphin. "Immortal Sewerage." In *Meliora; or, Better Times to Come*, ed. Viscount Ingestre. 1st series, 7–17. 1853. London: Frank Cass, 1971.

O'Sullivan, Patrick, ed. *The Meaning of the Famine*. London: Leicester University Press, 1997.

O'Toole, Fintan. "Going Native: The Irish as Blacks and Indians." *Études Irlandaises* 19 (autumn 1994): 121–31.

Otter, Samuel. " 'Race' in *Typee* and *White-Jacket*." In Levine, *The Cambridge Companion to Herman Melville*, 12–36.

Owens, J. M. R. "New Zealand before Annexation." In Oliver and Williams, *The Oxford History of New Zealand*, 28–53.

Parkman, Francis. *The Conspiracy of Pontiac*. 1851. New York: Collier, 1962.

Pearce, Roy Harvey. *The Savages of America: A Study of the Indian and the Idea of Civilization*. Baltimore: Johns Hopkins University Press, 1965.

Peck, H. Daniel. "James Fenimore Cooper and the Writers of the Frontier." In E. Elliott, *The Columbia Literary History of the United States*, 240–61.

Peel, J. D. Y., ed. *Herbert Spencer on Social Evolution*. Chicago: University of Chicago Press, 1972.

Peires, J. B. "The British and the Cape, 1814–1834." In Elphick and Giliomee, *The Shaping of South African Society, 1652–1840*, 472–517.

Penn, Nigel. " 'Fated to Perish': The Destruction of the Cape San." In Skotnes, *Miscast*, 81–91.

Philip, John. *Researches in South Africa: Illustrating the Civil, Moral, and Religious Condition of the Native Tribes*. 2 vols. 1828. New York: Negro Universities Press, 1969.

Pick, Daniel. *Faces of Degeneration: A European Disorder, c. 1848–c. 1918*. Cambridge: Cambridge University Press, 1989.

Pickering, Michael. "Consuming Doubts: What Some People Ate? or, What Some

People Swallowed?" In *The Anthropology of Cannibalism*, ed. Laurence R. Goldman, 51–74. Westport, Conn.: Bergin and Garvey, 1999.

Pieterse, Jan Nederveen. *White on Black: Images of Africa in Western Popular Culture*. New Haven: Yale University Press, 1992.

Pilger, John. *A Secret Country*. London: Jonathan Cape, Vintage, 1992.

Pitt-Rivers, Augustus Lane Fox. *The Evolution of Culture, and Other Essays*. Oxford: Clarendon, 1906.

Plomley, N. J. B., ed. *Friendly Mission: The Tasmanian Journals and Papers of George Augustus Robinson, 1829–1834*. Hobart: Tasmanian Historical Research Association, 1966.

——, ed. *Weep in Silence: A History of the Flinders Island Aboriginal Settlement*. Hobart: Blubber Head, 1987.

Póirtéir, Cahal, ed. *The Great Irish Famine*. Dublin: Mercier, 1995.

Polack, Joel Samuel. *Manners and Customs of the New Zealanders; with Notes Corroborative of their Habits, Usages, etc., and Remarks to Intending Emigrants*. 2 vols. London: James Madden and Hatchard, 1840.

Pool, D. Ian. *The Maori Population of New Zealand, 1769–1971*. Auckland: Auckland University Press, 1977.

Popkin, Richard H. "The Philosophical Bases of Modern Racism." In Walton and Anton, *Philosophy and the Civilizing Arts*, 126–65.

Pretorius, J. G. *The British Humanitarians and the Cape Eastern Frontier, 1834–1836*. Pretoria: Archives Year Book for South African History, 1988.

Prichard, James Cowles. "On the Extinction of Human Races." *Edinburgh New Philosophical Journal* 28 (1839): 166–70.

——. *The Natural History of Man; Comprising Inquiries into the Modifying Influence of Physical and Moral Agencies on the Different Tribes of the Human Family*. London: Hippolyte Bailliere, 1845.

Pringle, Thomas. *African Poems of Thomas Pringle*. Edited by Ernest Pereira and Michael Chapman. Durban: University of Natal Press, 1989.

——. *Narrative of a Residence in South Africa*. 1835. Cape Town: Struik, 1966.

Prucha, Francis Paul, ed. *Documents of United States Indian Policy*. Lincoln: University of Nebraska Press, 1975.

Quinn, Peter. Introduction to special issue on the Irish Famine. *Éire-Ireland* 32, no. 1 (spring 1997).

Rae-Ellis, Vivienne. *Trucanini: Queen or Traitor?* Canberra: Australian Institute of Aboriginal Studies, 1981.

——. *Black Robinson: Protector of Aborigines*. Melbourne: Melbourne University Press, 1987.

Rafferty, Terrence. "Brave Acts." *New Yorker*, October 5, 1992, 160–62.

Rawson, Claude. *God, Gulliver, and Genocide: Barbarism and the European Imagination, 1492–1945*. Oxford: Oxford University Press, 2001.

Reece, R. H. W. *Aborigines and Colonists: Aborigines and Colonial Society in New South Wales in the 1830s and 1840s*. Sydney: Sydney University Press, 1974.

Renan, Ernest. "On the Poetry of the Celtic Races." In *The World's Great Literature*, 60:411–55. New York: Collier, 1900.

Report from the Select Committee on Aborigines (British Settlements). Parliamentary Papers, 2 vols., 1836–37. Shannon: Irish University Press, 1968.

Reynolds, Henry. *Dispossession: Black Australians and White Invaders*. Sydney: Allen and Unwin, 1989.

——. "The Land, the Explorers, and the Aborigines." In Janson and Macintyre, *Through White Eyes*, 120–31.

——. *The Law of the Land*. 2nd ed. Ringwood, Victoria: Penguin Australia, 1992.

——. *Frontier: Reports from the Edge of White Settlement*. St. Leonard's, New South Wales: Allen and Unwin, 1996.

——, ed. *Aborigines and Settlers: The Australian Experience, 1788–1939*. Melbourne: Cassell Australia, 1972.

Ricardo, David. *The Principles of Economics and Taxation*. London: Everyman Library, n.d.

Ritchie, D. G. *Darwinism and Politics*. New York: Scribner and Welford, 1889.

Roberts, Stephen H. *Population Problems of the Pacific*. 1927. New York: AMS Press, 1969.

Robinson, George Augustus. "Report on the Aboriginal Establishment at Flinders Island." In *Report from the Select Committee on Aborigines (British Settlements)*. Parliamentary Papers, 1839, 396–411. Shannon: Irish University Press, 1968.

Robson, Lloyd. *A History of Tasmania*, vol. 1: *Van Diemen's Land from the Earliest Times to 1855*. Melbourne: Oxford University Press, 1983.

Roebuck, J. A. *The Colonies of England*. London: Parker, 1849.

Rogin, Michael Paul. *Fathers and Children: Andrew Jackson and the Subjugation of the American Indian*. New York: Knopf, 1975.

Romero, Lora. "Vanishing Americans: Gender, Empire, and New Historicism." *American Literature* 63, no. 3 (September 1991): 385–404.

Rosaldo, Renato. "Imperialist Nostalgia." In *Culture and Truth: The Remaking of Social Analysis*, 68–87. Boston: Beacon, 1989.

Rosenbaum, Alan S. *Is the Holocaust Unique? Perspectives on Comparative Genocide*. Boulder, Colo.: Westview, 1996.

Ross, Andrew. *John Philip (1775–1851): Missions, Race, and Politics in South Africa*. Aberdeen: Aberdeen University Press, 1986.

Ross, Robert. *A Concise History of South Africa*. Cambridge: Cambridge University Press, 1999.

Roth, H. Ling. *The Aborigines of Tasmania*. 1890. Halifax, Engl.: F. King, 1899.

Rousseau, Jean-Jacques. *The Essential Rousseau*. Translated by Lowell Bair. New York: Mentor, 1974.

Rowley, C. D. *The Destruction of Aboriginal Society*. Canberra: Australian National University Press, 1970.

Rubenstein, Richard L. *The Age of Triage: Fear and Hope in an Overcrowded World*. Boston: Beacon, 1983.

Rudwick, Martin. *The Meaning of Fossils: Episodes in the History of Palaeontology*. 2d ed. New York: Science History Publications, 1976.

Rummel, R. J. *Death by Government*. New Brunswick, N.J.: Transaction, 1994.

Ruse, Michael. *The Darwinian Revolution: Science Red in Tooth and Claw*. 2d ed. Chicago: University of Chicago Press, 1999.

Ryan, Lyndall. *The Aboriginal Tasmanians*. Vancouver: University of British Columbia Press, 1981.

Said, Edward. *Culture and Imperialism*. New York: Knopf, 1993.

Salter, Elizabeth. *Daisy Bates: "The Great White Queen of the Never Never."* London: Angus and Robertson, 1971.

Sayre, Robert F. *Thoreau and the Indians*. Princeton, N.J.: Princeton University Press, 1977.

Schaffer, Kay. *In the Wake of First Contact: The Eliza Fraser Stories*. Cambridge: Cambridge University Press, 1995.

Schneewind, J. B., ed. *Mill's Essays on Literature and Society*. New York: Collier, 1965.

Schoolcraft, Henry. *The American Indians, Their History, Condition, and Prospects, from Original Notes and Manuscripts*. Rev. ed. Buffalo: George H. Derby, 1851.

Schreiner, Olive. *Thoughts on South Africa*. 1923. Johannesburg: Africana Book Society, 1976.

——. "The Native Question." In *An Olive Schreiner Reader: Writings on Women and South Africa*, ed. Carol Barash, 186–97. London: Pandora, 1987.

Searle, G. R. *The Quest for National Efficiency: A Study in British Politics and Political Thought, 1899–1914*. Oxford: Blackwell, 1971.

——. *Eugenics and Politics in Britain, 1900–1914*. Leyden: Noordhoff, 1976.

Secord, James. *Victorian Sensation: The Extraordinary Publication, Reception, and Secret Authorship of* Vestiges of the Natural History of Creation. Chicago: University of Chicago Press, 2000.

Senior, Nassau William. *Journals, Conversations, and Essays Relating to Ireland*. 2 vols. 2d ed. London: Longmans, Green, 1868.

Sheehan, Bernard W. *Seeds of Extinction: Jeffersonian Philanthropy and the American Indian*. Chapel Hill: University of North Carolina Press, 1973.

Shelley, Mary. *The Last Man*. Peterborough, Ont.: Broadview, 1996.

Shiel, Matthew P. *The Yellow Danger*. 1898. London: Routledge/Thoemmes, 1998.

Sigerson, George. *Modern Ireland: Its Vital Questions, Secret Societies, and Government*. London: Longmans, Green, Reader, and Dyer, 1868.

Simms, William Gilmore. *The Yemassee, A Romance of Carolina*. 1835. Boston: Houghton Mifflin, 1961.

Skotnes, Pippa. Introduction to Skotnes, *Miscast*, 15–23.

——, ed. *Miscast: Negotiating the Presence of the Bushmen*. Capetown: University of Capetown Press, 1996.

Slotkin, Richard. *Regeneration through Violence: The Mythology of the American Frontier, 1600–1860*. Middletown, Conn.: Wesleyan University Press, 1973.

Smiles, Samuel. *Self-Help*. 1859. Chicago: Belford, Clarke, 1889.

Smith, Adam. *The Wealth of Nations*. Edited by Edwin Cannan. 2 vols. Chicago: University of Chicago Press, 1976.

Smith, Charles Hamilton. *The Natural History of the Human Species*. Edinburgh: W. H. Lizars, 1848.

Smith, Vanessa. *Literary Culture and the Pacific: Nineteenth-Century Textual Encounters*. Cambridge: Cambridge University Press, 1998.

Sorrenson, M. P. K. "Maori and Pakeha." In Oliver and Williams, *The Oxford History of New Zealand*, 168–93.

Spencer, Baldwin, and F. J. Gillen. *The Arunta: A Study of a Stone Age People*. 2 vols. London: Macmillan, 1927.

Spencer, Herbert. *The Principles of Sociology*. Vol. 1. 1874. New York: Appleton, 1910.

——. *The Study of Sociology*. 1873. Ann Arbor: University of Michigan Press, 1961.

——. "Progress: Its Law and Cause." In Peel, *Herbert Spencer on Social Evolution*, 38–52.

Spenser, Edmund. *A View of the State of Ireland*. Oxford: Blackwell, 1997.

Stannard, David E. *Before the Horror: The Population of Hawai'i on the Eve of Western Contact*. Honolulu: Social Science Research Institute, University of Hawaii, 1989.

——. *American Holocaust: Columbus and the Conquest of the New World*. New York: Oxford University Press, 1992.

Stanner, W. E. H. *White Man Got No Dreaming: Essays 1938–1973*. Canberra: Australian National University Press, 1979.

Stanton, William. *The Leopard's Spots: Scientific Attitudes toward Race in America, 1815–59*. Chicago: University of Chicago Press, 1960.

Stepan, Nancy. *The Idea of Race in Science: Great Britain, 1800–1960*. Hamden, Conn.: Archon, 1982.

Stevenson, Robert Louis. *In the South Seas: Being an Account of Experiences and Observations in the Marquesas, Paumotus, and Gilbert Islands in the Course of Two Cruises, on the Yacht "Casco" (1888) and the Schooner "Equator" (1889)*. London: Chatto and Windus, 1900.

Stockenström, Andries. *The Autobiography of the Late Sir Andries Stockenström*. 2 vols. Cape Town: C. Struik, 1964.

Stocking, George W., Jr. *Victorian Anthropology*. New York: Free Press, 1987.

Strzelecki, Paul Edmund de. *Physical Description of New South Wales and Van Diemen's Land*. London: Longman, Brown, Green, and Longmans, 1845.

Swain, Tony, and Deborah Bird Rose, eds. *Aboriginal Australians and Christian Missions: Ethnographic and Historical Studies*. Bedford Park, South Australia: Australian Association for the Study of Religions, 1988.

Swift, Jonathan. *Gulliver's Travels*. New York: Norton, 1970.

Taylor, Richard. *Te Ika A Maui; or, New Zealand and Its Inhabitants, Illustrating the Origin, Manners, Customs, Mythology, Religion, Rites, Songs, Proverbs, Fables, and Language of the Natives*. London: Wertheim and Macintosh, 1855.

Taylor, W. Cooke. *The Natural History of the Human Species*. 2 vols. 1841. Edinburgh: W. H. Lizars, 1848.

Tennyson, Alfred. *The Poems of Tennyson*. Edited by Christopher Ricks. New York: Norton, 1972.

Theal, George McCall. *The Yellow and Dark-Skinned People of Africa South of the Zambesi*. London: Swan Sonnenschein, 1910.

——. *History of South Africa*. 10 vols. 1915. 4th ed. Capetown: Struik, 1964.

Thompson, Leonard. *A History of South Africa*. New Haven: Yale University Press, 1995.

Thomson, Arthur S. *The Story of New Zealand: Past and Present—Savage and Civilized*. 2 vols. London: John Murray, 1859.

Thoreau, Henry David. *The Maine Woods*. New York: Penguin, 1988.

Threlkeld, L[ancelot] E. *Australian Reminiscences and Papers of L. E. Threlkeld*,

Missionary to the Aborigines, 1824–1859. Edited by Niel Gunson. 2 vols. Canberra: Australian Institute of Aboriginal Studies, 1974.

Torgovnick, Marianna. *Gone Primitive: Savage Intellects, Modern Lives*. Chicago: University of Chicago Press, 1990.

Totten, Samuel, William S. Parsons, and Israel W. Charny, eds. *Genocide in the Twentieth Century: Critical Essays and Eyewitness Accounts*. New York: Garland, 1995.

Trevelyan, Charles. *The Irish Crisis*. London: Longman, Brown, Green, and Longmans, 1848.

Trollope, Anthony. "Trollope's Letters to the *Examiner*." Edited by Helen Garlinghouse King. *The Princeton University Library Chronicle* 26, no. 2 (winter 1965): 71–101.

——. *Australia and New Zealand*. 2 vols. 1873. London: Dawsons, 1968.

——. *South Africa*. 2 vols. 1878. London: Dawsons of Pall Mall, 1968.

——. *Castle Richmond*. Oxford: Oxford World's Classics, 1989.

Turnbull, Clive. *The Black War: The Extermination of the Tasmanian Aborigines*. Melbourne: Cheshire-Lansdowne, 1948.

Turner, H. B. *A History of the Colony of Victoria*. 2 vols. London: Longman, 1902.

Twain, Mark. "The Noble Red Man." In *Collected Tales, Sketches, Speeches, and Essays, 1852–1890*, ed. Louis J. Budd, 1:442–48. New York: The Library of America, 1992.

Tylor, Edward Burnett. Preface to *The Aborigines of Tasmania*, by H. Ling Roth. 1890. Halifax, Engl.: F. King, 1899.

——. *Anthropology*. 1881. New York: Appleton, 1903.

——. *Researches into the Early History of Mankind*. Edited by Paul Bohannen. 1865. Chicago: University of Chicago Press, 1964.

——. *Primitive Culture*. 1871. 2 vols. New York: Harper and Row, 1970.

Vaughan, W. E., ed. *Ireland under the Union*. Vol. 5 of *A New History of Ireland*. Oxford: Clarendon, 1989.

Wagar, Warren. 1982: *Terminal Visions: The Literature of Last Things*. Bloomington: Indiana University Press.

Wakefield, Edward Gibbon. *A View of the Art of Colonization*. 1849. New York: Augustus M. Kelley, 1969.

Walker, Eric A. *The Great Trek*. 5th ed. London: Adam and Charles Black, 1965.

Wallace, Alfred Russel. "The Origin of Human Races and the Antiquity of Man Deduced from the Theory of 'Natural Selection.'" *Journal of the Anthropological Society* 2 (March 1, 1864): clvii–clxxxvii.

——. *The Malay Archipelago . . . A Narrative of Travel with Studies of Man and Nature*. 1869. London: Macmillan, 1898.

——. *A Narrative of Travels on the Amazon and Rio Negro, with an Account of the Native Tribes*. 1853. New York: Haskell House, 1969.

Wallace, Anthony F. C. *The Long, Bitter Trail: Andrew Jackson and the Indians*. New York: Hill and Wang, 1993.

Walton, Craig, and John P. Anton, eds. *Philosophy and the Civilizing Arts: Essays Presented to Herbert W. Schneider*. Athens: Ohio University Press, 1974.

Walvin, James, ed. *Slavery and British Society, 1776–1846*. Baton Rouge: Louisiana State University Press, 1982.

Washburn, Wilcomb E., ed. *The American Indian and the United States: A Documentary History*. 4 vols. New York: Random House, 1973.

Waters, Hazel. "The Great Famine and the Rise of Anti-Irish Racism." *Race and Class* 37, no. 1 (1995): 95–108.

Webb, Janeen, and Andrew Enstice. *Aliens and Savages: Fiction, Politics, and Prejudice in Australia*. Sydney: HarperCollins, 1998.

Wells, H. G. *Anticipations of the Reaction of Mechanical and Scientific Progress on Human Life and Thought*. 1901. New York: Harper, 1902.

——. *H. G. Wells: Early Writings in Science and Science Fiction*. Edited by Robert M. Philmus and David Y. Hughes. Berkeley: University of California Press, 1975.

——. *Seven Science Fiction Novels*. New York: Dover, n.d.

West, John. *The History of Tasmania*. 1852. Edited by A. G. L. Shaw. Sydney: Angus and Robertson, 1971.

Westgarth, William. *Report on the Condition, Capabilities, and Prospects of the Australian Aborigines*. Melbourne: W. Clarke, 1846.

White, Arnold. *The Problems of a Great City*. London: Remington, 1886.

——. *Efficiency and Empire*. 1901. Edited by George R. Searle. Brighton Sussex: Harvester, 1973.

White, Michael, and John Gribbin. *Darwin: A Life in Science*. New York: Penguin, Plume Books, 1997.

Williams, Thomas. *Fiji and the Fijians*. Edited by George Stringer Rowe. London: Alexander Heylin, 1958.

Wilson, Monica. "Co-Operation and Conflict: The Eastern Cape Frontier." In Wilson and Thompson, *The Oxford History of South Africa*, 1:233–71.

——. "The Hunters and Herders." In Wilson and Thompson, *The Oxford History of South Africa*, 1:40–74.

Wilson, Monica, and Leonard Thompson, eds. *The Oxford History of South Africa*. 2 vols. Oxford: Oxford University Press, 1969.

Winch, Donald. *Classical Political Economy and Colonies*. London: Bell, 1965.

Wittig, E. W. "Trollope's Irish Fiction." *Éire-Ireland* 9, no. 3 (1974): 97–118.

Wood, John George. *The Uncivilized Races of Men in All Countries of the World; Being a Comprehensive Account of Their Manners and Customs, and of Their Physical, Social, Mental, Moral, and Religious Characteristics*. Hartford, Conn.: J. B. Burr and Hyde, 1872.

Woodham-Smith, Cecil. *The Great Hunger: Ireland 1845–1849*. 1962. London: Penguin, 1991.

Woodward, Kenneth. "We Are Witnesses." *Newsweek*, April 26, 1993, 48–51.

Woolmington, Jean. "'Writing on the Sand': The First Missions to Aborigines in Eastern Australia." In Swain and Rose, *Aboriginal Australians and Christian Missions*, 77–92.

Wylie, Dan. *Savage Delight: White Myths of Shaka*. Pietermaritzburg: University of Natal Press, 2000.

Yarwood, A. T. *Samuel Marsden: The Great Survivor*. Melbourne: Melbourne University Press, 1977.

Young, Robert. *Colonial Desire: Hybridity in Theory, Culture, and Race*. London: Routledge, 1995.

Žižek, Slavoj. *The Sublime Object of Ideology*. London: Verso, 1989.

Index